College Research Papers

by Joe Giampalmi, EdD

for **dummies**®

A Wiley Brand

College Research Papers For Dummies®

Published by: **John Wiley & Sons, Inc.**, 111 River Street, Hoboken, NJ 07030-5774, www.wiley.com

Copyright © 2023 by John Wiley & Sons, Inc., Hoboken, New Jersey

Published simultaneously in Canada

For general information on our other products and services, please contact our Customer Care Department within the U.S. at 877-762-2974, outside the U.S. at 317-572-3993, or fax 317-572-4002. For technical support, please visit https://hub.wiley.com/community/support/dummies.

Wiley publishes in a variety of print and electronic formats and by print-on-demand. Some material included with standard print versions of this book may not be included in e-books or in print-on-demand. If this book refers to media such as a CD or DVD that is not included in the version you purchased, you may download this material at http://booksupport.wiley.com. For more information about Wiley products, visit www.wiley.com.

Library of Congress Control Number: 2023941184

ISBN 978-1-394-19110-9 (pbk); ISBN 978-1-394-19111-6 (ebk); ISBN 978-1-394-19112-3 (ebk)

SKY10050356_070623

Contents at a Glance

Table of Contents

Introduction

Reading this book shows your commitment to understanding research papers and their role in fulfilling your academic goals and career preparation. I've been helping students like you achieve academic dreams by teaching researching and writing for more than a half century, including more than three decades at the college level. I've evaluated more than 10,000 research papers, essays, and other research projects.

I started teaching a few years before Neil Armstrong walked on the moon with technology 13,000 times less powerful than the phone you carry with you. New technology has improved today's research process, and databases today store thousands of times more data than microfiche storage in the 1960s.

For you to write successful research papers, I am asking three things:

>> Commit to a mindset that you can achieve almost any academic goal if you work hard enough, including writing exemplary college research papers.

>> Use your research opportunities to satisfy your curiosities and develop new ones.

>> Increase your book reading (or start reading books) 15 minutes a day.

You're a busy college student, but busy people commit time to what's important to them. Researching and writing are skills common to almost everything you do academically. A commitment to researching, writing, and reading will fast-track you to achieving your college degree. It's yours for the earning.

About This Book

College Research Papers For Dummies emerged from my enjoyment writing research papers at Widener University in the 1960s — a time when databases were a dream in a researcher's file cabinet. I later taught students to write research papers to satisfy their curiosities. Some of those students pursued careers that resulted from their research.

Here's a look at how this book can help you write professor-pleasing research papers:

>> Analyzing, planning, and organizing your research paper assignment

>> Developing your topic, thesis, argument, rebuttal, and research questions

>> Searching and organizing sources to support your argument

>> Citing and integrating sources

>> Formatting your paper with the required documentation style

>> Writing a first draft in an academic writing style

>> Revising your draft at three organizational layers

>> Checking your paper before final submission

This book shows you classroom-tested skills for writing successful research papers such as the following:

>> Capitalizing on the full-service resources of your college library, especially meeting with a reference librarian

>> Writing with language that respects all people

>> Identifying what to cite and what not to cite

>> Converting sources into evidence

>> Creating an annotated bibliography

>> Writing sentences that emphasize action verbs and specific nouns, and branch in three directions

>> Writing a research paper portfolio

>> Writing research papers across disciplines

Other features you'll see in this book include

>> Example language modeling all parts of writing the research paper

>> Comparisons of major documentation styles

>> Planning strategies that prepare you for plagiarism allegations

>> Tips for reading academic journal articles

>> What to do with Wikipedia

- » Tips for asking professors questions and clarifications
- » Warnings for using citation generators
- » Information on writing reviews of literature and white papers
- » Tips for writing reports, reaction papers, and essays

Foolish Assumptions

You have a busy life as a college student, not an assumption, but a fact. From my decades' experience teaching students like you and enjoying your academic energy in the classroom, I offer the following assumptions, which may or may not be foolish:

- » You're committed to attending every class to learn about writing research papers, but stuff happens such as family emergencies that require you to miss a class. And if that happens, you'll never ask your professor: Did we do anything important last class?

- » You're most likely not committed to being a writer, and you may not be committed to being a researcher. But you're committed to giving your best effort to every research paper you're assigned to write.

- » Technology is one of your life commitments. It's a teacher, tool, and a toy — and sometimes a tireless waste of time.

- » Some social media sites are available for academic engagement, but they're not among the popular ones with college students.

Icons Used in This Book

Icons are legendary in *For Dummies* books, and some are candidates for the icon hall of fame (IHOF). They're used similar to calendar reminders on your phone. Here's an explanation of four icons used in this book to explore points of interest:

The tip icon highlights information that deserves special attention.

Think of the warning icon as cautionary action that may be necessary.

This icon represents a brief digression from the flow of content. This text is interesting but not essential to understanding my point.

The remember icon reinforces an important point.

Beyond This Book

For information on additional online sources for college research papers, see the Cheat Sheet at www.dummies.com. Just search for "College Research Papers For Dummies" for more information you can refer to whenever you need.

Where to Go from Here

This book includes research-writing skills you need to complement your professor and your syllabus. It's not a replacement for either but shows you another professor's way of teaching research papers — and a way that may not meet specific objectives of your course.

If you're working independently, this book can guide you, along with your research paper assignment and specifics of your required documentation style. In that sense, this is a reference book for writing research papers.

This book was designed like a contact list that overdosed on energy drinks — giving you quick access into depths of information you need to write research papers. Here's a quick guide for using the book:

>> Give a quick read-through Chapters 1 to 4 in Part 1 for background on expectations for writing college research papers, a survey of documentation styles, implications of plagiarism as a threat to academic integrity, and an overview of research-paper portfolios.

>> Read Chapter 14 for planning and organizing your paper and Chapter 5 for beginning your research.

>> Before writing your first draft (Chapter 15), review addressing your audience and purpose (Chapter 10); look over grammar and conventions as a review of language issues common to your writing (Chapter 12); and focus on elements common to an academic writing style (Chapter 11).

>> Revise your draft (Chapter 17) and check your writing and documentation style (Chapter 18) before submitting your paper.

1

Laying a Foundation for Writing a Research Paper

Fulfill your professor's research expectations by committing to course research requirements identified in the syllabus, accepting accountability for meeting all assignment requirements, persevering to figuring out the challenges of the assignment, and completing the assignment by meeting professional standards with an academic writing style.

Recognize the emphasis of major documentation styles such as APA's focus on writing style development, MLA's focus on literature and language topics, Chicago's focus on professional research publishing and book publishing, and AP's focus on writing for journalists and reporters.

Comprehend the seriousness of plagiarism such as learning your university's plagiarism policy, evaluating controversies of today's honor codes, identifying recent trends in plagiarism, recognizing why students cheat, and absorbing life-altering consequences of plagiarism.

Satisfy common research paper portfolio requirements such as writing a reflective statement that previews the organization of the portfolio, including artifacts that serve as supporting evidence for a successful portfolio, formulating language that validates artifacts as evidence, and formatting the portfolio consistent with the required documentation style.

Chapter 1

Understanding Expectations: College Research Papers

The signature activity of an educated person is reading academic materials. The amount you read corresponds with your success as a college student — especially your writing and research success. That belief is supported by self-educated successful readers who bypassed systems of formal education, including Wilbur and Orville Wright, Steve Jobs, and architect Frank Lloyd Wright.

These high achievers also researched — not in the sense of using databases and peer-reviewed sources — to answer formal research questions, but in a sense of satisfying their curiosities and answering questions such as: How can a self-powered machine fly? How can a pocket-size computer and a phone look like a piece of art? How can a functional building look aesthetically pleasing?

The answers require reading, researching, satisfying curiosities, and asking the right questions — questions that generate more questions than answers.

This chapter serves as your entry point into the world of research papers. Here I describe the research paper and its importance, explain the mindset of a college researcher, examine your professor's expectations of you as a researcher writer, and identify the research skills you'll carry into your career.

Looking Closer: The What and Why of College Research Papers

Although legendary innovators and creators obviously didn't write formal research papers, they did follow a similar research process that included planning, organizing, searching, evaluating, and formulating questions from which they discovered their information.

College research papers are your invitation to participate at the adult dinner table with other researchers. They're your passcode into the world of academic scholarship that answers the questions why and why not. Also, think of college research papers as your personalized extension of your course in the direction of new topics that you want to explore. Here I explain the what and why of writing research papers.

Recognizing what they're all about

Research papers are as basic to college life as Thirsty Thursdays. And you can quench your research curiosities similar to your thirst — responsibly.

In today's world of people sharing opinions based on gut feelings, research papers represent a non-opinionated position from evidence generated by the best experts in the field. As a college student, you represent a culture of people interested in explaining and adding new information to the body of research on a specific topic.

Research writing is scholarly inquiry that results in new information. It begins with developing an argument (see Chapter 7) and ends with drawing conclusions based on the findings, applying them to wider audiences (see Chapter 15).

The academic community accepts information that results from the research process of supporting an argument with reliable peer-reviewed sources and research methods reviewed by your professor and other experts. It's called scholarship.

REMEMBER

Characteristics of successful undergraduate research papers include the following:

» Citing and formatting information following the required documentation style (see Chapter 8 for citing and Chapter 13 for formatting)

» Creating an innovative topic that addresses the assignment question (refer to Chapter 5)

» Reviewing literature on the topic (flip to Chapter 9)

» Integrating reliable evidence (see Chapter 6) into the argument (see Chapter 7)

» Adding to the body of research on the topic (refer to Chapter 16) by drawing conclusions based on the evidence.

Realizing why research papers matter

Research papers are like a six-hour energy drink for your grade. They're usually weighted a higher point value than other assignments because they require more work. And writing a few successful research papers each semester boasts your GPA — and your academic confidence.

In addition to energizing your grade, here's a look at the benefits of research papers and why they matter. They

» **Broaden your knowledge base:** Curious people like you are driven to satisfy curiosities. New knowledge produces new questions to answer and new answers to questions. Research papers broaden and develop new interests.

» **Develop your scholarship:** Research papers are the primary academic activity of scholars-in-training like you. It's your apprenticeship for credentialing yourself as an educated person. More than any other academic assignment, research papers show your depth of understanding a topic.

» **Focus your expertise:** If your research writing reveals patterns of interests, such as an analysis of workplace issues, you may be developing an area of focus for career exploration. Trace your research topics from middle school through college and analyze what they reveal about your interests.

» **Develop problem-solving skills:** Captain Obvious (whom you meet throughout this book) reminds you that solving problems develops your problem-solving skills. Researching and writing are endless marathons of solving problems. Show me a research paper, and I'll show you an abyss of problems that need solving.

» **Expand career opportunities:** Research papers and grad school are a given. A research background also qualifies you for many business careers, including entrepreneurialism. Each paper you write represents an opportunity to explore a new career.

>> **Show your skills:** Research papers demonstrate a variety of academic skills such as synthesizing, analyzing, organizing, summarizing, and paraphrasing. They also show skills such as creating research questions, developing an argument, and drawing conclusions.

A number of studies show that students who write research papers develop the following **academic benefits:**

>> Preparation for the remainder of college and throughout their careers

>> Experiences for the workplace and applying for grad school

>> Confidence to work independently

>> Persistence toward achieving their degrees and other goals

>> Logical reasoning to support ideas

>> Complex research skills and knowledge of research resources

Writing research papers could easily be identified as the fourth "R" of basic skills and the first "R" of college learning.

Examining first-year college research papers

Your college experience includes a number of firsts:

>> Responsibility for your health and wellbeing

>> Accountability for your academic success

>> Reliance on your own transportation

First-year college also includes your first fully accountable scholarly research paper, which is often your first experience with the scholarship of higher education. First-year college writing courses frequently include essay writing, literature study, and research writing. Because of the importance of research and research-paper writing to college success, the second-semester course is usually dedicated to writing the college research paper.

Your first-year college courses are designed to give you hands-on experience with skills you'll need for research success throughout your college courses and eventually in the workplace.

RESEARCH IN TODAY'S INFORMATION AGE

Imagine life today without research that developed innovations for better lives such as the following:

- Safer auto and air travel
- Electronic devices that fit into the palm of your hand
- Fire retardant clothing and materials
- Arthroscopic surgery eliminating large incisions
- Texting and social media that improves communication — when used responsibly

If you're thinking like a researcher, you may also be formulating questions such as the following:

- What's the role of ChatGPT in college writing?
- Can global pandemics be prevented?
- What will be a replacement for invasive surgery?

Although the Internet has provided instant access to information to answer these questions today, college libraries and similar collections have made that information reliable and available — and very convenient for college students like you.

The challenge of undergraduate research today is locating reliable information among unreliable sources and information that some students prefer for convenience. Research for convenience earns you the grade that "convenience" begins with.

Throughout this book I encourage you to prioritize the resources that you're paying for and that includes support for using them. Your library databases are fields of dreams and reference librarians are available to help you fulfill those dreams. Chapter 6 helps you distinguish the 5- and 4-star sources from the 1- and 2-star sources.

A recent survey of college librarians revealed the following research deficiencies among beginning college students:

>> Depending on Google for sources

>> Lacking the skills to evaluate sources, especially authenticity of sources (refer to Chapter 6)

>> Using weak critical thinking skills such as drawing conclusions (see Chapter 15)

>> Misunderstanding plagiarism (check out Chapter 3)

>> Failing to integrate sources into writing (flip to Chapter 6)

Classifying research writing skills

Research paper writing requires these two distinct skill sets:

>> **Researching skills:** You need these skills to locate your information (refer to Part 2). They include the following:

- Creating research questions

- Developing key terms for searching

- Familiarizing yourself with library databases

- Citing sources

- Evaluating, annotating, and managing sources

- Exploring the library catalogue of materials

>> **Research writing skills:** You need these skills to incorporate your research into writing your research paper (refer to Part 3). They include the following:

- Sticking to a documentation style as you write (see Chapter 8)

- Integrating sources into the argument (check out Chapter 7)

- Drawing conclusions from evidence (refer to Chapter 15)

- Summarizing, paraphrasing, and quoting sources (see Chapter 6)

- Addressing an audience and purpose (flip to Chapter 10)

- Developing a topic and creating a thesis statement (see Chapter 5)

Searching from your strengths

You have your strengths as a person, and you have your strengths as a student. Your learning strengths can serve as an asset for your research skills.

Research papers usually include a number of required sources such as peer-reviewed articles and a number of optional sources. Choose your optional sources based on your strengths such as the following (they're generalizations created for the purpose of locating additional sources):

>> **Literacy-rich oriented:** Focus on additional primary and secondary sources (refer to Chapter 5) and library databases. Search reference entries in reviews of literature.

>> **Extrovert-gregarious oriented:** Focus on talking with people (librarians, professors, writing center staff) to gain more information about available and applicable sources.

>> **Audio-visually oriented:** Focus on academic podcasts and YouTube channels, speeches, and documentaries.

Writing research papers across disciplines

The sequence of your college courses usually includes a course designated as your research paper instructional course — followed by or simultaneous to — research paper requirements across the disciplines you are studying. See Chapter 9 for examples of research paper topics across disciplines.

Excelling at writing research papers

Tens of thousands of college students work hard and write successful research papers every semester, and most of them earn As and Bs. Yet many of those successful students lack confidence as college writers. By passing your essay writing course, your university validated you can write at the college level and fulfill college assignments.

In other words, you're enrolled in a research-writing course because you successfully completed the prerequisites of essay writing.

REMEMBER

Your essay-writing course is frequently designated as a *gatekeeper course*, meaning if you don't write successfully, you don't pass through the gate to the next level of college writing. For more information on college essay writing, see my *College Writing For Dummies*.

Writing research papers can be easier than writing college essays because research papers are more formulaic, meaning they include a built-in structure unlike essays.

Table 1-1 compares writing research papers and writing essays, showing the organizational advantages of research writing for college students.

The comparison doesn't say research papers are less work or easier to write. Rather, research papers require less creative design than essays.

TABLE 1-1 **Research-Paper Writing versus Essay Writing**

Writing Element	Research Paper	Essay
Topic selection	Develops a topic from a question asked in the assignment	Develops a topic from the theme of the assignment
Supporting evidence	Requires researched evidence to argue a position on the assigned question	Requires creating evidence to support a created thesis
Audience engagement	Addresses an audience of fellow researchers	Addresses an audience with a variety of interests
Writing style	Requires a style with the serious tone of research	Requires a style appropriate to the audience and that engages their interests
Writing structure	Follows a highly structured research format	Creates a structure that isn't five paragraphs

Take a look at these tips for writing professor-pleasing research papers:

>> Begin as soon as you're assigned the project (see Chapter 14).

>> Meet with your professor and a reference librarian at the beginning of the assignment (refer to Chapter 5).

>> Review your thesis, argument, and research questions (see Chapter 5) with your professor (or the writing center if your professor isn't available).

>> Plan your feedback sources, trial readers who will tell you strengths and liabilities of your paper (check out Chapter 17).

>> Commit to a three-layer revising plan that distinguishes revising from editing (see Chapter 17).

Applying Research Mindset: Way to A

Think of a research-paper mindset as preparing for a four-week study abroad program. You're initially overwhelmed with thoughts such as: How do I start? Where can I get information I need? How do I organize what I find?

You committed for study abroad when you paid your fee, and you committed to your research paper when you enrolled in the course. The mindset for writing a college research paper requires the commitment of a four-week relationship with your new love — researching, reading, analyzing, documenting, and revising.

REMEMBER

Writing a research paper requires a similar commitment and confidence that hard work will result in achieving almost all your academic goals. And when you face obstacles, support is available to help you. See Chapter 20 for a description of resources available to help you with write your research paper.

Approach research and other assignments with a mindset that hard work results in success and that you can figure out more than you think you can.

Here are characteristics of a growth mindset attitude that applies to writing college research papers:

>> **Commitment:** Allocate the time, energy, and mental resources required to write a successful assignment.

>> **Determination:** Work with the confidence that you can write a successful paper and that some assignments require more effort than others.

>> **Resilience:** Recognize that you'll face obstacles and that when you need support, help is available on campus.

>> **Progression:** Focus on accomplishing incremental steps that lead to the next step. You can't become a successful second-year college student unless you complete requirements for the first year.

REMEMBER

A plan for completing your college degree incrementally includes completing requirements one step at a time — one assignment at a time, one course at a time, one semester at a time, and one year at a time. In sports it's called "small ball."

>> **Reflection:** Reflect regularly on what was successful and unsuccessful and the lessons you learned to overcome obstacles.

Fulfilling Professors' Expectations

You're the successful person you are today because you've fulfilled expectations — those of the significant adults in your life and those you've set for yourself. Add your professors to the influential people in your life who set expectations for you, including their research expectations.

TECHNICAL STUFF

Your professors, as representatives of the academic community, are held to a high standard of research and professional development. If they fail to meet those expectations, they fail to earn promotions and other career advancements. They can also be dismissed from employment. Research is an integral part of their academic lives, and when they're teaching you research, they most likely are completing it themselves.

Research offers you an opportunity to connect with your professors on a scholarly level. Think of your research as planting ivy in front of the tower. The following sections show you the value of research and research expectations of your professors.

Professors' research requirements

Think of the disservice of professors — or any other instructors — who expect little from their students, and they get it. When professors expect more, students achieve more. If your professors expect a multifaceted research paper with extensive analysis and synthesis, you're going to write a better paper than a requirement to write about the history of an event.

REMEMBER

Here's a look at research expectations most college professors expect from their students:

>> **Commitment:** Professors expect a commitment to the course and research, which is displayed by attending and preparing for every class, following the syllabus, completing readings, meeting deadlines, checking course management sites, and showing academic enthusiasm for your research projects. They also expect your commitment to learning research strategies and the designated documentation style.

>> **Accountability:** College students accept accountability for performing at their best level. Professors expect you to be accountable for selecting a topic that addresses the assignment and interests you, understanding the structure and purpose of the research, locating scholarly sources that argue your thesis, and citing and formatting as determined by the required style.

>> **Perseverance:** Researching includes many movable parts which sometimes malfunction and cause frustration — similar to most complex projects. Your professors expect you to persist through problems, access available support when you need it, and utilize office hours as necessary.

>> **Professionalism:** Your professor expects professionalism that includes formal writing, not only with the assignment, but also with all course communications. Your professor expects academic writing that includes clarity, conciseness, sentence variety, and use of academic verbs and nouns.

See Chapter 11 for detailed information on writing in an academic style, including elements described in the previous paragraphs.

>> **Scholarship:** Scholarship represents the difference between high school academics and college academics. Most professors were serious scholars from the time their parents read Shakespeare to them as a two-year-old. Forgive them for expecting similar scholarship form you, especially if you only

had Chaucer read to you as a two-year-old. Professors' scholarship expectations from you include a passion for knowledge, an unquenched thirst for inquiry, near-perfection in your academic work, and a desire to re-read the classics when you're not working on assignments. Thank them for such scholarly expectation.

REMEMBER

Professors design assignments based on their education background, research, and teaching experience — which is very demanding for you as a student. Follow the program. You're not going to understand the whys of the assignment, and don't ask. Remember who's the professor and who's the student. You'll figure out the assignment, and if you work hard, you'll earn a good grade.

Undergraduate mentored research

For many undergraduate scholars, working with a faculty research mentor is a memorable experience in their undergraduate education. It's almost as exciting as scoring a backstage pass for a Taylor Swift concert.

Mentored research is an asset for applying to graduate school and also shows initiative and leadership on a workplace application.

Here are some tips for pursuing mentored research opportunities:

>> If your university has an undergraduate research office, stop there to ask about opportunities. If your campus doesn't have one, stop by the faculty research office and talk with them.

>> Talk with your academic advisor about opportunities.

>> Look for a professor who shares similar research interests as yours.

Before you meet with anyone to talk about mentored research, develop your research idea by completing the following:

>> Detail your research plan, including an investigation of funding.

>> Complete a preliminary review of literature.

>> Draft preliminary research questions.

If formal mentored opportunities aren't available, consider asking to volunteer with a professor.

Building Career Assets: Forever Research Skills

When many college students are first assigned a research paper, their thoughts include questions such as the following:

- >> What do I need to do?
- >> Where do I get the information?
- >> How do I start?
- >> How much time do I have to do it?

Then they commit their best effort to the paper and earn an A or B. The one question students don't ask is more important than the ones they do ask: What did I learn from the project that contributed to my career-preparation skills? The answer is more academic value than students imagined.

The skills that students learn from writing research papers could fill a resume. Here's a look at lifetime academic skills students learn from a regular diet of writing research papers:

- >> **Project management:** Planning and organizing a research paper and delivering comprehensive results within the structure of a formal style

- >> **Research:** Applying research strategies by developing keywords that answer the research questions

- >> **Data collection:** Collecting, organizing, and preparing data into an informational format

- >> **Source evaluating:** Evaluating source information according to its currency, relevance, accuracy, and appropriateness to the topic

- >> **Communication:** Writing information into a documentation format understandable by the audience

- >> **Supporting an argument:** Converting sources into evidence that supports an argument

These skills, for example, can be applied to business or a number of other careers by performing workplace activities.

Chapter **2**

Certifying Consistency: Documentation Styles

Your dreams and goals as an educated person may be centered in the fields of marketing, management, science, technology, law enforcement, or the arts. Each discipline of study contains its own standards, expectations, and formatting preferences.

Research in those and other fields also has their standards and formatting preferences — and they're called *documentation styles*. Standards of crediting the works of others represent the language of professional scholars as they communicate with one another and the remainder of the academic community.

In this chapter I explain documentation styles common to college writing: APA (American Psychological Association), MLA (Modern Language Association), CMOS (Chicago Manual of Style), and a few others. I also explain differences in cultural philosophies of crediting sources and debunk myths associated with documentation styles.

What and Why: Documentation Styles and Academic Standards

My experience with some scholars is that they lack a sense of humor; they eat plain pizza; they brew their morning beverage from recycled herbs; and they read thick books sometimes written in foreign languages. Scholars thrive on academic consistency — for example, some have been using the same book marker since the invention of paper.

Scholars dislike inconsistencies such as three different styles of documentation using three different terms for lists of sources: references (APA), works cited (MLA), and bibliography (Chicago). Scholars prefer style consistencies when they read, write, and teach research.

You may ask: Why not one super-style documentation style system for all academic disciplines? Scholars are very protective of their disciplines and believe that the style for their discipline is the one true style. It's like all owners of Golden Retrievers thinking they have the best pet — and they're all correct.

Data and information differ among disciplines and require unique formatting of information. For example, a style for formatting statistical values differs from a style that displays historical documents. Documentation styles are as different as college students' creation of playlists.

Certifying Sources: Documentation Styles

They aren't the lines of sportswear endorsed by college athletes as part of their NIL rights. *Documentation styles* are a set of standards for documenting the works of others and formatting pages of research specific to a field of study.

Scholars have been thinking about and working on standards since a group first met to discuss them on a cold December day at the University of Pennsylvania on Walnut Street in Philadelphia in 1892. (No, I wasn't in attendance.)

REMEMBER

A documentation style provides consistent (and sometimes logical) methods of documenting and formatting information for readers and researchers in the same field of study. For example, MLA readers expect the list of citations at the end of a research paper will be labeled "Works Cited," logical wording for a list of cited works in the research.

The documentation style chosen by your professor or the department is based on its compatibility with the type of data common to the topics being studies.

Documentation styles such as APA and MLA are compatible with most research topics studied in high school and first-year college. Those styles are adaptable to research in literature, language arts, history, psychology, economics, sociology, mass media, business management, and many others.

THE HISTORY OF POPULAR DOCUMENTATION STYLES

More than a hundred years ago, three popular documentation styles were developed and continue to be used today for writing college research papers. Here's a look at how they began:

- **APA (American Psychological Association):** More than 120 years ago, approximately at the time when Orville and Wilbur were dreaming of flying, a handful of psychologists organized with a dream of promoting scholarship and standards among academicians in psychology and related disciplines.

  Their official seven-page writing and style guide from the early 1900s evolved into the 2020 *Publication Manual of the American Psychological Association, 7th Edition*, a 427-page document.

- **MLA (Modern Language Association):** Advocates for study of language and other humanities (literature, history, and philosophy) first met in the late 1800s for the purpose of studying modern languages and focus on the teaching of those languages.

  MLA survived a period of disagreeing on the objectives of the organization (scholars will be scholars) and eventually refocused to become a leading professional resource for the promotion and teaching of language and literature study.

- **CMOS (Chicago Manual of Style):** In the late 1800s, the University of Chicago Press (affiliated with the University of Chicago), began notating style inconsistencies from handwritten manuscripts submitted by professional scholars. The development of that list of style issues continues today.

  The Chicago Manual of Style, a publication of the University of Chicago Press, has been revised and published continuously since 1906. That initial publication title was a mouthful: *Manual of Style: Being a Compilation of the Typographical Rules in Force at the University of Chicago Press, to Which are Appended Specimens of Type in Use.* Chicago followed its advice on eliminating wordiness and reduced the 27-word title to 5: *The Chicago Manual of Style.*

  The 17th edition was published in 2017. Chicago stands out among other style-books for its detailed sections on grammar and usage. In addition to its use by students, publishers use Chicago for novels and trade books.

REMEMBER

If you're writing a research paper as a major in a field of study such as literature and language study, MLA is the best style. If you're a psychology or social science major, APA is the best style for research. And if your field of study is publications, Chicago is your best choice.

The full versions of your documentation styles are created for professional scholars who usually intend to publish their research. The documentation style offers presentation formatting for complex information such as tables of statistical data that exceeds first-year college research.

Because most college research doesn't need complex formatting, your research papers are adaptable to APA, MLA, or Chicago.

Surveying Documentation Styles: APA, MLA, and CMOS

These sections describe documentation styles older than dirt — and all three major styles adapted and survived controversy. Today they're commonly used in college and high school research writing, more than a century after small groups of scholars first met and eventually resolved their differences.

REMEMBER

In full disclosure, note that I'm the author of *APA Style & Citations For Dummies*. As a former high school English teacher, I taught Turabian and MLA styles. As a college professor, I taught both MLA and APA. Eventually APA became the designated style in the department I taught at Rowan University in Glassboro, New Jersey. These sections detail background on documentation styles common to college research writing.

American Psychological Association (APA)

APA ranks among the oldest documentation styles and held its first organizational meeting in the late 1800s. Philadelphia hosted a couple dozen psychology scholars who started an organization that claims more than 120,000 members today.

The documentation and formatting guidelines in APA's seventh edition focus on features for professional scholars. The latest edition introduces a sample student research paper for college and high school scholars. The student paper includes a title page that differs from the professional title page.

The APA manual includes several undergraduate examples and many professional examples.

Scholars-in-training, like you, can benefit from an APA version written to the undergraduate audience — one that models writing the basic structure of a research paper and includes strategies for revising. Are you listening, APA?

APA features guidance for college and high school audiences that includes the following:

>> **Writing style development:** APA includes elements of an academic writing style such as flow, conciseness, clarity, and tone. It explains the importance of reducing wordiness and avoiding contractions, colloquialisms, and jargon (see Chapter 11).

>> **Respectful language guidelines:** APA details language that shows respect for all people and provides guidelines for reducing bias. The guide includes excellent examples of inclusive language (refer to Chapter 10).

>> **Grammar and mechanics guidelines:** Similar to other major manuals, APA reviews grammar, usage, and mechanics that are fundamental to academic writing (see Chapter 12).

Modern Language Association (MLA)

MLA is appropriately named and it's the only popular documentation style that includes the word "language" in its name. When your research topic is language related, think MLA.

TECHNICAL STUFF

MLA's popularity in high school can be partially attributed to generations of high school teachers who were weaned on MLA as liberal arts majors in college and became well-versed in MLA style and documentation. The standards of MLA were developed to serve scholars in the humanities, especially language and literature study.

MLA's professional development and student support materials exceed their style and citation guidance for scholars-in-training. MLA provides more instructional materials for students than APA and Chicago.

Beyond MLA's guidance for writing research papers that focus on literature and literary works, the MLA offers extensive language instruction such as the following topics that appear in the *MLA Handbook 9th Edition*:

>> **Literature-research topics:** MLA documentation style focuses on referencing literature-based sources that support language and literature topics.

>> **Language study:** The study of language is fundamental to the MLA manual. It's the best language review of any of the major styles.

>> **Respectful language principles:** Similar to APA, MLA emphasizes language that respects all people and all groups of people.

>> **Language-based citations:** MLA offers extensive examples for referencing language-based sources.

See Chapter 8 for additional information on MLA.

AP AND OTHER DOCUMENTATION STYLES

The Associated Press (AP) news organization was created about 80 years ago. The resulting *AP Stylebook* was developed to standardize grammar and usage initially among news organizations in the New York City area. Popularity of the style guide extended to other journalists and reporters as a basic reference for rules of usage.

The first public editions of the *AP Stylebook* became available in the early '50s, and since then the AP style has become the standard in news, broadcasting, public relations, and magazine publication. In recent years, the *AP Stylebook* has been sold worldwide with annual sales exceeding 2 million copies. AP Style is also the standard for college majors in the fields of journalism, public relations, and marketing.

AP is a major style guide along with the others compared in this book (APA, MLA, and Chicago). AP isn't used as a comparison style because it's exclusively used by journalists and other media representatives, and journalists don't commonly write college research papers.

Other documentation styles in specific fields of study include the following:

- **American Anthropological Association (AAA):** Used in the field of anthropology

- **American Chemical Society (ACM):** Used in the field of chemistry and related sciences

- **American Medical Association (AMA):** Used in medicine and related fields

- **American Political Science Association (APSA):** Used in the field of political science

- **Colombia Online Style (COS):** Used in the humanities and sciences

- **Legal Style (The Red Book):** Used in the legal field

- **Vancouver:** Used in the field of biological sciences

Chicago Manual of Style (CMOS)

If you're a publication-focused major, your favorite song could easily be (with respect to Frank Sinatra) "Chicago, My Kind of Manual." When publishing houses think publication, they think Chicago and the University of Chicago Press.

Chicago's emphasis in publication began more than a century ago and continues today. It's the publication style of the *For Dummies* series that you're currently reading. Chicago lists more examples of style and usage than any other style. Because of that feature, a copy of Chicago has been a reference book in my office library for more than half a century. It's my go-to source for questions of usage.

Chicago's appeal to language lovers is that it includes chapters of topics such as the following:

>> Mathematics in type

>> Numbers

>> Distinctive treatment of words

>> Quotations and dialogue

>> Indices

See Chapter 8 for additional information on uses of Chicago.

Your professor's style

The documentation style for your course and research is sometimes as complex as a recipe that has more chefs than ingredients. For example, the department that houses your course may have a preferred documentation style. But your professor may determine that a specific research assignment is more adaptable by a different style. The professor's choice rules.

REMEMBER

Professors' choices may be influenced by the documentation style they're more experienced with reading and researching. Or, if professors preferred style isn't adaptable to the assignment, they may adjust the assignment to meet the research needs. The options may result in the required style you're most familiar with.

Professors' documentation style is shaped by the documentation style they teach and their personal preferences of what they value. Professors' adaptions to assignments frequently include the following:

>> Avoiding tables and figures (see Chapter 6)

>> Requiring use of sources found exclusively in library databases (refer to Chapter 5)

>> Requiring an annotated bibliography (check out Chapter 5)

>> Requiring an appendix (see Chapter 16)

These options offer you flexibility of presenting your research ideas.

Table 2-1 shows features many professors value and undervalue in a documentation style:

TABLE 2-1   **Professors' Value and Undervalue of Style Features**

Professors Value	Professors Undervalue
Accurate citations	Footnotes (unless Chicago style)
Table of content	Creative title page
Page numbers (see Chapter 13)	Running heads (see Chapter 13)
Punctuation in text (see Chapter 12)	Internal punctuation in unusual reference entries (see Chapter 8)
Formatting accuracy of reference page (see Chapter 8)	Citation and reference accuracy of unusual sources (see Chapter 8)
Library database sources (see Chapter 5)	Open Internet sources (see Chapter 5)

TIP

Professors frequently adapt documentation requirements to assignments. For example, a professor may accept an informal reference to a source in an essay or short reaction paper, such as naming the source in the text and not requiring a formal list of sources at the end of the essay. For more information on informal sources in essays and writing essays, see my *College Writing For Dummies*

Professors don't memorize documentation styles. (But they do know how to research answers to questions if they need to.) If you ask a question in class about documenting an unusual source, professors usually respond with the following: "Choose a format consistent with similar entries."

The point is don't fear minor formatting errors in unusual citations and references entries. Professors may sometimes confuse unusual reference entries, and they frequently give you the benefit of their doubt.

Your preferred style

You're the product of your experiences, and your successes created confidence in your academic skills such as the documentation style you're comfortable with.

In college many students are generally required to use APA more than MLA — except for language and literature majors who still use MLA. Between high school and college, you may have experience with Chicago.

When you have style choices, use the style you're most familiar with. If you're having a can't-make-a-decision day about style, think APA first, MLA second, and Chicago third.

Differentiating between the East and West When Documenting

The two major hemispheres of the world include more than a thousand cultures, with each culture having its unique beliefs. Some of those belief differences include documentation styles, more specifically, lack of need for a documentation style. Academic writing on a global scale has become culturally centered in audience, content, tone, and especially crediting sources.

Two opposing positions of writing discourse have developed in the past few decades, styles that can be generally classified as Eastern philosophy and Western philosophy. The following sections explain cultural differences in writing and documenting.

Grasping cultural differences in writing

Saying that English is a difficult language to speak and write is an understatement. Think of nonnative language learners trying to make sense of expressions such as *learn by heart, pass with flying colors, hit the books,* and *brainstorm.*

And with a belief that language is a gift to be shared by all, Eastern culture students lack understanding of crediting sources. Their misunderstanding of citing frequently results in unintentional plagiarism. Table 2-2 shows major areas of differences of Eastern and Western styles.

Research-writing tips for nonnative English students

Students don't learn an additional language by speaking and writing alone. They learn the skills when they have the help of a team. Most college campuses commit to providing the resources that nonnative speakers need to succeed.

TABLE 2-2 ## Differences in Eastern and Western Academic Culture

	Eastern Philosophy Beliefs	Western Philosophy Beliefs
Writing clarity	Vague, general written description	Specific, detailed description
Writing style	Indirect and reader figures out the point	Direct and to the point
Literary criticism	What's written by cultural experts is right and not to questioned	Respectful formal tone with justifiable disagreement
Documentation	Belief that creative work doesn't need citing	Strict, formal crediting of sources
Intellectual ideas	A gift to be shared and enjoyed by all, owned by society	A gift to be shared by all with formal recognition to the source originator
Support of ideas	Supported by cultural beliefs	Supported by evidence and data

TIP

Here are tips for helping nonnative English speakers learn documentation styles, and many of them include working with others:

>> **Team up.** Build your own class review team. Create your team with students similar to you or with students taking the same course. Schedule weekly meetings to talk about class activities and class assignments. Chapter 17 suggests questions that provide feedback for writing assignments.

>> **Learn course vocabulary.** Create study sheets to help you understand the language of the course. Focus on instructional research words such as the following: key words, database, citations, references, sources, formatting, evidence, argument, and so forth. List writing-related words such as the following: writing process, drafting, revising, feedback, comments, brainstorm, and so forth. Also learn vocabulary related to the syllabus such as the following: syllabus, prerequisite, requirements, and deadlines.

>> **Use campus resources.** Remember that universities that admit nonnative speaking students are committed to help you graduate and offer resources to assist you. Use these resources available from the start of the semester. Support includes your professor, the writing center, the academic support center, and reference librarians and other support available within the library. These resources are referenced in almost every chapter in Parts 2, 3, and 4.

>> **Focus on documentation basics.** Learning documentation styles can be overwhelming for even the best of students. You can be successful with your research paper without learning everything about your research style. And most of the information in the documentation manuals is for professional scholars. Focus on learning basics, which include limiting your sources to books, journal articles, and academic websites. Learn how to cite these sources and enter them in reference lists. Also, get early help to develop your topic, thesis, and research questions.

>> **Use course resources.** Regularly visit your course's website or learning platform. Explore it like you're shopping online. You'll find links or tabs to pages such as the syllabus, weekly schedule, assignments, handouts, and so forth. Prioritize assignments' due dates and information about assignments that may include sample sections of assignments. You may also find links to help you learn the required documentation style.

>> **Create personal models.** Make models of citations and references entries for books, journal articles, academic websites — and any additional resources you use for your research paper.

Debunking Documentation Style Myths: The Whole Truth

If you've been on a college campus for a week, you've figured out that stories become exaggerated at the rate of the number of students who repeat them. Every campus has its myth about the haunted building on campus, the student who never attended a class and earned an A in every course, and the professor who recited books from memory — in Greek.

Documentation styles are fertile soil for student myths. The following sections reveal the whole truth — from a professor who has heard more myths than excuses for late papers. Here are some of the more popular myths about documentation.

Documentation styles are for nerds

If you're reading a book like this, you're a nerd. College is a nesting grounds for nerds, so be proud of it.

Nerds are synonymous with being a scholar, and the world needs more nerds. Documentation styles are for nerds and non-nerds They're for anyone who doesn't want to lose tuition money for failing a course.

And on the brighter side, they're for any student who wants to enter the conversation of scholars and show respect for the scholarship of others. Call yourself a nerd or a scholar, but be sure to follow guidelines in your required documentation style.

My sources are accurate: I don't need a documentation style

The thinking is half right, and being half right is better than being half fast. The need for accurate and reliable sources (see Chapter 5) isn't a myth. Thinking that accurate sources don't need documenting can result in plagiarism (see Chapter 3).

Documented accurate and reliable information is the foundation of any conversation, especially an academic conversation. Accurate use of sources includes citing the source and entering it into the references.

Accuracy and documentation aren't mutually exclusive. Your sources need documenting (see Chapter 8) because they belong to a rightful owner, the scholar who created them. Taking someone's intellectual property without recognition is like taking their laptop. One form of theft is called stealing, the other is called plagiarism (see Chapter 3). Both forms have serious consequences.

Search for reliable and accurate sources, and document them because they're the property of others.

My professor doesn't talk about a documentation style

Silence may be golden, but it's also expensive for your grade if you interpret your professor's silence as an indifference toward following a documentation style.

Documenting sources became a necessity for you as soon as you wrote your first research paper. Your professor doesn't talk about it much because it's an academic expectation of the academic environment you're part of.

Hers's a list of other topics your professor doesn't talk much about, but they remain high priority for the classroom:

>> Attending every class

>> Being prepared for and participating in every class

>> Committing your best effort to every requirement

>> Word processing every assignment you're required to submit

>> Completing assignments in the standard language of the classroom

Documenting sources and following the required documentation style is as much an expectation as paying your college tuition.

My combination of documentation styles worked in the past

The good news is that you recognize the importance of documenting sources, but combining styles is like combining your schools' basketball and volleyball teams and asking them to compete in a swim meet.

Combining styles is likely to result in a grade preventing you from remaining above water. Learn the documentation style you're required to follow. And if you want to complete in a swim meet, take swim lessons.

Chapter **3**

Preventing Plagiarism: Endorsing Academic Integrity

Picture this: You wrote a research paper you're excited to submit because you started early, planned it with your professor, met with a reference librarian, and revised it with the writing center. You've never felt so confident about an assignment, and you need a good grade to maintain your partial scholarship.

You emailed it to a friend in the same course who asked to see it because they got a late start on the assignment. Your friend does a quick find-and-replace and submits it to your professor — in their name. What do you do? Is this a story about friendship? Are you possibly implicated in plagiarism?

Forget the friendship. This is plagiarism, representative of more than half of college students who said they cheated on an assignment or misrepresented their work in some form in the past year. Academic dishonesty is like an infestation of termites destructively eating their way through the foundation of higher education.

Students who cheat are devaluing degrees of hard-working and committed students who earn them honestly and fairly. Plagiarists are causing whispers by CEOs of Fortune 500 companies saying, "Cheaters graduate from that university."

This chapter explains plagiarism's threat to academic integrity, recent trends in academic dishonesty, and six-easy-steps for avoiding plagiarism. This chapter also includes an honest look at two forces on a collision course — plagiarism and academic integrity — and describes a recent court decision that supports honest students.

Defining Academic Integrity: A Win-Win Approach

Academic integrity is like guardrails on a winding mountain road that keep you headed in an honest direction. Accidents do happen, but awareness and knowledge of the road helps keep you safe — also safe from plagiarism.

Academic honesty is all students doing their own work in a fair manner. It's following assignment rules for collaboration and use of resources. It's universities and professors ensuring a level playing field for academic accomplishment.

These sections dive deeper into understanding academic integrity and its implication on learning and earning degrees.

Colliding integrity and plagiarism

The foundation of a family is the unselfish trust of its members to help and support one another. When distrust replaces trust, the family structure fails.

Educational institutions are built on similar trusts of all stakeholders — trust in the honor of all participants that degrees and certifications are earned respectfully and fairly, not earned falsely and awarded indiscriminately. Academic integrity is the protector of the fruits of hard-working committed students who educate themselves based on the principles of decency, integrity, determination, and respect for others.

Institutions of higher learning ensure fair academic behavior by implementing procedures such as the following:

>> Policies that promote honest work and address forms of academic misconduct

>> Training that clarifies acceptable and unacceptable academic behavior

>> Venues for addressing cases of alleged violations of policies

>> Regular reviews of policies based on current trends of dishonest work

>> Commitment of resources to fight plagiarism and other forms of cheating

Discovering your university's policy

Academic integrity policies on campuses are as common as tuition payment plans — they include a variety of options, but payment remains due and academic honesty remains required.

REMEMBER

Plagiarism policy committees usually include student participants. If your university committee lacks a student voice, argue (see Chapter 7) the importance of one and volunteer to serve.

University committees develop policies for academic honesty. They include definitions of dishonesty, examples of cheating, and procedures for addressing violations. Plagiarism examples usually include issues that occurred recently on campus.

University policies usually begin with a statement describing the importance of academic honesty and include language such as the following:

Every shareholder in the academic community is expected to demonstrate standards of academic honesty and avoid dishonest behaviors such as (but not inclusive of) the following . . .

The opening of the policy continues with specific information such as the following:

>> Examples of academic dishonesty (refer to the section "Reviewing Forms of Academic Dishonesty: It's on You" later in this chapter)

>> Professors' procedures for reporting allegations

>> University procedures for addressing plagiarism

>> Disciplinary consequences for dishonest practices

>> Reminders of policies in place to discourage cheating

HONOR CODES' GROWING CONTROVERSIES

Honor codes began in the Colonial Era when William and Mary College established ethical standards for students in the classroom — and in some instances — in the community outside the classroom. Here's a look at honor codes, their adaptions, and their influence on academic honesty on campuses today.

Early honor codes

Formal honor codes were established at U.S. service academies during the mid-20th century. Controversies with honor codes originated with the word "tolerate" in some codes, meaning that students who witnessed code violations were obligated to reveal names of those students who cheated — under penalty of committing a violation themselves.

In some schools with honor codes, students take nonproctored exams, and students are required to reveal academic misconduct by any student taking the exam.

Traditional honor codes have included violations such as disrespecting property of others and disrespecting students, faculty, and staff. "Respect" clauses are considered unenforceable by many educational leaders today and are being deleted from honor codes.

Honor codes and collaboration

Another honor code issue is collaboration on academic projects — unauthorized and authorized. Collaboration such as writing a team paper represents a skill required in most workplaces. Yet collaboration is unacceptable in many honor codes because it represents work done by someone other than the assigned author.

Some schools have attempted to manage their honor codes, identifying only misconduct related to plagiarism and cheating — and not violations such as self-plagiarism, fabrication, and unfair test advantages. An inconsistency of collaboration is that some professors permit it and some professors don't.

Uncovering recent online plagiarism trends

Disturbingly, incidents of academic dishonesty are increasing, and it's identified as a worldwide problem in education. Post–Covid data shows an increase in online plagiarism, leading some experts to say that "plagiarism threatens the future of online learning."

Here's a look at research findings on academic dishonesty in the past few years:

>> **New detection tools:** New and improved software continues to be developed, such as Turnitin's improved detection of copy-and-paste cheating. Turnitin also released a version AI-detection software.

>> **Protective assignment development:** Professors' staff development includes designing assignments that challenges pro-cheating software, such as requiring assignments reference specific classroom activities.

>> **Increased disciplinary action:** Data shows that more schools are taking disciplinary action against dishonest students, and the number of disciplined students has doubled in the past five years.

WARNING

In spring 2023, the Supreme Court of Texas voted to revoke degrees from students who graduated but received diplomas through academic misconduct. The state said the degrees weren't earned and that they shouldn't have been awarded. This is a landmark court decision in the fight against plagiarism.

>> **Increased litigation:** Data also shows increased litigation against dishonest academic behavior. Colleges are taking their cases to the courts.

>> **Increased financial commitment:** Colleges continue to invest more funding to fight the plagiarism epidemic, including forming consortiums to maximize funding. One expert said, "Students cannot compete with resources of combined universities to fight plagiarism," and that we should continue to see data showing decreases in plagiarism.

Reviewing Forms of Academic Dishonesty: It's on You

I don't need to tell you about the extent of cheating on college campuses. You know the people, their methods, their justifications, and the resentment of ethical and hard-working students who fairly earn their academic grades. You have also most likely heard the stories of how students cheat.

The following sections explain the whys and hows of students cheating, including classifications of academic dishonesty. It also includes a look at the new bot on the block — artificial intelligence.

Recognizing why students cheat

Some students spend more time plagiarizing a paper than they would writing the paper. Research shows students are motivated to cheat by peer pressure that "everyone cheats" and also by overconfidence that they won't get caught.

Here's a look at the range of reasons why students cheat:

>> **Poor planning:** Cheating for many students results from poor planning that leads to behavior such as buying an online paper as their only option to pass. Research shows delayed or poor planning is the major cause of underachievement on almost any assignment.

REMEMBER

File this in your brain's hard drive: The earlier you start an assignment, the better your grade. The early bird not only gets the worm, but it also earns the A.

>> **Overconfidence:** Many traditional-age college students believe in their invincibility and that they can do just about anything, including outsmarting the intellectual capability of their university and thus gain an academic advantage. Cheating attempts of risk-taking students include changing grades electronically, accessing notes hidden in a calculator, collaborating electronically during a test, sharing answers during a synchronous online test, and contract cheating.

>> **Underestimate implications:** Some students see plagiarism as innocuous and not harmful to anyone and cite the Eastern culture belief that scholarship is an open-market commodity not needing citations (see Chapter 2). They don't see the big picture of dishonest students earning grades they didn't earn and honest students not earning similar grades. Academic dishonesty is a multibillion-dollar industry fueled by students spending millions to cheat without getting caught and universities spending money to catch them cheating. And students who don't cheat are paying tuition money to prevent cheaters from cheating.

>> **Peer pressure:** This isn't the first time, and it won't be the last time, you hear about peer pressure. Friends (you don't need friends who pressure you) may ask you to help them with a paper, see your paper, or recommend sources for you to use in your paper. Depending on your course collaboration guidelines, all these examples could be plagiarism. You need to make a hard adult decision when friends ask for unauthorized collaboration.

REMEMBER

Sometimes plagiarism is identified as *unintentional* or *inadvert*, meaning a formatting error that misidentifies your intended document source. See more informational on unintentional plagiarism in the section "Did I inadvertently plagiarize?" later in this chapter.

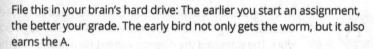

Identifying variations of academic misconduct

Academic dishonesty includes many labels and classifications of misrepresenting work. All definitions of dishonesty have one thing in common: They're all wrong.

Here's a look at classifications of cheating and academic dishonesty:

>> **Contracting:** One of the most extensive forms of dishonesty includes purchasing papers from online mills. Other forms of contracting include paying someone to write a paper, complete an assignment, or take a test.

>> **Fabricating:** Fabricating or falsifying academic work includes inventing elements of citations and references, creating false data, misrepresenting evidence, and designating false dates on sources.

>> **Dishonesty:** Dishonesty has many faces and none of them are attractive. It includes accessing unauthorized sources for a paper or test, talking with students who previously took a test you're scheduled to take, using unauthorized notes, and speaking with unauthorized authorities.

Academic dishonesty also includes self-plagiarism — submitting a paper you wrote for one course to another course without receiving authorization from the professor you're submitting the paper to.

>> **Facilitating:** This form of plagiarism includes participating in dishonesty such as helping someone write a paper and coordinating materials used for cheating.

REMEMBER

Other forms of academic dishonesty include selling tests and answers, forging a faculty member's signature, changing answers before a regrade, and having parents do the work.

Looking closer at artificial intelligence

ChatGPT, an AI chatbot, was launched in November 2022, with the primary purpose of duplicating human conversation. Experts in the field of writing and education have praised and condemned it.

AI detection software remains a possibility because AI's conversational language differs from written language, the language expected in college writing assignments. See my *College Writing For Dummies* for more information distinguishing spoken language from written language.

ChatGPT's successes include passing a state bar exam and passing an MBA test. It has also successfully written computer programs, composed music, and played a children's game.

Education experts project that AI can successfully write reference lists, research abstracts, and first drafts. It also contains the capabilities to brainstorm for writing.

TECHNICAL STUFF

AI reactions from educators have been mixed. Some have praised its ability to help nonnative English learners to apply nuances to their writing; others have suggested that AI will result in the downfall of college writing. Critics of AI also identify its inability to use respectful language (see Chapter 10). The current version of ChatGPT shows patterns of using cultural biases and discriminating language. AI's role in higher education includes many uncertainties at this time.

Knowing life-altering consequences of plagiarism

The consequences of plagiarizing have a ripple effect throughout universities. The half of college students who cheat affect the education of the half that don't cheat. For example, when professors evaluate their teaching, they analyze results of student assignments, which includes dishonest results. These sections look at plagiarism's consequences and implications.

Celebrity consequences

Some celebrities have survived accusations of plagiarism such as journalists misusing a source or neglecting a source. They were reprimanded by their supervisors and required to apologize to their readers but retained their positions.

Celebrity careers don't usually survive two incidents of plagiarism. Similarly for college students, one incident of plagiarism doesn't usually result in dismissal from college. But two incidents are one too many.

Forms of dishonesty such as cheating by purchasing papers or falsifying records are considered more serious and usually result in academic or career dismissal. Some celebrities have experienced career-altering consequences for actions such as falsifying academic degrees or fabricating academic accomplishments.

Similarly at the college level, students have been dismissed at prestigious institutions for actions such as participating in systematic cheating, large-scale cheating on tests, and attempting to hack software and alter final grades. In many of these situations, universities (with their available legal counsel) are prosecuting students.

Consequences for honest students

When students perform well on tests, which includes results of students who cheat — professors conclude their teaching is successful. But when success includes students who cheated, professors are making judgments based on flawed student data. Professors could better assess their teaching and adjust their courses for all students if they had accurate data.

TECHNICAL STUFF

Administrative decisions are based on student performances. For example, when data shows students performing poorly, institutions make decisions to fund more academic support. Cheating diminishes revealing the support that some honest students need to succeed. Also students who cheat and earn academic honors reduce recognition of honest students such as students who honestly earn cum laude honors.

Research shows that cheating in college increases incidents of cheating in the workplace. In other words, deceiving a professor on a test translates into deceiving a colleague or customer in the workplace. Evidence shows that cheating and deceiving becomes a growing mindset of believing that wrong is right. Deception isn't only a threat to education but also to society as a whole.

Interpreting plagiarism in your syllabus

What's defined as plagiarism in one class by one professor isn't plagiarism in another class by another professor. Both professors are right, and both professors are required to clarify their guidelines in their syllabus.

Think of your syllabi (in all courses) as your professor's interpretation of your university's plagiarism policy. And like receiving a driving violation, you can't plead you didn't know the rule. If you drive, you're responsible for knowing the rules, If you're enrolled in college, you're responsible for knowing the rules.

Your syllabi in all your courses reveals professors' experiences with plagiarism and their students and how they choose to clarify possible violations. For example, if professors warn you in the syllabus about unauthorized collaboration, falsifying citations, and purchasing papers online — they're telling you they had student violations in the past and are concerned about addressing them.

Avoiding Plagiarism in Six Easy Steps

The word "plagiarism" sounds like a disease, one that can be detrimental to your academic health. Worse than that, it can be academically fatal and in some instances a violation of the law. You can avoid it like the plague and remain academically healthy by sticking to the following steps.

Step 1: Plan and organize

The number one step is also the number one reason why research papers crash and burn — and why some students make the poor choice to plagiarize. Begin major assignments the day they're introduced in class, or at least four weeks before the due date. Work on assignments regularly so that they remain in your mind. Keeping them in your working memory allows your brain to flash you ideas when you least expect them.

REMEMBER

If you're unfairly accused of plagiarism, your main defense will be your notes, so begin notetaking with planning and organizing. As you record notes and write your paper, remember this importance of notetaking.

Step 2: Cite as you search and write

Not citing sources as you write is like trusting your memory to recall assignment due dates. Your brain wasn't designed for that function. Cite sources (refer to Chapter 6) and complete reference entries as you write. Locate a reliable citation generator to expedite citing as you write (see Chapter 8).

If you delay citations and references, you risk losing source elements and some sources, resulting in some students entertaining thoughts of falsifying documentation, which is a form of plagiarism.

Step 3: Master documentation basics

If you can't document accurately, you can't avoid plagiarism. Chapter 8 explains documenting sources and shows you models in three popular documentation styles.

Start learning documentation fundamentals by creating model citations of summaries, paraphrases, and quotations. Then create citations from books, academic journals, and academic websites. Build your library of models you can plug into citations. If you don't accurately document, you may be guilty of unintentional plagiarism, explained the section "Did I inadvertently plagiarize?" later in this chapter.

Step 4: Use reliable sources

Here's a tip to fast-track your search for sources. Prioritize library databases and other library sources recommended by reference librarians. See Chapter 5 for more information on library databases.

Reliable sources eliminate the use of questionable sources that raise plagiarism questions. When professors see library sources in your paper, they mentally check off the box for excellent sources.

Step 5: Personalize models

Create a full set of templates from which you can add examples for required styles. Personalize models for all your documenting and formatting needs including a title page, table of contents, abstract, references, annotated bibliography, and so forth. A set of personalized models also shows you're proactive in preventing plagiarism.

Step 6: Dedicate a revision to documentation

Documentation is its own foreign language that you don't speak every day. It needs its own revision, a dedicated session of reviewing formatting accuracy such as the following:

>> Parenthesis located within sentence-ending punctuation

>> Inclusion of all citation elements

>> Page numbers when required

>> Citations corresponding to reference entries

>> Hanging indentations in references (works cited and bibliographies)

Avoiding the worst kinds of plagiarism

Honest and hard-working students need not fear plagiarism. But at the collegiate level, knowledge is your security to avoid incidents of plagiarism.

Here are four actions to help you avoid encounters with plagiarism of the worst kind:

>> **Study your university's plagiarism policy.** Read and reread your university's policy as you would analyze a writing assignment (see Chapter 14). Focus on examples of plagiarism because they usually represent recent infractions. Underline examples that you never imagined would be plagiarism, such as suggesting a research topic to a friend. Focus on recognizing examples of unauthorized collaboration.

>> **List unauthorized examples of collaboration for each course.** You can't survive in a high-risk environment without knowing the rules. Memorize (okay, maybe that's a tad hyperbolic) authorized and unauthorized collaboration for each course. For example, may you talk with other students about the assignment? Are you restricted to use any sources?

UNSCRUPULOUS WEBSITES AND UNSUSPECTING STUDENTS

Responsible students frequently search for online information on topics such as research paper introductions, research paper organization, academic arguments, college research strategies, and so forth. But among highly-reputable academic websites — such as Purdue OWL and writing centers at Harvard, North Carolina, Texas A&M, and Boston College — your results will yield credible information.

But some sites that appear to offer creditable information include uncreditable intentions such as links or a pop-up chat asking if you want help with your search or help writing your paper. Their intentions exceed wanting to help you; they want to sell you a paper and help you plagiarize.

They promise you the moon, but don't deliver the light of day — they deliver the potential to devastate your academic career. They guarantee you a "plagiarism proof" paper, a reference used by many students to argue they didn't plagiarize. Think about that: The company that you purchased an illegal paper from telling you that you purchased a plagiarism-free paper.

Alternatives to cheating include the following:

- Commit more time to learning the material.
- Adapt a growth mindset that success results from hard work and that people *become* smarter.
- Take advantage of the help resources available in campus.
- Believe in your ability to continue to be successful.
- Recognize that success includes setbacks and that successful legendary people overcame failure before they were successful, such as Abraham Lincoln who experienced political defeat more than a half dozen times before being elected president of the United States.

>> **Learn rules for team assignments.** Team assignments raise new concerns for plagiarism. Collaboration for individual assignments usually differs from team assignments. Clarify collaboration by asking questions in class and learn guidelines for self-plagiarism in every class. What do you do if a team member plagiarizes part of an assignment? Make sure you know your professor's collaboration rules for team assignments and ask questions at the beginning of the course. When you begin team assignments, discuss team plagiarism and the possibility of all team members being accused if one member plagiarizes.

>> **Advocate for academic honesty.** Learn your university's rules for plagiarism well enough that you can answer student questions. Let your peers know that you're an advocate for academic integrity.

How professors protect academic integrity

Academic integrity is the most valuable commodity of an academic institution and needs to be fully supported by every member of the community, especially first-line defenders such as professors.

What follows are examples of how professors prepare students to complete honest work and avoid situations conducive to considering plagiarism:

>> **Encourage planning and organizing.** Professors' staff development includes designing assignments that prevent plagiarism, offers clear directions, and reduces student frustration. Professors frequently introduce research paper assignments a month or more before the due date and provide class time for assignment questions and discussion. These planning and organizing strategies keep students on track and eliminate thoughts about dishonest work.

>> **Emphasize accurate notetaking.** Professors emphasize accurate notetaking of sources, including elements of citations, which prepare students to cite as they write their first draft. Easy access to notes and citations helps students achieve regular progress on their paper and assures them they have the knowledge and understanding to complete their papers.

>> **Focus on documentation basics.** Professors in basic-level research courses emphasize fundamentals of documenting, providing you the confidence to cite and reference basic sources such as journal articles, books, and websites. Knowledge of these skills eliminates plagiarism temptations.

>> **Ensure reliable sources.** Professors encourage the use of reliable sources — such as those found in library databases — which eliminates most source-issue problems, keeping students on track. Continuous research progress reduces student frustration and thoughts of dishonest approaches.

>> **Advocate collecting models.** Many professors encourage their students to use models of documentation formatting, which provide personalized examples to plug and play into their research papers.

REMEMBER

This chapter's introduction tells a story about a student emailing his paper to a friend in the same course who asks to see it, and the friend changes the name and submits the paper. According to the syllabus language in the second bullet, both students may be guilty of plagiarism. Obviously, the person who falsified their name and submitted the paper committed academic misbehavior. The original author participated in potentially unauthorized collaboration by agreeing to share the paper with their friend — their former friend.

Frequently Asked Questions About Plagiarism: Final Answers

You'll have as many questions about plagiarism as you do about your remaining requirements for graduation. Here's a look at frequently ask questions about plagiarism.

Is it that big of a problem?

When state supreme courts are protecting academic honesty, it's that big of a problem.

Many students underestimate the problem and consequences of plagiarism. It results in devaluing degrees earned by hard-working students. Plagiarism eliminates the "earn" from "earning a degree" and replaces it with "receive a degree."

Isn't it similar to high school plagiarism?

The difference between high school plagiarism and college plagiarism is similar to playing school as a child and going to college as an adult. College is a new level of personal responsibility. If you doubt that, look at your tuition bill.

The consequences of academic misconduct are more severe in college than high school. Have you ever heard of a high school student dismissed from school for plagiarism?

You'll also recognize the difference by the attention that plagiarism receives at the college level. Colleges have university policies, course policies, and assignment policies. And processes are in place to address allegations.

Can I be safe and cite everything?

Can you create one all-purpose username and password for every site you visit? Obviously, you can't. Neither can you *supercite* once for a page full of references. You're unlikely to be accused of plagiarism, but you may easily fail the paper because of misunderstanding citations (see Chapter 8).

You're not required to cite common knowledge (refer to Chapter 5), and you're not required to cite your own words when you interact with sources (see Chapter 7). You *are* required to cite sources (words and ideas from others) that you use in your paper as evidence to support your argument and you *are* required to cite background information on your topic.

May I plead ignorance?

You lost the right to plead ignorance for not citing sources as soon as you left middle school. Misusing sources and plagiarism aren't child's play. Colleges are allocating resources and fighting against students who cheat and devalue every graduate's degree.

The Texas Supreme Court case (see "Uncovering recent online plagiarism trends" earlier in this chapter) that revokes degrees will likely spread to other states. The court's decision is strong evidence against plagiarism. You can plead ignorance of knowing the law.

REMEMBER

With the new Texas law and similar laws in other states, students who cheat to receive their degrees live their daily lives in fear of knowing that their degrees (and most likely their employment) could be revoked any day. Think of it this way. The $150 you spend buying a paper may have been the most expensive purchase in your life.

What if I'm accused?

When it happens, many students initially generalize that everyone cheats. Everyone doesn't cheat. Research shows that almost half of students don't cheat.

TIP

If you're accused, meet with your professor as soon as possible (within days) and honestly explain what happened. Remember that your professor has already met with an administrator. If you bought a paper, explain the circumstances that lead to that poor decision. When you're finished explaining, listen and take notes. After that initial meeting you'll have many hours to prepare what to do next because you won't be getting much sleep.

Here's a look at various scenarios involving cheating.

Did I cheat?

Academic misconduct includes any type of cheating, plagiarizing, or breaking rules for an assignment. If you violated a rule, admit it and hopefully it's your first (and only!) offense.

As a first offender with no history of plagiarism, you're likely to be disciplined with a major grade deduction and recording of the offense without a suspension. It's like strike one, but with plagiarism it's two strikes and you're out of school.

Was I wrongfully accused?

If you didn't commit academic misconduct accordingly to university policy and syllabus guidelines, offer a logical explanation for the issue you're accused of. If you're suspected of plagiarism, show your notes from your research and explain how you used them in your paper.

If, for example, your professor suspects you didn't write the assignment, show the paper trail of notes that resulted in your paper. Also show drafts you revised.

Did I inadvertently plagiarize?

If you're suspected of unintentional plagiarism — meaning, for example, you neglected a citation when you integrated sources or when you engaged with a source — explain how you arrived at what you wrote and the note trail that support what you did. Inadvertent plagiarism is frequently accepted from first-year students. It's unlikely to be accepted by second-year and upper-level college students.

Chapter 4

Fulfilling Requirements: Research Papers and Portfolios

Which of the following two approaches better shows understanding of a math problem?

» Submitting an answer to a math problem — an answer without an explanation

» Submitting an explanation to solving the problem — an explanation without an answer

The second choice demonstrates thinking toward solving the problem. The process that results in an answer is more evidence of thinking than the answer itself. Similarly, a research-paper portfolio shows thinking during the research process from gathering information to submitting the final paper — the thinking that can be applied to future research papers.

This portfolio may be the first time you're required to submit one — but it won't be the last time. The principles of portfolios displaying examples of artistic achievement dates back almost a thousand years and represents a practice that continues today. And portfolios are becoming common practice, as evidence of work in courses across the curriculum and in fields such as teaching and the arts.

This chapter explains the what, why, and how of research portfolios. It discusses the advantages and challenges of them, details completing their requirements, and shows their applications to careers.

Taking a Closer Look at Portfolios

Think of research portfolios as the post-game review show — they argue and reflect how good your research paper was. If your research paper earned a good grade, reflect and credit your process for your success. If your paper didn't make the grade, beg for mercy, explain what went wrong, and explain your new and improved plan for your next paper.

Yes, it's that simple if you're reflecting on a good research paper. But if you have a problem research paper, a portfolio is another opportunity to show your knowledge as a researcher and sell your committee of readers what you learned following the research-writing process.

REMEMBER

Your portfolio assignment isn't a traditional write-a-paper assignment. It's a read-think-write assignment. It's read your research paper, think about your process for completing it, and evaluate the research skills to complete it.

TECHNICAL STUFF

The idea of portfolios dates back at least to the late 15th century when artists and craftspeople traveled with evidence of their creations that showcased their work to potential customers. Portfolios of artists at the time included art samples they would show to perspective clients in hope of securing a commission for their work.

You aren't earning a commission with your portfolio of research materials. Your objective is to earn a grade representative of your understanding of the research process. These sections explain research portfolios in greater detail.

Understanding the ins and outs of portfolios

Portfolios are like raising a vegetable garden. They need care, nurturing, and a little love. Portfolios need attention regularly throughout the semester.

The goal of your *portfolio* is to show a broad range of research skills and experiences that resulted in your research paper. Writing your research paper required completion of a series of research skills — as complex as the network of software and hardware that connects your digital watch to your digital phone.

Those research skills include the following:

>> Selecting a topic and discussing it with a research librarian

>> Developing an argument, thesis, and research questions

>> Identifying key search terms

>> Searching reliable sources

>> Preparing sources as evidence

>> Citing sources and formatting a paper

>> Writing your introduction, body, and conclusion

>> Obtaining and evaluating feedback for revising drafts

Guided by the specifics of your professor's assignment, your portfolio will include a selection of these skills to argue the success of your paper.

Identifying the advantages and challenges of portfolios

Portfolio evaluations are like making a short story long, resulting in a best-selling novel with many characters avoiding conflict. The major advantage of portfolios for students is that they provide second opportunities to argue a successful research paper.

Research portfolios include the following advantages. They

>> Offer a reflective look at the research process with the opportunity to revise and improve future papers.

>> Provide critical analysis of the research-writing process.

>> Improve understanding of the research-writing process.

>> Give practice experience for future portfolios.

>> Show student performance over a length of time compared with a one-time test.

>> Represent an authentic evaluation based on what students actually do.

>> Provide practice arguing an academic position.

>> Enter students into the conversation of evaluation.

The challenges of portfolios include the following:

>> Long-term studies haven't as yet validated the effectiveness of portfolios, but the collection process and time requirements to evaluate portfolios hinders long-term studies.

>> The effectiveness of student arguments is dependent on research process materials — and sometimes students make poor choices of materials.

>> Some students are challenged with the collection and organization of the extensive number of documents.

Assembling Your Portfolio: Completing Requirements

The two major parts of the portfolio assignment are the reflective statement and the supporting artifacts or evidence that shows your thinking. A revised draft or notes from a meeting at the writing center are examples of artifacts. The assignment usually includes options of artifacts to choose as evidence.

Think of your portfolio assignment as showing the evidence that resulted in a successful research paper. The sections that follow explain how to complete a research–portfolio assignment. I show you how to write a reflective statement, select supporting artifacts, assemble portfolio evidence, format all requirements, organize your materials for presentation, and prepare an e-portfolio if one's required.

The reflective statement

The *reflective statement* (sometimes called the *reflective letter*) explains the format, direction, and contents of the portfolio. It explains why you choose each artifact for your portfolio. The explanation of how the artifact improved your paper is reserved for the body of the portfolio that follows the reflective statement. The length of the reflective statement ranges between two and three pages.

TIP

Begin your reflective statement with an opening statement similar to this:

> After completing my research paper for Professor Zeller, I thought I was finished with research papers for the course. But when I began my reflection portfolio, I saw that this was different from any assignment I have written in the past.
>
> The portfolio was an opportunity to think about my research process, evaluate it, and explain the artifacts I chose as evidence to track my success — how cool, thinking about my thinking.
>
> The artifacts I choose were my meeting with the reference librarian (Dr. Hauser) and a research session searching library databases.
>
> This reflective statement explains why I choose to include them in my portfolio assignment.

Artifacts requirements

Portfolio assignments usually include your choices of artifacts to use as supporting evidence. Two or three pieces are commonly required from the following list:

>> **Material development:** Write a brief description tracing the development of research paper elements such as the topic, thesis, argument, research questions, introduction, and key search terms. The artifact is the description of the element.

>> **Search sessions:** Detail your strategies during a period of searching. Identify key search terms, parameters, databases searched, and results yielded. The artifact is the description of the session.

>> **Support meetings:** Describe a meeting and include your notes from a session with one of the following: a reference librarian, your professor, or writing center staff. The artifact is the description and your notes.

>> **Section drafts:** Describe how feedback resulted in a revised draft of a major section of your paper, such as the evidence section (see Chapter 6). Refer to Chapter 17 for an explanation of revising. The artifact is the draft with changes and your notes.

Portfolio content

The *portfolio reflection* document follows the reflective statement document (refer to the section "The reflective statement" earlier in this chapter). The portfolio shows the evidence that supports the success of your research process. You're explaining how each artifact contributed to the development of your paper.

Language commonly found in the portfolio content section includes the following:

» My meeting with . . . resulted in . . ., which improved my argument as follows . . .

» My revised draft included . . ., resulting in . . ., which shows the reader that . . .

» I learned the importance of using search parameters such as . . . when I changed . . . to . . ., resulting in search findings such as . . .

» Professor Zeller suggested to . . . in my conclusion, resulting in . . ., which is important to my readers because . . .

» The most valuable feedback I received was . . . from . . ., which resulted in changing ". . ." to ". . ."

» I had difficulty creating my research question, until I . . ., which resulted in changing my research question from . . . to . . .

» The portfolio assignment made me realize that . . . and improved my research writing from . . . to . . ., which is important because . . . . For example, I . . .

Tips for writing your portfolio content include the following:

» Write from the point of view of you as the writer of research.

» Reference summaries, paraphrase, and quotations from your research paper.

» Identify skills and knowledge each artifact represents.

» Explain how feedback (see Chapter 17) contributed to your success as a writer.

» Focus on the research process.

Formatting requirements

Some professors can be freaky about formatting. (You may have already learned that.) If your professor is in that category, take extra care in your formatting. Chapter 13 details formatting for all parts of a research paper. These sections identify the following requirements in your portfolio assignment.

Title page

Design a title page following the formatting principles of your documentation style. Figure 4-1 shows a title page accepted by most professors.

```
[One-inch margins on all four sides]

[Position title four double spaces from top of page, bold and center]

                        Research Paper Portfolio

[Two double spaces below the title, center your name and contact information]

                            [Student's name]
                            [Course name]
                            [Professor's name]
                            [Assignment due date]


              [Leave blank the remaining three-quarters of the page.]
                   [End this page with a hard page break.]
```

FIGURE 4-1: A sample portfolio title page.

REMEMBER

Remember that your professor's guidelines supersede those of your documentation-style guidelines and those used throughout this book.

Table of contents

A table of contents adds organization and professional appearance to your portfolio assignment — and most college assignments that exceed six pages. Your professor may not say anything about a table of contents, but add one (unless, of course, your professor says not to). See Figure 4-2 for a table of contents that most professors find acceptable.

```
                    [one-inch margins of all sides]

                          Table of Contents

Reflective statement...........................................................1

Portfolio reflection...........................................................3

    Developing materials.......................................................4

    Revisions..................................................................5

References.....................................................................6

Appendix A: Artifacts..........................................................7

Acknowledgement forms..........................................................8

           [End the contents page with a hard-page break.]
```

FIGURE 4-2: A sample table of contents.

References

If you want to exceed your professor's expectations, include a reference section (APA terminology) in your portfolio. Reference a source in your portfolio and include that source in your references.

Obviously, if you professor tells you to include a list of references, it's mandatory. Your portfolio reference formatting duplicates the reference in your research paper. See examples of references in Chapter 8.

REMEMBER

In your portfolio reference section, be sure to delete sources you don't reference in your portfolio.

Appendices

Use an appendix page for each artifact you include in your portfolio. The second appendix is labeled as Appendix B, followed by the title. Be sure to reference each appendix in your portfolio. See Chapter 16 for more information on appendices.

REMEMBER

Throughout this book I remind you to insert hard-page breaks at the end of a section and at the beginning of a major section such as the abstract, reference section, and appendix (see Chapter 16). To insert a hard page break in Microsoft Word, position the curser where you want the hard-break to occur. Go to Insert in the main menu, and then Break ⇨ Page Break. If you neglect to insert a hard-page break, you risk a reference section beginning in the middle of the page.

Presenting your portfolio

The grade of almost any complex college assignment is influenced by its organization and appearance. If your professor can't locate major requirements, you'll get burned with your grade, and it can easily be toast.

In addition to the presentation guidelines in Chapter 18, here's a list of tips for presentation:

>> Proof your title page for an aesthetic appearance and accurate spelling of key words and names such as your professor's name and the course name.

>> Review the accuracy of your table of contents page, ensuring that your content wording duplicates the wording of the heading in your paper and that the page number identifies the page where the content begins.

>> Be sure all pages are presented in the required sequences and numbered.

>> Check that any authorization forms are signed and included.

> ❯❯ Be sure you're submitting the assignment to the email address (or portal) or hard copy location identified in the assignment. Don't assume the email address is your professor's class email. Don't assume anything in higher education or in life.

Preparing an e-portfolio

A form of electronic portfolios is required in almost every university today. E-portfolios require another level of organization and presentation. They've been known to be easy assignment-napping targets for gremlins and other electronic creatures of ill repute.

Here are tips for preparing your e-portfolio:

> ❯❯ Check the digital format you're required to convert your document to, usually a PDF.

> ❯❯ Ensure that your pages are properly sequenced before the file conversion, and be sure all pages are included, such as authorization forms.

> ❯❯ Be sure to include hard page breaks to stabilize headings that should begin at the topic of a page.

> ❯❯ Perform a trial run and email the document to yourself to ensure it emails and opens upon arrival. You're responsible for an attachment that your professor can't open. Most professors will email you when it happens — but only the first time.

> ❯❯ Review the editing and formatting checklists in Chapter 18.

Reaching Portfolio Success: Step by Step

You can't reach your destination until you identify where you're headed and plan your steps to get there. Before you complete a successful research portfolio success, you need to identify your requirements and how to complete them.

You can complete the portfolio assignment the easy way or the difficult way, the stressless way or the stressful way. The stressful way includes completing all requirements the week before the due date, when you're also stressed with finals and end-of-the-semester requirements. The steps that follow explain the stressless approach to reaching portfolio success, starting early and working in small increments.

Step 1: Analyze the requirements

Portfolio success begins with understanding the assignment, identifying the deliverables (see the section, "Assembling Your Portfolio: Completing Requirements," earlier in this chapter), and establishing the time frame for completion. Analyze the assignment and begin to-do lists during the first week of the course. The early starters eliminate the stress.

Step 2: Identify any deliverables

Portfolios include choices of deliverable documents (the artifacts for your portfolio). For example, you may have a choice of submitting an analysis of a meeting with a reference librarian or analyzing a search session. Choose options you have more information on — and plan to develop them early in the course. About week three in the course, identify every deliverable and required part of your research portfolio, including the title page, table of contents, reflection letter, references, and so forth.

TIP

Separate the portfolio requirements into major tasks and minor tasks. Major tasks include writing the reflective letter, addressing the identified audience. Minor requirements include creating the title page, outlining the table of contents, and creating the reference list.

Step 3: Develop the requirements

By the third week on the course, begin notations on your artifacts, such as annotating improvements in your writing, describing successful revisions, evaluating a searching session, and recording suggestions from support people you met with (your professor, a reference librarian, or writing center staff).

Step 4: Create organizational headings

About week four, create organizational headings for your portfolio. Create your title page, outline your table of contents, and write subheadings for individual requirements such as "meetings with support people," "developing research questions," and "developing drafts."

Step 5: Outline your reflective statement

About a month before the portfolio due date, outline your reflective letter (refer to the section, "The reflective statement," earlier in this chapter). About three weeks before the due date, record any notations of content to be included in each section.

Preparing for Career Portfolios: Future Investments

A goal of most college students is converting their education into a career that offers a lifetime of financial stability. Your portfolio reflection assignment prepares you for the grown-up game of show and sell. Show your work-related accomplishments during an interview and sell your skills to a company you want to work for.

Most employers believe that past performances predict future performances, and your portfolio accomplishments in your workplace portfolio are indicators of your past accomplishment and what you can offer to an organization.

Showing and selling earns you the grade in the classroom, and the same strategy offers you an opportunity to sell your skills in the workplace. The career portfolio collection process for the workplace is similar to the one for the classroom. Assemble a career portfolio by completing the following:

>> Collecting artifacts representative of your workplace accomplishments

>> Writing a brief description of each, describing its importance to your skills as an employee

>> Organizing your materials into a manageable digital document

>> Introducing your portfolio with a one-page reflective statement, similar to your research portfolio

>> Adding a table of contents

>> Preparing it for electronic dissemination or availability

Here's a list of what to include in your workplace portfolio:

>> **Resume:** A one-page resume (for entry level) that includes a list of skills, degrees and certifications, and biographical information

>> **Letters of recommendation:** At least two current letters that have contact information (or the contact information from two people)

>> **Professional awards:** Recognitions such as high-performer award, employee-of-the-month award, and president's recognition award

>> **Work samples:** Projects spearheaded such as an employee training program, annual reports, new product rollout, and five-year projection plan

>> **Community service:** Community volunteering programs such as food bank organization, playground building, and local fundraising

>> **Technology skills:** Technology experiences such as videoconferencing, audio and video production, social media experiences, data analysis, and online customer service

Portfolio presentation skills are applicable also for entrepreneurs to showcase talents to perspective buyers.

Remember to clean up your social media. Expect prospective employers to search you before they hire you.

2

Building Essentials of Research

Address searching prerequisites by identifying an innovative topic, developing a thoughtful thesis, creating insightful research questions, and forming sub-questions from the major question.

Capitalize on your library's full services by meeting with a reference librarian, figuring out the library catalogue computer, focusing on library database sources, accessing academic search engines, and utilizing a source-management tool.

Identify sources that your professor expects by determining relevancy of publication dates, authority of the author, and relevancy of information to the topic.

Analyze academic journal articles by skimming for a sense of content, reading the abstract, identifying the argument and its implication, reviewing literature on the topic, and studying citations and references.

Build a compelling argument by clarifying the position on the topic, applying supportive evidence, addressing counter-evidence, arguing from academic disciplines, and drawing conclusions and offering insights.

Master principles of citing sources including crediting every source referenced, learning emphasis of the required documentation style, focusing on summary and paraphrase, recording a page number with quotations, coordinating reference entries for every citation, and recognizing common knowledge that doesn't need citing.

Examine major structures of organizing research writing such as synthesis that shows interrelationships of elements of a problem or process, analysis that examines parts of a problem, problem-solving that results in more solutions than problems, and persuasion that convinces readers to take action.

Chapter **5**

Managing Information: Gathering and Organizing Sources

B efore the age of mass computers, research was like locating a lucky flake in a family-size box of cereal. The research process included locating the library's one copy of the *Readers Guide to Periodical Literature*, searching your topic, recording periodical biographical information, submitting your source requests, and returning in a week to see if your requests could be fulfilled. Occasionally, an overzealous peer would irresponsibly rip out the periodical page you needed for research.

Gathering scholarly sources today lacks yesterday's drama, but not yesterday's importance. Sources may not be as significant to you as your phone and Wi-Fi, but without research skills to locate them, your academic life will crash like an over-heated device. Research skills, such as gathering and organizing sources, are as relevant to your college life as surfing and sleeping.

This chapter explains prerequisites for searching: topic selection, thesis creation, and research question formulation. It also shows you how to search and manage sources that will determine your paper's success. I offer you tips for maximizing the brain center of your college experience — the library — and also show you five steps for researching college papers.

Put on your academic game face, alert your friends you're taking a short sabbatical from social media, and commit yourself to the type of research that decreases the distance toward your college graduation goal.

Identifying What Makes a Good Topic

Let this idea live rent free in your head: As a college professor who has graded more than 10,000 research papers, I assure you the most important grade-influencing decision you make — before you write word one in draft one — is identifying the topic. Innovative topics encourage your professor to reward your initiative with a grade of B or better, and it's usually better.

Innovative or outlier topics show your audience, and your professor, that your thinking surpasses the status quo and recognizes the importance of engaging writing and interesting content. Here's a look at creative topics that professors want to see more of and are willing to reward you for:

>> Culinary trends in Shakespeare's plays: What they say about nutrition at the time

>> Nineteenth century literary characters who would blow up Twitter — and today's First Amendment implications

>> Is a "good" dictatorship better than a bad democracy?

These topics combine unexpected elements: Shakespeare themes and nutrition, literary characters and the First Amendment — and arguing against the grain (a good dictatorship).

REMEMBER

Your initial topic, research questions, and thesis are called *working* because they usually require revising during background research and early writing of the assignment.

The following sections walk you through the process of selecting your topic.

Recognizing topic elements

In addition to novel and uncommon approaches, elements of professor-pleasing topics include the following:

>> **Addresses assignment question:** Professors design research assignments to allow you broad interpretations of the topic, but not limitless approaches. Professors expect your topic to fulfill the major purpose of the assignment, usually a form of argument. Chapter 14 details analyzing the assignment and identifying the major question asked in the assignment.

>> **Connects to course content:** Connect your topic to course content by surveying your syllabus, reviewing tests, perusing notes and readings, and recalling class discussions. Identify major themes of the course and determine how one of them connects with the assignment. Professors expect a psychology research paper in a psychology course, an education research paper in an education course, and so forth.

>> **Contains a debatable issue:** Be certain that your topic has an element of disagreement. If you're arguing that government should partially repay student loans, be sure to address reasons for disagreement (refer to Chapter 7).

>> **Appeals to scholarly audience, including your professor:** Connect your topic to the scholarly audience by analyzing it through an academic discipline such as economics, health, psychology, sociology, and works of literature. Also consider integrating interests of your professor who represents that audience.

>> **Identifies with your academic interest:** Within the context of the assignment, choose a topic that will sustain your interest for three or four weeks. Consider a topic in your major field of study, a topic you want to explore, or a topic you think about and talk about.

>> **Includes available research:** An early red flag to abort your topic is lack of easily available research. If you can't locate 15 to 20 sources on your first search, and if the reference librarian can't direct you to topic sources, reboot your topic.

REMEMBER

Successful topics add new information to the body of knowledge on the subject. They may include approaches researchers neglect to consider, considerations that need to be addressed in light of new information, and data that needs further explanation.

Generating topic ideas

Topic ideas surround your everyday academic life. Here are some resources for developing your research topic:

>> **Background reading:** Read extensively and deeply on the topic. Read for who, what, when, where, how, and why. Read for ideas explained, implied, understated, and omitted. See Chapter 14 for details of background reading.

- **Your professor and other faculty:** Talk with your professor about your planned approach to the topic and ask about other professors who may be a source for your research.

- **Content from other courses:** Professors value interdisciplinary thinking. Consider topics from another course that apply to the assignment.

- **Library resources:** A walk through the library or a scroll through the library website may generate topic ideas. Note displays and special interest exhibits and consider their connection to your topic.

- **Campus and community issues:** Consider campus and community issues that may connect to the assignment such as campus resources that can address community problems.

- **Your phone's AI:** Ask your phone's artificial intelligence for a suggested topic. The answer may surprise you.

- **Social media:** Is a topic trending on social media that's academically applicable to the assignment? What topics are going viral?

TIP

Identify a working topic within hours after analyzing your assignment and completing background reading. Avoid topic paralysis that bankrupts your time-management budget. Topic indecision is the enemy of a successful assignment.

Avoiding topic pitfalls

Your goal as a student is to fulfill your professor's expectations for the assignment, which includes researching scholarly evidence to argue a thesis. Avoid topics that present unnecessary obstacles for achieving those objectives, such as the following:

- **Too intricate:** Steer clear of complex topics that exceed assignment length and increase difficulty of the assignment, such as the following:

  - Causes of declining GPAs among first-generation college students who commute and work full time, reducing available study time

  - All about AI: Uses and abuses, position in the workplace, and potential to replace college writing

- **Non-arguable:** College students thrive on defending a belief. But when a belief lacks defense, they're speechless — or wordless. Here are examples of topics that lack a logical argument:

  - Cancer is a leading cause of death worldwide and needs a cure.

  - Colleges that have large endowments offer more resources to students than colleges with smaller endowments.

>> **Values:** College students feel strongly about their personal values (honesty, authenticity, compassion, service, and so forth). But research papers and most other college assignments (except in a course that studies values and ethics) aren't the platform to defend them because they're too difficult to argue with scholarly sources. Defend your values with how you live your life and argue them in dorm-room discussions — with the door closed tightly. Here are a couple of examples of a values topic difficult to write a research paper about:

- X (fill in the name) is the most morally corrupt world leader of all time.

- The most important trait of a college president is compassion.

>> **Too technical:** Avoid topics that exceed the technical knowledge of your audience and require too much terminology to explain. For example:

- Unfair advantages of high-tech swimwear in collegiate competitive swimming

- The energy efficiency of an HVAC system is directly related to its air exchange capabilities

>> **Personal obsessions:** Avoid topics focused on personal obsessions you're passionate about, such as politics, religion, and personal health. The emotional "you" will overpower the logical "you," and your argument usually includes personal opinion rather than scholarly sources and a thesis based on logic.

WARNING

As soon as you begin accumulating information for your research project, back up files and back up your backup. Universities usually provide adequate student storage. Self-emailing represents another form of back up, in addition to an external hard drive backup. Avoid embarrassing yourself with the excuses almost all professors will decry: "I lost my files" or "My computer crashed."

Creating a Thesis Statement

Your most important sentence as an academic writer is the *thesis statement*, which states the position your paper will take and the direction it will develop. It's like system settings on your devices, controlling every function of your research. If one part of your thesis malfunctions, your research assignment is toast.

Think of the thesis like sentence ground zero. The development of every idea in the assignment flows through the thesis statement. In research writing, thesis statements are called *claim statements* because they claim or assert the argument of the paper.

Thesis statements require more thought than any other sentence you write. And when the thesis fails, the assignment fails. These sections explain the what and how of writing thesis statements and illustrate five steps for drafting a research paper thesis.

Focusing your thesis on a problem within the topic

After analyzing the assignment and background reading, identify a problem related to the topic. Here's an example on the topic of earning college degrees:

> Almost 60 percent of first-year college students neglect to graduate within six years.

The topic's problems include millions of students who fail to achieve their college dream and the financial opportunities that accompany it and drop out of college with approximately $15,000 in student-loan debt.

REMEMBER

The thesis offers a research-supported solution to the problem. When thesis statements neglect to focus on a problem, they lack reader drama and audience interest. How much interest do you have in a thesis statement such as the following?

> When large numbers of students are admitted to college, everyone is happy — parents, students, professors, and administrators.

Writing a thesis: The how-to

The thesis identifies the purpose of the research paper and references the argument the paper will defend. Here's an example of a thesis:

> The college admission process should include students' demonstrating an understanding of at least three classic books.

The sample thesis asserts that students should demonstrate critical reading skills before admission to college. The thesis argues that the almost 60 percent college attrition rate six years after enrollment is attributed to poor reading skills. It will be supported by research showing that reading is a fundamental skill for success in college.

REMEMBER

As a general rule, a thesis statement is completion of the sentence: The purpose of this research paper is to argue that . . . Here's a look at theses that complete that sentence:

>> The cost of producing electric vehicles often exceeds energy saved over lifetime operation of the vehicle.

>> Music improves the benefits of exercising.

>> Colleges bear some responsibility for the student loan crisis.

Here's a look at successful thesis statements:

>> Responsibility for the student loan crisis should be shared by borrowers and colleges, especially the college admission process.

>> Female characters in Shakespeare are representative of today's "Me Too" movement.

>> NIL (Name, Image, and Likeness) has had a positive influence on college academics.

The most common error writing thesis statements is writing sentences too narrow or too broad. Here are examples of those errors and their revisions:

Too narrow: College students' academic performance is limited by eating unhealthy snacks.

Revised: College students perform better academically when they exercise and develop good nutrition habits.

Too broad: Everyone should go to college.

Revised: Everyone qualified and motivated should attend college, but many other routes leading to career success and financial stability are available, such as the trades and entrepreneurialism.

Drafting a research paper thesis in five easy steps

Thesis statements preview the argument the research paper supports. Here are five easy-to-follow steps for writing a thesis statement for research papers:

1. Determine your topic.

After analyzing the assignment and reading background information, list the topic that interests you, which includes an argument and support by available research. (See the section "Identifying What Makes a Good Topic" earlier in this chapter.)

2. **Identify a problem.**

   Identify a major problem related to the topic that the research paper will address.

3. **Interrogate your topic.**

   Identify a variety of meanings of the problem by asking questions such as:

   - Whom or what is affected by the problem?

   - Who benefits and who doesn't?

   - So what? and What if?

   - What do the answers suggest about content needed to address the topic?

4. **Write a research question.**

   The question you write is answered by the thesis.

   Here's an example of a research question: How does NIL affect college athletes?

5. **Convert the question into a position statement.**

   A thesis statement takes an arguable position that offers a solution to the problem, such as: NIL provides college athletes with the same social media financial opportunities as non-athlete students.

Here are a few tips for writing your thesis:

>> Generate the thesis language from key terms and topics in the assignment and background reading.

>> Write using the active voice, the subject and action verb sentence pattern as I describe in Chapter 11.

>> Prefer specific nouns and active verbs common to the topic also explained in Chapter 11.

>> Eliminate unnecessary and overused words as I explain in Chapter 17.

Developing Research Questions

When I was working on my doctoral dissertation at Temple University in the 1980s, my advisor gave me this advice about writing research questions: A smart person knows the answers; an educated person knows the questions that result in answers that solve problems.

As a college student, you thrive on knowing answers. But the value of answers is dependent on addressing the right question. The body and argument of your research paper is dependent on asking the appropriate research question and sub-questions. In research, and in the workplace, questions are more important than answers.

REMEMBER

Your answer, your research paper, can't be successful unless it answers the right research question. Remember that a number of research questions can result in successful research papers. But a research project that begins with a bad question is destined for failure.

These sections explain coordinating your research questions with your writing purpose (see Chapter 19 for more information).

Fulfilling your research question purpose

Writing your research question is like completing a required course. It moves you closer to fulfilling your purpose of earning a college degree. The purpose of developing a research question includes the following:

>> Offers a starting point for research

>> Establishes keywords and concepts needed for searching

>> Focuses and identifies the purpose of your research

>> Sets boundaries for the limitations of your research

>> Identifies information needed to research your topic

Bad research questions are usually too broad or too narrow. Here's a look at bad research questions revised as good ones:

Bad question: Is NIL good or bad for college athletics?

Revised question: How does NIL affect college athletics?

Bad question: Are teenagers affected by social media?

Revised question: How do social media "likes" affect self-esteem and academic performance of high school students?

Writing successful research questions

Research questions and thesis statements are siblings sharing the same parents. Your research paper's the answer to your research question.

TIP

Write your question by formulating your thesis statement into a question. Table 5-1 shows thesis statements and research questions side-by-side.

TABLE 5-1   ## Thesis Statements and Resulting Research Questions

Thesis Statements	Major Research Questions
Regular aerobic exercise improves blood flow that increases the brain's capacity to learn.	How does exercise enrich blood flow and increase the brain's capacity to learn?
Colleges accept too little responsibility for the nearly 60 percent dropout rate.	What can colleges do to improve student retention?
Some communities across the country have been successful in reducing gun violence and offer a model for other communities.	What can communities do to reduce gun violence?

Most college research papers can be written by answering one question. But longer paper assignments frequently require answering a few additional subquestions.

The following shows a subquestion developed from a major research question:

Major Question	Subquestions
What responsibilities for the student loan crisis are attributed to the various shareholders?	Do students make the best economical decisions to finance their educations? Does the college admission process contribute to the student loan crisis? Are student loan costs reasonable for students?

REMEMBER

Captain Obvious would say: The answer to a research question is grounded in research — and your opinion isn't research.

Searching and Discovering: Sourcing Your Paper's Success

Life is about building relationships and no relationship is as important to you as your commitment to your scholarly sources that argue your thesis. That statement may be a stretch about relationships and commitment, but it's not an exaggeration about the importance of scholarly sources whose absence could result in a fallout with your GPA.

As the demands of college research assignments increase, the skills needed to locate scholarly sources also increase. The sections that follow show you how to classify sources, identify their purpose, and locate them — skills that require a commitment almost similar to the most important relationships in your life.

Identifying types of sources

Source availability is like a free meal plan that gives you access to a smorgasbord of items. But unlimited food availability can also result in overindulgence, unhealthy choices, and unknown health consequences.

Similarly, your academic source selections depend on healthy source choices that support your thesis. Thinking like a researcher means: If your mom says she loves you, you'll ask her for the scholarly citation.

REMEMBER

Sources provide an academic authority's credibility to a topic, called *scholarly source*. Your academic audience expects you to support your argument or position with the findings and validated opinions of academic experts. Without scholarly sources your argument is the unsubstantiated opinion of a scholar-in-training, sometimes an academic wannabe. A research argument without validated sources is like an unsupported opinion that your mom loves you.

Sources for academic research are classified as primary, secondary, and tertiary — similar to how you grouped your college acceptances. Each group of source serves a specific research purpose. The following three sections explain those classifications.

Primary sources

Primary sources are original creations, such as artistic performances and artifacts, from which secondary and tertiary sources are developed.

Categories of primary sources include academic creations (literature and works of art), museum collections (Roman tools and Egyptian pottery), historical documents (*Declaration of Independence* and *Magna Carta*), and artifacts (diaries and original photos). If you're writing a first-year research paper, a primary source impresses your professor. Primary sources are more commonly used in upper-level and graduate research.

Research topics dependent on primary research include the following:

>> Historical events such as 19th century presidential election campaigns

>> Art analysis such as Egyptian frescoes

>> Ancient civilizations such as Roman city planning

Most primary sources lack meaning without the interpretation of secondary sources, especially works of art.

Secondary sources

Secondary sources explain, analyze, and synthesize primary sources, such as a scholar's evaluation of a classic novel or an interpretation of ancient eating utensils found in a container. Secondary sources are the foundation of most undergraduate research papers. They're the focus of most college courses that teach research and research papers.

Examples of secondary sources commonly used in college research include the following:

>> Database collections and academic search engines (ASE)

>> Peer-reviewed journal articles

>> Books analyzing literary authors and works of literature

>> Reviews and critiques of performing arts

>> Biographies

>> Newspaper articles from credible newspapers

>> White papers (see Chapter 9)

Tertiary sources

Tertiary sources are general overviews of a topic such as specialized dictionaries, encyclopedias, handbooks, and indices. They're generally used as background, such as providing an expert's definition of a term. Use tertiary sources as garnish on research papers, never as the main course. Dependence on tertiary sources tells your professors more than you want them to know about your research effort.

Using high-yield research resources

Imagine if searching sources were as simple as searching on your phone and asking Siri or Alexa. But artificial intelligence isn't that smart — yet. The challenge of academic research remains identifying scholarly sources appropriate for your argument, then locating them, and blending them into your thesis. (Refer to the section "Creating a Thesis Statement" earlier in this chapter for more about thesis statements.)

Here I explain the riches of your college library, including reference librarians and subscriptions to premium databases. I also focus on the role of academic search engines and familiarize you with the tools to locate the sources that'll populate your thesis.

REMEMBER

The term *peer reviewed* frequently describes scholarly sources. The peer-review process includes experts in a specific field validating the content of a research article that appears in a scholarly journal. For many academic journals, peer reviewing is required before an article is accepted for publication.

Liking your college library

If you value saving time and working efficiently, cultivate a connection with your college library. If you love your library, your library will love you back and reward you with independently vetted, high-yield scholarly sources that are the foundation of five-star research grades — a relationship that duplicates the loyalty of your favorite pet.

Your library also has completed a major part of your research for scholarly sources by eliminating almost all sources your professor would disapprove (see Chapter 6). Your library contains your largest available collection of resources to help you with your research. And for your convenience, almost all resources are available to you remotely with your university login.

Connecting with reference librarians

The sentence that follows is the most important piece of research advice in this book: Meet (face-to-face) with a reference librarian at the beginning of every research project.

That's not a suggestion, it's a necessity that increases your research skills, saves you time and stress, and provides hands on experiences with your college library that will improve your research skills throughout college. Your GPA will also thank you because you'll earn better grades, using more efficient work habits, on your college research assignments.

When you meet, have your assignment with you. Reference librarians are familiar with many research assignments at your university and have most-likely helped other students with similar projects, possible your exact assignment.

REMEMBER

Many libraries designate discipline-specific reference librarians. Ask if one is available in your field of study.

Reference librarians, sometimes called research librarians, offer you their expertise on the complete collection of databases in your library and other library resources, including the following:

>> Subject-matter content in each database

>> Database filters for searching such as peer-reviewed, full-text, citation formatted, and PDF availability

>> Specialized library resources on your topic, such as museum exhibits, experts on campus, and artifacts

>> Consortiums that may have additional helpful resources on your topic

>> Tips for using academic search engines (see the section "Positioning academic search engines" later in this chapter)

Capitalizing on academic databases

The person you are today is the product of the choices you've made over your lifetime. As a college student working on a research project, you have another choice: Internet sources or library database sources. Take the choice you're paying tuition for — your library, especially the databases.

The differences between searching databases and the Internet sources — including some academic engines — is like the difference between assembling a meal and being served a gourmet meal prepared by an award-winning chef. Databases in your library are like a meal that's paid for as part of your tuition. The ingredients have been chosen by a team of experts in their field. Your results from the Internet and some academic databases are sometimes potluck. Learn to acquire a taste for databases as your go-to sources.

Databases are self-contained collections of sources of information on one or more academic disciplines. Sources are carefully vetted and designated as scholarly by a team of experts. Libraries can pay up to $50,000 for a one-year subscription to one database.

Library databases include books, academic articles, news articles, journal articles, media, and a library of other resources.

Two major classifications of databases are as follows:

>> **Bibliographic:** A description of sources using citation elements

>> **Full-text:** A downloadable source

Prefer full-text sources when available. Internet use has its role with academic search engines (ASE), as I discuss in the section "Positioning academic search engines" later in this chapter.

EYEING THE BENEFITS TO USING LIBRARY DATABASES

Here's a detailed look at the benefits of library databases:

>> **Convenient:** They're available on demand in the library or remotely with your university login. Databases are convenient research opportunities waiting for you to take advantage of. Don't disappoint them.

>> **Reliable:** Database reliability means you've nearly eliminated sources questionable, incomplete, inaccessible, and likely unrecognizable by your professor — major causes of frustration and unproductive work hours.

>> **Fully cited:** Databases ensure inclusion of all source citation elements. A team of academic experts ensure source inclusion of all bibliographical elements. In addition, many databases generate citations in popular styles including APA, MLA, and Chicago.

>> **Fully supported:** Have a question about a database source, including a question about supporting your argument? A team of library experts trained in databases is available to help you.

REMEMBER

Prioritize library databases for your research needs. Think of databases for sources as often as you think about the location of your phone and keys. And unlike your phone and keys, databases never get misplaced. They're always in your library.

FOCUSING ON THE FEATURES OF LIBRARY DATABASES

Because libraries purchase databases as part of a consortium, each library database usually includes the following high-end features that are unavailable through almost all free Internet choices:

>> Almost exclusively peer-reviewed journal articles

>> Sources selected by a team of scholar experts

>> Sources updated as new information becomes available

>> Full-search parameters such as full-text, abstract, citation, PDF, time frame, and email capability

>> Tutorials for database support

>> Librarians professionally trained to support databases

TIP

Databases can save you time, reduce your academic stress, and establish your status as a nerd. A body of research shows that students who use databases and other library resources have higher GPAs.

WARNING

Your access to the full services of databases requires connecting through your library login, either on campus or remotely. When you access through off-campus Wi-Fi, your free database features are limited and many sources hide behind paywalls.

IDENTIFYING THE DIFFERENT DATABASES

Libraries have hundreds of database choices to choose from, selections based on curriculum support and budget. Popular multidisciplinary academic databases common to many college libraries include the following:

» **Academic Search Complete:** An all-purpose multidisciplinary database, Academic Search (as it's sometimes called) includes filters or search parameters for title, author, peer reviewed, publication date, and full-text. The database includes magazines, journals, and newspapers.

» **Directory of Open Access Journals (DOAJ):** DOAJ stores sources for journals in the disciplines of the arts, humanities, technology, science, and social sciences.

» **JSTOR:** Short for Journal Storage, JSTOR is an almost three-decade-old database that stores full-text e-books and journal articles in the social sciences and humanities. It's one of the most popular databases.

» **ERIC:** The Educational Resources Information Center is the major database (sometimes called a search engine because it includes limited Internet resources) for education majors and professionals in the field. ERIC includes almost a million and a half bibliographic entries, including peer-reviewed journals, abstracts, books, conference papers, government reports, and organization policies. Searching an educational topic without ERIC is like educating yourself without reading.

» **Research Gate:** This exceptionally popular hybrid database and social network site attracts the Twitter and LinkedIn crowd by combining social networking with researching. It offers opportunities for searching information and sharing research and provides an opportunity for getting questions answered in fields such as science, psychology, writing, and computer science.

» **Web of Science:** Also known as Web of Knowledge, this database provides sources for science, social sciences, and the humanities.

» **Scopus:** This large multidisciplinary database stores more than a billion references and scholarly articles in almost every field of study. Sources generally include abstracts, citations, and full-text articles.

In addition to these multidisciplinary databases, Table 5-2 lists databases specific to academic disciplines:

TABLE 5-2   ## Databases Specific to Academic Disciplines

Discipline	Database
American history	America: History and Life: History and cultural articles related to the United States and Canada
Art	Art Full-Text: Abstracts and full-text articles related to art
Business	ABI/INFORM Collection: Includes sources on companies and business topics
Communication and mass media	Communication and Mass Media Complete: Provides sources for communications, linguistics, and mass media
Government	Congressional Research Service Reports: Government reports on a variety of topics
Health	Consumer Health Complete: Articles related to consumer healthcare
Law	Lexis Web: Go-to site for law-related topics
Medicine and biology	PubMed: Includes abstracts, summaries, and full-text in medicine and biology
News	U.S. Newstream: Stores full-text news and archives from *The New York Times* and *Wall Street Journal*
Psychology and sociology	PsycINFO: Sponsored by the American Psychological Association (APA), provides sources for psychology and sociology

Positioning academic search engines

If databases are the main dish of your source searches, think of academic search engines (ASE) as the appetizers and occasional memorable desserts. Unlike databases whose sources live in a sealed container — formerly a CD-ROM (ask your oldest available friend) — ASEs actively search the Internet for results of your search terms (refer to Table 5-3). Their strength is that they return results based on *web crawlers*, algorithms that filter and prioritize search results, sometimes using AI and frequency of cited sources.

Because academic search engines search in real time, unlike databases, the major advantage of ASEs is that they produce prime-time results for current topics such as current events, social media, law, and politics.

TABLE 5-3 — Comparisons of Databases and Academic Search Engines

Features	Library Databases	Academic Search Engines
Cost	Library databases are included with cost of tuition.	Free online version offers limited sources.
Source collection	Sources vetted by academic experts.	Sources filtered from expanse of Internet.
Citation elements	Excellent reliability, includes citation generator.	Inclusive elements and citation generator questionable.
Filters	Library versions include premium filters	Filters limited with online versions.
Timeliness	Sources current up to time of database release.	Sources current up to time of download.
Support	Available librarians are experts in your library's databases.	Librarians can help you problem-solve ASEs generally.
Reliability	Sources are almost one hundred percent reliable.	Some sources unavailable and inaccessible.

LISTING POPULAR SEARCH ENGINES

Here's a look at popular academic search engines used by college students:

>> **Google Scholar:** Google Scholar is the name recognition academic search engine for searching online and a formidable source for topics more recent than sources available in databases. Search results include articles, books, websites, and dissertations. For a deeper look into evaluating Google Scholar, flip to Chapter 6.

>> **Wolfram Alpha:** Called an *answer engine,* Wolfram Alpha responds to computational questions as well as factual questions in a variety of disciplines. It response to naturally phrased language.

>> **CORE:** This ASE offers access to more than 250 million research papers — almost all submitted to Turnitin — so don't even think about it. Check out plagiarism in Chapter 3.

>> **BASE:** BASE, which stands for Bielefeld Academic Search Engine, is a multi-mega multidisciplinary search engine that contains more than a hundred million vetted documents in a variety of disciplines including the humanities, social sciences, and natural sciences.

>> **Sematic Scholar:** This futuristic search engine is one of the first searches to introduce artificial intelligence by interpreting sematic meaning of your search phrases. Its searches exceed locating keywords and their Boolean variations. Sematic Scholar contains almost 2 million scientific papers.

- **Infotopic:** Infotopic describes itself as a "Google alternative safe search engine" of vetted multidisciplinary sources.

- **Science.gov:** Described as "a gateway to U.S. government science information," it searches databases and scientific websites. It offers full-text documents with citations and is an excellent tool for all things science.

- **CiteSeerx:** This public search engine sponsored by Penn State University stores online journals and databases in the fields of computer science and includes citation generation in popular styles.

Use discipline-specific search engines to supplement your library databases. ASEs are especially effective for topics requiring sources dated within a year.

CONSIDERING ADDITIONAL SOURCE COLLECTIONS

Collections of sources are like discovering all your favorite music at one location. Here are locations where you can find multiple sources on a similar topic:

- **Bibliographies:** When you locate sources, search for additional topic materials in the bibliography, also called reference (APA) and works cited (MLA).

- **Reviews of literature:** In addition to reviews of literature used for advanced research (see Chapter 9), they contain a focused collection of sources on a topic. Their bibliographies are a rich deposit of resources on a specific topic. Reviews of literature are also included in master's thesis and doctoral dissertations.

- **Book collections:** Hardback books on similar topics like to hang together on library shelves. When you find one book, look for similar titles nearby. Book collections online include JSTOR eBooks, eBook Central, eBook Collection, Safari Books Online, and Library E-Books.

- **General reference sources:** General references of specialized sources are listed as dictionaries, encyclopedias, indices, handbooks, guides, and so forth. Many are available in your library; others are available online.

TIP

Many online libraries offer the same scholarly resources as your college library. For example, Wiley's Online Library offers multidisciplinary resources in the fields of agriculture, architecture, economics, law and criminology, and veterinary medicine.

REMEMBER

An *index* is a subject listing of a topic such as business, science, education, and psychology. An *abstract* is a brief summary of a report or study. See the following reference sources.

Reference Sources

Dictionary of Literary Symbols	Encyclopedia of Romantic Literature	USA.gov
Dictionary of Shakespeare	Cambridge Guide to Literature in English	ReferenceDesk.org
Henderson's Dictionary of Biology	World Fact Book	The Times Index (The New York Times)
Oxford English Dictionary	Stanford Encyclopedia of Philosophy	Library of Congress

Strategic searching: Tips for better search terms

Regardless of how well you analyze your assignment, read background information, and design your thesis question, the search results you receive are the result of your keywords and other search terms.

Designing a search isn't a process you want to farm out to the lowest bidder. It's a topic to ask questions about in class and discuss with your peers.

Here are four steps for designing better searches:

1. Summarize and identify.

From your preliminary reading and analysis, identify key nouns and verbs related to the topic. (See Chapter 12 for a review of nouns and verbs.)

2. Question.

From your keywords and concepts, create additional questions you need answered.

3. Filter.

Use available filters searching databases and online, such as full-text, publication date, and citation. Use Boolean Operators such as AND and NOT, quotations for exact wording, and parenthesis to group keywords.

4. Evaluate.

After each search, evaluate results produced by your search terms. What changes in keywords could have produced more desirable results?

Researching College Papers in Five Easy Steps

You've completed the preliminaries: analyzing your assignment, selecting a topic, creating research questions, developing a thesis statement, and identifying key search terms. Let the researching begin.

Here are five steps for the core activity of your assignment — the research.

Step 1: Focus on the research question and subquestions

Your research questions are your project's GPS. It shows where you were, where you are, and what's remaining to be completed. Your questions help evaluate your progress by revealing what's completed and what remains.

Step 2: Meet with a reference librarian

As soon as you complete the assignment analysis and background research in Step 1, schedule a face-to-face meeting with a reference librarian. Prepare a one-sentence statement explaining the purpose of your research. Ask permission to audio record and take appropriate screenshots. Plan to immediately practice what you learn. Refer to the section "Connecting with reference librarians" earlier in this chapter for guidelines for meeting with a reference librarian.

Step 3: Search strategically

Begin searching with library databases. Use additional collections of sources as necessary. Concentrate on sources that provide evidence for your argument and background information. Focus on academic search engines (see the section "Positioning academic search engines" earlier in this chapter) if your topic is current. When search filters are available, use them especially for publication date and full-text.

Step 4: Categorize and process sources

Develop a collection, process, and retrieval management system as I describe in the section "Using source management tools" later in this chapter.

Step 5: Identify counter-evidence for rebuttal

Identify counterevidence for your rebuttal (see Chapter 7). Search exclusively for counterevidence by reversing searches, such as reversing "advantages of working from home" to "disadvantages of working from home."

Finessing Sources: Making Arrangements

If your desktop is wall-papered with icons from searching sources, you lack a system of organizing your research — and you're a lost icon away from an academic panic attack.

The length and complexity of research projects requires an organizational research plan. College research doesn't love you back unless you have an organizational plan for locating sources, identifying their purpose, extracting their bibliographical elements, and labeling them for retrieving.

Here I explain an organizational process for collection sources, labeling them, processing them, and storing them for retrieval — with a minimal number of folders and subfolders on your desktop.

Identifying an organization problem

You can judge your ability to organize your research sources by evaluating how well you organize other parts of your life: finances, social media, housing, and technology for example. If you misfile your research paper on your desktop, and you lack a system of retrieving it, you have an organization problem — in addition to an academic problem of locating your paper.

Academically, your courses are your major organizational challenge, which includes storing and retrieving administrative and instruction materials as well as assignments and projects in progress.

Research writing increases the challenge of organizing — but not as daunting as organizing your college class for a flash mob. Research writing also requires organization of many movable elements: sources, citations, evidence, introduction, conclusion, writing style, and citation style.

If your academic organization needs an upgrade, the following sections offer you tips for evaluating your research organization.

If you need support managing your academic affairs, help is available on campus (and online) at your writing center and academic success center. You only need to supply the initiative and effort.

Handling your research

Organizational strategies are unique to each person. Albert Einstein, for example, organized his work into piles stored on his desk and the floor. His technique was good for his science, but not for a teaching position that he was allegedly denied because of organizational deficiencies.

To ensure you aren't denied an opportunity like Einstein, stick to these steps and following this organizational process for a reasonably clean desktop and managing your research sources:

1. **Search and skim.**

   Using keywords and questions (refer to the section "Developing Research Questions" earlier in this chapter), search databases and other five-star collections of information. Skim (see Chapter 6) sources for timeliness and content relevancy.

2. **Label and cite.**

   After determining usefulness of the source, evaluate its fit into your research. Identify elements for citing and referencing in the required documentation style.

3. **Process and position.**

   Extract information from the source as summary, paraphrase, or quotation (see Chapter 6). Identify page numbers and the research paper position for each piece of information, for example background, introduction, body and conclusion.

4. **Store.**

   Use your inboxes or create folders for short-term parking. Label folders for "New Sources to Process," and after processing move them into "Sources to Retrieve."

Back up, and back up your backup.

Using source management tools

If you're successfully organizing with notecards and manilla folders, and it works for you and your grade, continue to work that way. But also take a look at new source management technologies, some of which may be available to you through your school's institutional licensing.

Features available in source management apps include the following:

>> Collect, organize, cite, store, and share sources

>> Citation generation in popular styles

>> Online storage

>> PDF and e-book highlighting, annotating, and mind-mapping

>> Mac and Windows compatibility

>> Synchronization across Mac devices

>> Google Docs compatibility

>> Accessibility from any computer

Here's a look at free or inexpensive apps to help manage your research:

>> **Mendeley:** A source organizing and sharing software, Mendeley offers citation generation and online storage.

>> **RefWorks:** A premium version of RefWorks is available on many campuses. It includes many common features.

>> **MarginNote:** A commercial version of MarginNote organizes large files, allows PDF highlighting and includes compatibility across Mac devices. It's used in many professional offices.

>> **Zotero:** Zotero gathers sources, organizes, shares, and cites in popular styles. Versions are available for Mac and Windows.

Chapter **6**

Evaluating and Preparing Sources

Your success in college has depended on problem-solving and figuring out how to navigate the academic maze. You've successfully learned to register online, interpretate syllabi, question a test grade, and land in the courses of your preferred professors.

An additional requirement for your academic success is figuring out acceptable sources to support your argument in your research paper.

In this chapter I show criteria for evaluating sources, illustrate converting sources to evidence, and explain difference-makers for earning good research grades. The only effort required on your part is turning pages and getting involved.

Figuring Out Acceptable Sources: Earning Credibility

Without good evidence, you lack a good argument (see Chapter 7). The following sections explain criteria for evaluating the sources you research and identifying the sources that please your professor. I also examine using Wikipedia as a starting point — but not as an ending point.

Evaluating sources

You can't prepare a good meal with bad ingredients, and you can't enjoy good takeout without reliable delivery. Similarly, the strength of your academic entrée, your argument, is based on quality source ingredients and reliable evidence.

The source evaluation process starts when you begin searching — and if you begin with library databases and similar sources, you're as good as getting measured for your cap and gown. Many searches expedite the source evaluation process by including filters for publication dates, peer-reviewed materials, and full-text articles.

REMEMBER

If you're using library resources, the following guidelines are a review. If you're using the open Internet or academic search engine resources, the guidelines are a necessity.

Here's a look at guidelines for evaluating sources your professors expect:

>> **Currency:** Review your assignment for professor restrictions on dates of sources. Publication dates are relevant to your topic, especially current topics. Academic search engines usually contain more current sources than databases. Age matters when selecting sources. For example, current topics (technology and current events) need current sources. Literary topics (classic literature and art) may be supported with eight-to-ten-year-old sources.

Verification of the publication date answers the question: When was the source published and does the data have relevance to the topic?

>> **Credibility:** Author credibility includes demonstrating knowledge on the topic as well as being truthful, objective, and ethical. Credible authors are usually affiliated with credible institutions. Further investigate sources you're unfamiliar with.

Author credibility also includes the author citing similar credible authors and answers the question: Does the author demonstrate the credibility that's necessary for the success of the paper?

REMEMBER

REMEMBER

REMEMBER

» **Accuracy:** Read a few paragraphs in the middle of the text and determine the accuracy of information. Ideas should appear academic, documented, and well supported.

Information accuracy answers the question: Is information accurate and presented fairly, and does it fulfill the purpose of the paper?

» **Writing:** Authors of scholarly sources should write like scholars. If they don't, question their credibility — and also question the credibility of the source because scholarly journals are professionally edited.

Validity of the author's writing style answers the question: Is the information written in a scholarly documented style that contributes to understanding ideas in the source?

ANALYZING WEBSITES AS SOURCES

Many websites lack the vetting and quality control of databases and many academic search engines. Although most criteria for evaluating sources also apply to websites, one significant criteria of evaluation remains: the eye test or appearance of the website.

Here are questions to ask to evaluate the appearance of websites:

- Is it regularly maintained and updated?

- Are links relevant and functional?

- Does it appear professional and express an academic tone (see tone in Chapter 10)?

- Does it contain an academic, noncommercial extension such as .org, .gov, or .edu?

- Does the text avoid promotion of outlier claims such as the 9-11 attack on America never occurred?

- Is ownership of the website identified and credible?

- Is information supported with cited sources and active links to those sources?

- Is information sponsored by an organization with an unbiased interest in beliefs expressed?

Studies show that students lack evaluation skills to distinguish between factual sites and fictional sites. Critically evaluate every website you search.

> » **Relevance:** Even though your source information may check all boxes, it's useless to you if it lacks relevance answering your research questions.
>
> The relevance of information answers the question: Does the information contribute to the argument of the paper?

REMEMBER

REMEMBER

If you're using library databases, almost all sources have been vetted for accuracy and credibility of information. Use database sources as models for what to expect from other sources.

Avoiding sources displeasing to professors

Evaluating sources is critical to the source selection process and to ensuring academic evidence that supports your argument.

TIP

Look at your source choices this way: You have about 12 to 15 source opportunities in a research paper to impress your professor. Why choose a nonscholarly questionable source that displeases your professor? Why chose Wikipedia when you're also likely to find a scholarly library database (refer to the next section for more about Wikipedia)?

Sources that your professors generally dislike, as much as they dislike students walking into class late during a lecture, include the following:

- » Articles from nonscholarly popular magazines
- » Definitions from general dictionaries
- » References from your textbook
- » References from some self-published books
- » Unscholarly blogs, websites, and social media
- » Information-sharing sites that include open editing
- » Biased, unethical, and nonmainstream sources

Reckoning with Wikipedia

Since its inception in 2001, Wikipedia may be the most controversial research source among professors in college classrooms. The issue is that information is edited by a community of volunteers — meaning the information lacks clear accountability. It's like not having the adult in charge in the room.

My suggestion as a professor is to use Wikipedia (and sometimes AI) as background reading and fact check information before considering it. I prefer not to see Wikipedia in a citation in a college course because it doesn't show much skill as a researcher. It requires as much effort as enjoying a sunset on Clearwater Beach.

Clarify with professors their approval or disapproval of Wikipedia. Like all matters of authority in higher education, professors' word is as final as your final course grade.

Uncovering Stones: Foundations of Evidence

You may have learned that when you're looking for the truth you should go directly to the source. But did you ever learn what to do at the source when you arrive there? The following sections show you how to convert sources into evidence and make meaning — when you get to the source.

Reading for determining evidence

Reading is not only fundamental to your education, but it's also fundamental to converting your sources into evidence.

REMEMBER

Making meaning from your sources begins with skimming for evidence to evaluate usefulness of the source. In other words, read for information that answers your research questions and supports your argument. Here are some skimming strategies you can use for initial source evaluation:

>> **Read large print.** Survey the field of material by reading the title, major headings, and pullouts. Skim supplemental sections such as abstracts and appendices. Identify headings related to your argument.

>> **Read subheadings.** Read subheadings in the middle sections that connect to your purpose and look for cited sources in subheadings related to your thesis.

>> **Get graphic.** Identify graphic organizers (bullets, numbers, letters, and steps) that connect with your purpose.

>> **Review the thesis and evidence.** Determine if the thesis and argument show a connection with your questions.

>> **Accept or reject.** If the source shows value for your research, annotate and take notes as described in the sections that follow.

READING JOURNAL ARTICLES

Recall your first day on campus, trying to locate buildings where your classes were held. But after a few days, your quickly figured out the paths and eventually the shortcuts to arrive at class on time. Reading most journal articles requires similar practice to become familiar with a unique style of reading.

Here's the point about journal articles: You read scholarly articles for the purpose of answering your research question and acquiring information you can apply to your research. You're looking for the thesis the author's arguing and the connection between the author's evidence and your argument (see Chapter 7 for argument). As you read, you're deciding on the article's value as evidence, background information, or new insights on your topic.

Preparation for reading a journal article begins with studying your research question and identifying the information you're looking for. Here's a plan for reading scholarly articles:

- **Skim the complete article.** Skim the article. Look for headings that identify major sections such as abstract, introduction, statement of the problem, review of literature, and so forth. Look for author authority and affiliation as identified in the beginning of this section. As you read, add to your list of key terms.

- **Read the abstract.** From the summary of the article in the abstract, identify the thesis, argument, and the importance of the topic.

- **Identify the audience.** Journal articles are written for the academic audience, and college undergraduates can consume most articles. But some journal articles are written for professional scholars whose reading background surpasses that of some undergraduates. If the topic is too complex and requires a technical background, give it your best effort and move to another article. Some scholars write exclusively to an audience of other professional scholars.

- **Read the conclusion.** Reading the conclusion helps you understand the argument and its implications. Look for analysis and synthesis and points you may want to support and defend in your argument. Look in the conclusion for the greater application of the topic. What does the article add to the knowledge of the topic being studied?

- **Read the introduction.** Look for background information in the introduction that adds to your understanding of the topic. Locate the thesis near the end of the introduction. Create a research question that the article answers.

- **Read the review of literature.** The review of literature may appear as a separate heading or as a text discussion in the introduction. Literature reviews represent one of your best sources for identifying new evidence to support your argument. A review of literature includes analysis and synthesis of sources (see Chapter 9).

- **Read the discussion.** The discussion (found in the body or middle section) illustrates the evidence that supports the argument. Look for evidence and sources that may apply to your research.

- **Read citations and references.** Dedicate a reading to studying citations and references. Note the authors and publications of sources and file them as potential evidence for your research.

- **Identify the argument.** Journal articles are academic arguments (check out Chapter 7). Evaluate each argument's importance and application to your research.

An additional purpose of reading journal articles is familiarizing yourself with research writing and organizational structure.

Annotating sources

Do you enjoy talking to yourself? If you do, annotating your reading is the thinking activity made for you. *Annotating*, generating questions from reading sources, improves your understanding of what you read. It also keeps you involved in your reading.

The purpose of annotating is answering the question: What does the author want me to take away from the reading? Determining the answer to that question requires the process of engaging with the text by evaluating, analyzing, prioritizing, and questioning — critical thinking skills developed by annotating.

REMEMBER

I use the term annotating in this section to describe the process of thinking about what you read. It's also a form of notetaking used in the following section to describe the process of taking notes from sources as preparation for creating evidence.

Recognizing the advantages of annotating

Annotating, recording notes about the text, generates new ideas, just as the process of creating a to-do list primes the brain to remember additional items to do.

The advantages of annotating include the following:

>> Engages you, the reader, with understanding the text

>> Creates a record of key ideas and your reactions to them

>> Prepares for analyzing and synthesizing ideas (refer to Chapter 9)

>> Focuses on a deeper understanding of sources

>> Organizes ideas for their integration into the writing

>> Identifies information needing more investigation

Annotating: The how-to

Annotating is a pen-and-paper or digital process of applying your thinking to your reading and is usually completed in the margins. Annotate by processing what you're thinking about as you read. Here are strategies for annotating:

>> Ask questions such as: Why? Why not? How? So what? and What if?

>> Circle names and terms the first time they appear and list their traits in the margin.

>> Identify ideas that compare and contrasts with other readings.

>> Paraphrase major sections (see Chapter 6).

>> Identify information that connects to course projects and discussions.

>> Highlight information needing further explanation.

Designing annotation and notetaking abbreviations

You learned early in your academic career that you can't record notes verbatim — you can't write or type at the speed of sound (of words). But you can annotate and take notes with the help of abbreviations, your own abbreviations that make meaning to you.

Table 6-1 shows examples of annotation and notetaking abbreviations used by some college students.

TABLE 6-1

Abbreviations Used by Many College Students

Abbreviation	Meaning	Abbreviation	Meaning
!	Surprisingly good	?	Needs evaluation
AP	Ask professor	Ex	Example
5-S (star)	High value	C	Needs citation
Au	Author	Qt	Quotation
Ou	Outlier idea	P	Punctuation

Notetaking from sources

Notes are your external storage for information that exceeds space in your working and short-term memory. When you think of notetaking from sources, think of preventing plagiarism (see Chapter 3). Your notetaking is the foundation of information that identifies your sources and credits used for citations and evidence.

These sections expand notetaking from sources — the why, the how-to, and the wherefor of notetaking.

Understanding the importance of notetaking

Because college students have busy academic, social, and working lives, they can't remember everything. Notes are their memory assistance device. Here are three reasons why notetaking is important to you and your research:

>> **Prompts ideas:** Notes prompt the brain into generating more ideas, similar to how beginning an essay prompts you to think of additional ideas for your essay.

>> **Processes information:** Notetaking begins the process of writing ideas in your own words, the same language that will appear in your paper. Note the emphasis on "your own words."

>> **Initiates organization:** Notetaking begins the process of assembling puzzle pieces for completing your research — because you can't assemble the puzzle without the puzzle pieces.

Taking notes: The how-to

When you identify a potential source for your paper, record biographical information for citations including page numbers, chapter titles, and names of section headings. The latter is used when page numbers are omitted from PDF documents.

REMEMBER

More importantly, write in your own words a one-sentence summary of the source and a one-sentence importance of the source. Also write a sentence identifying where you plan to use the source in your paper, such as the introduction, body, or conclusion. Language in your own words saves you time when you apply those ideas to your paper.

Source notes may appear like this:

One-sentence summary: Herman Melville's *Moby-Dick* tells the story of Ahab, captain of the *Pequod*, and his obsession to chase the whale who bit off his leg.

One-sentence importance of source: Melville represents a notable American author who uses the revenge theme.

Location in paper: Position as evidence in the body section.

Purpose in paper: Use as primary evidence to support use of the revenge theme in American Literature.

Use your research questions as guardrails for information you take from your sources. They'll keep you headed in the direction of developing your thesis.

TIP

Turning sources to evidence

You have three common choices for extracting notes and preparing them as sources. Here's a look at notetaking suggestions for each of them.

>> **Quotation notetaking:** Label quotations from sources with quotation marks and — in addition to recording elements for citations — record page numbers, chapter numbers, and names of headings and sections. The following section provides detailed information for using quotations in your paper.

When you begin taking notes from your sources, create your bibliography page (see Chapter 8) that lists all sources in your paper and appears following the conclusion of your research paper.

REMEMBER

>> **Paraphrase notetaking:** Mark off each section of information you plan to paraphrase with parenthesis and label with a capital "Pa." Remember "Pa" begins both paraphrase and parentheses.

>> **Summary notetaking:** Bracket each section of text you plan to summarize or highlighting.

After compiling your notes from your sources, complete the following:

>> Read and clarify unclear abbreviations, words, and ideas.

>> Organize notes into designated sections of your research: introduction, body, and conclusion.

>> Begin analyzing and synthesizing sources (check out Chapter 9).

Knowing your options when notetaking

Choose a notetaking organization system that works for you. Here are three common options that many college students use to organize research notetaking:

- **Index cards:** Earlier generations of students were taught to organize research with 3 x 5 (read "three by five") and 5 x 8 index cards. The smaller card (the 3 x 5 if you're not a math major) was used for elements of citations and referencing sources. The larger cards (note cards) were used for notes including quotations, paraphrases, and summaries.

- **Word processing files:** The principles of the source and note system can be applied to word processing files. A variation includes listing source elements and recording notes under it. Sources are also copied and pasted to a works cited page, reference, or bibliography.

- **Source management apps:** For students willing to upgrade to new technologies, source management apps (see Chapter 5) offer the organizational convenience of tap technology.

Converting Sources: Supporting Assertions

When I was teaching quotations and asked a student why he positioned a quote in the middle of a paragraph like it parachuted in, he replied, "The quotation speaks for itself." Quotations, paraphrases, summaries, and other pieces of evidence don't speak for themselves. Writers speak for them by giving them context — meaning that makes them relevant to the paragraphs they live in.

The sections that follow explain giving context or meaning to source references you merge into your research.

Paraphrasing

When you think paraphrase, think of speaking to another person on behalf of a source, telling the source's experiences — in your own words, not the source's exact words.

REMEMBER

Paraphrasing is a go-to tool for integrating source ideas into your text. Unlike quotations, paraphrases allow you writing flexibility to support an idea in your own words — while giving credit to the source (see Chapter 8 for citing paraphrases).

Using paraphrasing: When to

Use paraphrasing to convert sources into evidence. Utilize paraphrasing in research writing situations such as the following:

>> Referencing a paragraph or two of the source's ideas

>> Combining your ideas with the source's ideas

>> Engaging in an intellectual conversation with multiple sources

>> Introducing source positions in an analysis and synthesis (refer to the section, "Becoming Controversial: Engaging with Sources," later in this chapter)

Creating a paraphrase: The how-to

Creating a paraphrase is as simple as 1, 2, 3. Just follow these steps:

1. **Read the source you want to paraphrase from.**

2. **Put it aside and write the major ideas you want to paraphrase — in your own words.**

3. **Check that you included major ideas but avoid replacing your language with exact language of the source.**

REMEMBER

Avoid plagiarism when you paraphrase by not looking at the source when you write.

Here's an example of paraphrased evidence taken from the *Declaration of Independence*:

> **Original language:** It becomes necessary for one people to dissolve the political bonds . . . a decent respect to the opinions of mankind requires that they should declare the causes which impel them to the separation . . . unalienable rights, that among these are life, liberty, and the pursuit of happiness . . . That whenever any form of government becomes destructive to these ends, it is the right of the people to alter or abolish it . . . But when a long train of abuses and usurpations . . . it is their duty, to throw off such government, and to provide new guards for their future security.

> **Paraphrase:** Jefferson's *Declaration of Independence* identifies reasons the colonies broke away from Great Britain and the rule of George III. Causes of rebellion included excessive taxation, stationing troops in private homes, and lack of trial by jury.

Chapter 8 explains documenting paraphrases, summaries, and quotations.

Avoiding patchwriting when paraphrasing

Like any tool, paraphrasing needs to be used correctly to avoid being abused — a hammer isn't the tool to repair a pair of glasses.

WARNING

A paraphrase isn't replacing the author's words with synonyms or switching the order of the author's words. That's called *patchwriting* — and also called plagiarism. Chapter 3 explains patchwriting and other forms of plagiarism and their career-altering consequences. Patchwriting is a bad choice.

Summarizing

When you summarize you show understanding of the content you summarized — which impresses your professor. Summaries are like the "lite" version of a larger source, and they avoid the use of the exact language of the original source. Summary is a response to your friend's question: How was Professor Chein for your philosophy course? Summarize by making a long story short.

Use summaries in situations such as the following:

>> Referencing quantities of information for background, such as books, court cases, and historical events

>> Comparing books or other large pieces of writing

>> Making large bodies of information manageable to incorporate into your writing

Here's an example of a summary sentence from the *Declaration of Independence*, explaining why independence was declared:

Jefferson's *Declaration of Independence* identifies reasons why the Colonies declared independence from England and include stationing troops in private homes, increasing taxes, restricting international trade, and refusing trial by jury.

TIP

Summaries frequently begin with identification of the author and title of the source, as shown in the previous sample.

Quoting

Have you ever had an experience in a class discussion where another student prefaced a question complimenting you with words you previously said? You felt honored that someone referenced your words.

In research, referencing a quotation is the highest form of recognition you can give an authority. Using a quotation says you as the writer can't make a point better than the author's exact words.

REMEMBER

Use quotations sparingly because people who talk more are frequently listened to less. Use quotations in a research paper when the expert's words make a point clearly, concisely, and directly. Quotations should sound like a media sound bite.

Use quotations in research in situations such as the following:

>> Highlighting an authority's exact words because they're perfect for the writing purpose

>> Demonstrating an expert's authority on a topic

>> Showing the tone (Chapter 11 explains tone) appropriate for the situation

A quotation isn't an isolated act. It requires an entrance and exit to set up and follow up content. Here's an example of what a quote looks like with an entrance and exit:

> To explain why the United States declared independence from Great Britain, Jefferson wrote, "We have petitioned for redress in the most humble terms: or repeated petitions have been answered by repeated injury." Those repeated injuries lead to the first Revolutionary battles at Lexington and Concord.

The language, "To explain why . . ." sets up the quote, and "Those repeated injuries . . .," closes out the quote — like an opening and closing curtain at a play.

Chapter 12 explains quotation rules for punctuating quotations.

Using visual and statistical data

Visual and statistical data may be worth — as the saying goes — "a thousand words," but that's much too wordy for college writing. Visuals highlight information better than text. They instantly show information in the form of trends, comparisons, and contrasts. Word processing programs include user-friendly features for creating tables, figures, and graphics.

Statistics and tables are commonly used for master's and doctoral research. Figures that include photos are sometimes used in college research papers in disciplines such as business, psychology, and the sciences.

REMEMBER

Figures, tables, and other forms of visual data require labeling and referencing in the text — they don't speak for themselves — and usually require a citation (see citation uses in Chapter 8).

Check with your professor for guidelines using visuals in research, and check with your stylebook for formatting.

Becoming Controversial: Engaging with Sources

No one has the right to ask you to be controversial, such as disagreeable, contentious, and skeptical. But if you want to earn high grades with your research, taking such positions with your sources represents a required skill. And it's not called being contentious, it's called engaging with sources.

The purpose of source engagement is to demonstrate source knowledge such as the following:

» The general point of each source

» Positions in relationship to other sources

» Patterns among sources

» Writing skills integrating sources into text

The following sections explain how to engage with sources.

Author and source

Author and source engagement represents a basic form of source interaction. It shows your position with a source. Here's an example in APA:

Gibson (2023) argues that the student loan crisis was created exclusively by the rapid rise in college tuitions. I disagree with Gibson's use of "exclusively" because he underestimates the role of college admittance of unqualified students who are likely to drop out of school with unmanageable student loan debt.

The source engagement begins with Gibson's position on the student loan crisis and the signal phrase "Gibson argues." (Refer to the section, "Sending Out Signals: Phrases Identifying Source Intentions," later in this chapter for more about signals.) The student author's position of disagreement begins with the signal phrase "I disagree." The author engages in a conversation with the source.

Author, source, and source

An author and two-source conversation add a third source position — similar to a three-person conversation. It looks like this example in MLA:

> McAdams questions a government-sponsored plan to partially relieve students from student loan obligations (83). Swain agrees with McAdams personal responsibility position, but also adds that lenders share responsibility in the crisis because of "charges above average lending rates" and beginning interest charges upon load distribution (232). I understand McAdams personal responsibility belief, but Swain's position shows that student loan rates were unreasonable and contributed to unmanageable amounts to repay.

Source, source, and source

Sometimes sources talk among themselves, and you, the author, listen. Here's an example of a three-source discussion in APA:

> Johnson (2023) examined the student loan crisis and concluded that the nearly 60 percent college dropout rate, compounded by the 14 percent student loan default rate, was precipitated by the acceptance of underqualified college students. Dryson (2023) disagrees with Johnson's underqualified belief, explaining that "giving college opportunities to students" is an American principle (p. 42) Carter (2023) disagrees with Dryson's nearly open-door policy and added, "College opportunities that include high financial risks lack sound economic judgment" (p. 27).

Chapter 8 explains documenting sources.

TIP

Prepare for source engagement by fully understanding the author's position, not merely to understand a point or two to reference. A recent study of student citations showed that students pick a source point they want to discuss, without an overall understanding of the source.

Sending Out Signals: Phrases Identifying Source Intentions

Signal phrases are like road signs that help direct readers to their intended destinations. They're used in research writing to identify the owner-author of the source and show their intention to express a position.

REMEMBER

Signal phrases introduce quotes, paraphrases, summaries, analysis, and synthesis. They identify author intentions such as agreeing, disagreeing, speculating, questioning, and verifying.

The purpose of signal phrases includes the following:

>> Signal use of a source

>> Designate the student-author as the speaker

>> Clarify a position as agreeing, disagreeing, questioning, and so forth

>> Identify the need to cite a source and prevent plagiarism

>> Separate source positions from your position as student-author

Here's a look at guidelines for creating signal phrases and referencing sources:

>> **Begin the sentence with the possessive form of the author's last name, followed by the name of the source:** Zinkoff's "Is College the New Casino?"

>> **Indicate a signal phrase verb:** Zinkoff's "Is College the New Casino?" *questions . . .*

>> **Add the source reference in the form of a summary, paraphrase, and so forth:** Zinkoff's "Is College the New Casino?" *questions the addictiveness of college students' gambling.*

>> **Include the required citation:** See Chapter 8 for applying the three major citation styles.

Here are examples of signal phrase verbs:

Agrees	Disagrees	Questions	Introduces
acknowledges	contradicts	doubts	says
argues	counters	questions	speculates
confirms	argues	contests	suggests

Agrees	Disagrees	Questions	Introduces
concurs	rejects	challenges	analyzes
supports	opposes	suspects	emphasizes
endorses	disputes	cross-examines	writes

Stepping Up Search Strategies: Beyond First-Year Research

Creating topics, thesis, and research questions. Check.

Distinguishing databases and academic search engines. Check.

Learning limitations of Google Scholar. Check.

Managing research sources. Check.

With these basics of research understood, you've earned rite of passage into surveying research strategies from projects that exceed undergraduate research papers. Some of the resources that follow support some traditional research papers. They also show you research sections for advanced research projects, including certification-earning supervised research and capstone projects.

Chapter 5 shows you how to locate sources from reference collections in the research projects that follow. These sections show you how to extract organizational information from advanced research.

Extracting from higher authorities

Taking information from advanced projects is like earning the right to eat at the adult table and its upgraded food choices. Advanced research projects offer research organizational strategies infrequent to undergraduate projects but common to advanced projects.

As you progress in your college research, your requirements will include the use of advanced strategies. The sections that follow familiarize you with research headings common to reviews of literature and advanced degrees.

Reviews of literature

Reviews of literature are as common to researchers as afternoon classes are to college students. In first-year research papers, formal reviews are frequently replaced with a summary of current research on the topic. Chapter 9 details reviews of literature as an advanced assignment.

In research papers, reviews of literature are summarized and incorporated into the introduction. In advanced research reviews are integrated into the essay that's included in the introduction.

Thesis

A thesis is a major, near book length document that fulfills requirements for completion of a master's degree or certification program such as an honors thesis or senior thesis. They model to you the research project of an experienced scholar at the end of a program.

In addition to including a dedicated review of literature, a thesis also commonly includes the following formal research sections:

>> **Abstract:** A brief one-page summary of the project

>> **Introduction:** Usually including subheadings such as statement of the problem, purpose of the study, theoretical base, limitations of the study, sample size, and list of terminology

>> **Methodology:** An explanation of the research design and collection of information

>> **Analysis:** Also referred to as a *discussion,* the explanation of the importance of the information

>> **List of tables and figures:** A list of visuals that support the research

>> **Original research:** A self-designed study that collects original information

Chapter 16 further explains some of these advanced features.

Dissertations

A dissertation is a book-length degree-granting requirement for earning a PhD or EdD, called terminal degrees. Research requirements exceed those of thesis candidates and include studies completed by the best researchers in their fields of study — offering you the epitome of scholarly research.

Creating original research

Are you a problem solver, which usually requires an original solution to a complex issue? Show your creativity and innovation with original research in your research projects, such as the following.

Surveys

Consider designing a one-page, four item, forced-response survey to collect data from a random population on a topic directly related to your research. For example, if your topic argues a tuition reduction by reducing campus amenities, ask a series of questions that can be simplified in a research paper. Your professor will appreciate the initiative and creativity. Remember to check with university guidelines that may require survey approval.

Observations

Primary research also includes observations, collecting data while studying participants performing an observable action, such as studying college students' recycling patterns on campus. Observations result in a reference in your research text such as the following:

> A personal observation in my research showed that 62 percent of students within proximity of recycling containers recycled empty plastic water bottles.

Interviews

Interviews represent another method of information gathering that can easily be used in research papers. Professors on campus represent a variety of expertise on various topics, and many are honored to be interviewed and help you with your research.

Chapter **7**

Going on the Offensive: From Evidence to Argument

I f you enjoy an environment where an argument is part of everyday life, then you're in the right place, college. But it's not — usually not — the type of argument where people shout, point fingers, and type capital letters to display their disdain. In higher education participants argue intellectually, not emotionally.

Academic arguments represent an opportunity to gain new knowledge and insight. Academicians evaluate the viewpoint and evidence of their rivals. For example, opponents of forgiving student loans recognize the validity of two issues with student loans: increased tuition drives up loans and the costs of excessive loan services add to the debt. Argumentative writing is your admission into the scholarly conversation — sometimes referred to as *academic discourse*.

This chapter explains transforming evidence into argument and addressing evidence that refutes your argument. You can also find how to build a compelling argument in six easy-to-follow steps and how to avoid fallacies that discredit an argument.

Silence your devices. Get ready for an argument.

Scholars Scuffling: Analyzing Argument

In an academic-safe space where argument is indigenous to higher education, runners run, dancers dance, writers write, and scholars' scuffle.

Almost all scholarly writing and presenting is an academic argument. But think of that argument as an emotionally controlled discussion where the goal of participants is gaining knowledge, not losing face.

The ideal outcome of argument is everyone walking away with insights of new knowledge and questions of old knowledge. Disagreement strengthens an academic argument because it results in reflection and evaluation.

Academic argument is amicable, thoughtful, and enlightening. It's the language of higher education and the foundation of academic writing and speaking. Scholars thrive on argument that develops intellectual growth — it's the talk of the tower, the ivory tower of learning.

These sections explore argument and its implications.

Defining argument

An academic *argument* is evidence-based defense of a debatable position on a complex issue with serious considerations to contrary views, called the *rebuttal*. Scholars celebrate a good academic argument, and the only losers are unsupported and illogically framed positions. (See the section "Approaching Argument Logically: Busting Fallacies" later in this chapter.)

An argument isn't a debate, disagreement, discussion, consensus, or defense of a position. It's a scholarly celebration of new ideas, new revelations, and opportunities for new thinking.

Here are examples of academic arguments (Chapter 5 shows arguments in the form of thesis statements):

>> Online dating is inherently dangerous and can sometimes turn deadly.

>> YouTube content is mostly unregulated and can result in unsafe outcomes for many people.

>> Vaccines should be mandatory for children entering public schools.

>> Social media contributes to loneliness and depression in many people.

>> Academically talented students share an obligation to use their talents for the improvement of society.

REMEMBER

The noun "argument" and the verb "argue" are used academically to mean reasons and evidence in support of an idea. Academic argument lacks the vernacular meaning of exchanging ideas with anger and contempt.

Identifying parts of an argument

Classical formal arguments come dressed in a variety of clothing styles. Research paper arguments are more casually attired and can be simplified into the following major parts:

>> **Assertion:** Your claim or argument, position on the issue

>> **Evidence:** Scholarly sources that support your argument, also including counter-evidence, a position contrary to your assertion

>> **Relevance:** The importance of your topic to the academic community and its broader implications to extended audiences

Beyond major elements of argument, characteristics include the following:

>> **A debatable thesis:** See Chapter 5 for thesis development.

>> **Logical presentation of evidence:** See Chapter 6.

>> **Recognition of opposing positions:** Refer to the section "Counter-Punching: The Rebuttal" later in this chapter.

Making your argument scholarly

Your professors are well-experienced with academic argument. They practice it in their professional life as they prepare for classes, design assignments, serve on committees, write reports, research, and produce a voluminous professional document for career advancement.

As experts in scholarly argument, professors expect similar competency from you. Research shows that when professors expect more from students, students achieve more. Celebrate professors who have the highest expectations for you. They're your allies, not your adversaries.

APPLYING PRINCIPLES OF ARGUMENT TO EVERYDAY LIFE

The skills of argument extend well beyond writing and the classroom walls. Argument skills used for daily and life decisions include evaluating evidence, rebutting contrary evidence, considering implications, and assessing new information and insights created by the argument process.

Those skills are used dozens of times in daily life for reaching decisions such as the following:

- **Purchasing morning beverages:** How many ounces is too many? What are long-term health costs and financial implications? Are better choices available?

- **Ordering products online:** What's the cost of convenience? What's the cost of available options? Is the purchase a want or a need?

- **Daily traveling:** Is the travelling a convenience or necessity? What are open and hidden costs? What are travel alternatives?

Skills of argument also apply to more consequential decisions such as the following:

- **Choosing a life partner:** Does criteria for choosing friends apply? What are the assets and liabilities of the person? What issues are dealmakers and dealbreakers?

- **Choosing a field of study:** What fields of interest also generate income needed or wanted? What are uncompromisable requirements for a career? What are career restrictions such as relocating?

- **Applying for a student loan:** What are consequences of getting and not getting a student loan? What are short-term and long-term consequences? What are less expensive educational alternatives?

REMEMBER

The purpose of your argument incudes convincing your academic audience that your position is academically valid. A research paper becomes academic when it's framed through content disciplines. Here's what scholarly argument looks like supported through a selection of disciplines:

> **» Economics:** An economic argument includes business and finance concerns with answers to questions such as: How does profit and loss affect the topic? What are controlled and uncontrolled costs? How does money affect performance? What's the economic future of the topic?

» **Psychology:** A psychologically developed argument includes references to attitudes, behaviors, social pressures, customs, and motivations. Consider answers to questions such as: Is the topic based on current psychological research? How have psychological beliefs on this topic changed in recent years? What are various motivations?

» **Literature:** Literary arguments reference works of literature associated with the topic. They also include literary movements, authors, and critical evaluations. Consider answers to questions such as: How does this piece of literature compare to others of the same period? What are its assets and liabilities? Are critical evaluations of the work justified? What are themes and their extended applications?

» **History:** An argument based on history references the origin, evolution, milestones, and current news on the topic. Consider answers to questions such as: How is the topic historically significant? How does it rank among similar topics of its time period? Who are the proponents and opponents of the topic? Who are the winners and losers?

Here's an example of non-academic language that doesn't belong in argument or most types of college writing:

» Everyone's entitled to an opinion . . .

» Because that's what I think . . .

» From my experience, that's how I see it . . .

» That's what I have always been taught . . .

» Because it can't be anything else . . .

Pleasing professors with your arguments

Prior to addressing your professor's argument requirements, think of yourself as a motivated and responsible college student whose behaviors include the following:

» Attends all classes

» Prepares for classes and participates in discussions

» Completes required assignments

» Accepts responsibility for initiating self-help when necessary

The following sections explain your professor's expectations for your argument.

Connects beyond the thesis

When you think of professors' expectations for your argument, think relevance — and connecting with the following:

>> **Professor:** Connect your assignment with your professor's academic interests such as research, publications, or specialty topics. Connecting with your professor is creative and flattering and shows your broad application of the topic.

>> **Course:** Align your topic with course-related requirements such as other assignments, tests, presentations, and classroom discussions.

>> **Campus debates:** Academic arguments are as common to campus life as volunteer organizations. Consider campus topics that connect to your argument.

>> **Current events:** Consider topics argued in the national debate such as climate change and immigration and their relevance to your argument.

Fulfills expectations

What are professors looking for in your research argument? Here's a look of what they expect to see within the context of your research paper:

>> An understanding of the assignment, its value, importance, and application to the course

>> Scholarly sources transformed into evidence

>> Connections between evidence and the thesis

>> Insight on the topic that shows a broader meaning of the information discovered

>> Documentation skills in the required documentation style

Building Your Compelling Argument in Six Easy-to-Follow Steps

Building your argument is like stacking a pile of blocks, each firmly positioned step serves as the foundation of the step that follows.

REMEMBER

Arguments are the literary foundation of college academics. When you're writing a college assignment, think of the argument. When you're reading a college assignment, think of the argument.

The following steps illustrate how to build an argument that earns the grade.

Step 1: Clarify your position

Develop your argument from your topic, thesis, and background reading. Clarify your position on the topic. What exactly is your argument that fulfills the requirements of your assignment? In the introduction (see Chapter 15) explain your argument and its importance to the academic community. Explain why your audience should care about it.

REMEMBER

If you're writing a first-year research paper, a summary of research on the topic follows your thesis. If you're writing an upper-level research paper, check with your professor on guidelines for including the review. See Chapter 9 for details about writing a review of literature.

Step 2: Research the issue

After identifying your argument, search for additional background information that provides a broader foundation of its implication. Read background for information and look for answers to questions such as the following:

>> What's the history of the issue?

>> What are the assets and liabilities of the issue?

>> What are landmark events on the topic?

Chapter 5 explain research collections of concentrated sources.

Step 3: Apply your supporting evidence

Apply your evidence to support your argument in the body section of your paper. Present your evidence; explain how it supports your argument; and connect it to your thesis (Chapter 5 explains thesis development). Also see Chapter 5 for searching sources and Chapter 6 for converting sources into evidence.

Apply your evidence to argue your point similar to how you used evidence to argue the best college that meets your academic needs. Use a variety of evidence (see Chapter 6), but focus on scholarly sources you locate in your library.

Step 4: Argue academically

Your professor and the academic community expect an academic argument, which requires evidence from the academic disciplines that I explain in the section "Making your argument scholarly" earlier in this chapter. An academic argument is also supported by academic sources.

Step 5: Address counter evidence

Counter evidence adds to the complexity of your argument, as well as shows your objectivity of your position. The later section "Counter-Punching: The Rebuttal" details counter evidence and its role in your research.

Step 6: Draw conclusions and offer insights

This step earns you your scholarly wings. Explain new information and insights you're concluding as a result of your argument. Consider answers to questions such as: What's the importance of your conclusions? What are you adding to the body of information on the topic? What's the extended meaning beyond the information. How does the argument apply beyond your class, on the local, national, and international levels? Chapter 15 explains writing the conclusion for your research.

REMEMBER

In advanced research projects, the conclusion section is often labeled "Results" and "Discussion."

Counter-Punching: The Rebuttal

The *rebuttal* is like demolition that precedes renovation. Rebuttal is the issues you need to address before you remodel and build a credible argument. It shows you have a comprehensive understanding of your argument and that you can discuss the strengths and weaknesses of contrary evidence. It's full disclosure.

Like a good trial attorney, anticipate objections to your argument and research to address them. Avoid fallacies (see the next section) and avoid discrediting counter evidence when it disagrees with your argument. Argue calmly, intelligently, and unemotionally.

Also recognize the importance of respectful language when addressing he rebuttal. Chapter 10 explains language appropriate for your audience. Avoid language you wouldn't use in front of your grandparents.

TIP

If you can't locate sources that oppose your argument, your topic may lack a debatable issue. You'll most likely need an adjustment to your argument.

If you agree with a piece of counter-evidence, explain why and reaffirm your position on the argument.

Rebuttals show the following:

>> In-depth understanding of the topic that includes contrary opinions

>> Opposition to your position

>> Responsibility as a researcher

>> Knowledge of understanding the topic

Present your rebuttal with a three-part approach:

>> Identify the opposing point of view.

>> Identify your point of view.

>> Explain your disagreement, middle ground, or overall strength of your argument.

Here's an example of what a rebuttal looks like in MLA:

The review of research shows that a number of sources support interest-free and low-cost student loans for first-generation college students. Raeger argues that low-cost loans continue to perpetuate the problem of increasing tuition rates. Her point is valid, and high tuitions continue to prevent millions of students from attending college (55).

But low-cost loans will offer a college opportunity to a population of first-generation students whom research shows will result in more family members going to college because of the success modeled by the first-in-the-family to graduate (Sheetz 124).

TIP

If your preliminary research indicates stronger rebuttal sources than evidence, consider reversing your argument.

Approaching Argument Logically: Busting Fallacies

If you're unfamiliar with illogical thinking, here's an example:

Your university decides to raise tuition. They argue that raising tuition will not only increase graduation rates but will also result in graduates receiving entry-level salaries averaging $100,000.

Here's their thinking: A group of colleges in the northeast section of the country increased their annual tuition to $80,000 annually and the following year improved graduation rates and entry-level salaries of graduates.

Are you buying it? Don't. A reasonably thinking person recognizes the fallacy. The tuition increase represents a cause-and-effect fallacy. Raising tuition doesn't result in increased graduation rates and increased starting salaries.

False logic or logical fallacies represent errors in thinking that can undermine your argument, pollute your evidence, and damage your argument. It's like sand in your laptop.

Here's a list of other fallacies that, unfortunately, frequently appear in college research papers:

>> **Anecdotal evidence fallacy:** The fallacy is based on applying an anecdotal experience as evidence of a trend. For example, throughout my teaching, a number of students told me they wrote assignments out-of-doors, and nature inspired them to earn As. Enjoy nature; it may inspire you, but it's illogical to believe that nature improves your GPA. Nature will help you earn an A, if you're an A student.

>> **Authority fallacy:** The authority fallacy is thinking if a person in authority endorsed a product, it must be good. For example, if the CEO eats pizza daily, it must be healthy for you. Don't buy the thinking, but do enjoy healthy pizza.

>> **Bandwagon fallacy:** Everyone's doing it; therefore, it must be good. For example, if colleges are implementing programs to accommodate student pets on campus, it must be a good program. Research shows pets on campus help reduce stress. Unfortunately, Golden Retrievers aren't smart enough to write your papers. They'd rather eat them.

>> **Either-or fallacy:** Life and academic performance isn't an either-or choice. The fallacy is that you're eliminating all options except two. The fallacy is like saying your education after high school includes either a private college or state supported college. That thinking eliminates choices such as community colleges, the military, trade schools, or even gap-year travel.

>> **Evidence absence fallacy:** This fallacy follows the thinking that you can't think of a reason why tuition shouldn't be reduced; therefore, it should be reduced. Don't bank on it.

>> **Generalization fallacy:** The generalization fallacy takes one experience that applies to all experiences. For example, if students who swim before a math test earn an A, swimming is the solution to improved math grades.

>> **Middle-ground fallacy:** The middle-ground fallacy believes that the solution to a problem is always compromise. For example, if a college needs a new technology infrastructure, the solution is to install half this year and half when funding is available. Enjoy your swimming, but it's not a substitute for studying.

>> **Straw fallacy:** The straw fallacy is a misrepresentation of evidence — evidence as unstable as a straw building. It's like a person saying, "I believe in supporting public education," the opponent saying, "You don't believing in supporting senior citizens because you want to prioritize supporting children."

Debunking Myths about Argument

When college students socialize in an informal setting, expect to hear exaggerated stories. When inaccurate stories are repeated often enough, uninformed listeners believe they're true. But no number of inaccurate stories add up to an accurate story. The math doesn't add up, and the stories are called myths. Here's a list of myths about arguments and their myth busters.

My goal is to convince my professors of my position

Your goal isn't to convince professors of your position, but to convince them of your argument. Professors have little interest of your position on topics you write about. But you get their attention by developing your argument, supporting it with reliable sources, analyzing it, and adding new knowledge and insights to the topic.

Your professor will remember you if you write a memorable conclusion with original thinking about your argument.

I can earn good grades with a middle-of-the road approach

A middle-of-the-road position is like remaining in neutral and never making progress. This thinking conflicts with the objective of an argument, which is to take a position on an arguable issue, refute the opposition, and discuss what you learned and its implications.

Neutral positions may have worked for you in high school, but they won't earn you a passing grade in college. Go find yourself an argument.

I should argue topics I personally like

Before you chose a topic based on personal preference, address the following criteria and answer the following questions for selecting a topic:

>> Does the topic fulfill the assignment's major requirement?

>> Does the topic include an arguable academic issue?

>> Does the topic contain a body of available research?

>> Does the topic connect to course content?

>> Does the topic appeal to the interest of the academic audience?

After those prerequisites are met, choose a topic you like and one that will sustain your interest for the weeks you will be working on it.

I'll never write a research paper in my career

You're correct that you may never write a research paper after your formal education. But you will be using principles of argument in your daily life and throughout your career. See everyday applications of arguments explained at the beginning of this chapter.

The principles of argument explained in this chapter represent skills applicable to almost every decision you make in your life.

I earned a 5 on my AP Lit test: No sweat

Congratulations on your AP score. Your AP skills are impressive. But analyzing argument is another set of skills. And mastering a documentation skill to support your research requires additional skills.

The AP exam is based on reading a literature prompt and responding to a series of questions requiring you to offer a literary analysis and add your reading background. The exam measures your reading and writing skills. It's an excellent assessment of your qualifications to get you in to college.

But it's not representative of the skills you're required to demonstrate to get you out of college. The AP writing response isn't argumentative (although the AP people may argue it is), doesn't require researching and evaluating evidence, and doesn't require a rebuttal of evidence.

Your perfect 5 is an impressive score only achieved by a small percentage of test-takers. You'll do well in college, and you'll do well taking argumentative writing and research.

Chapter **8**

Citing Sources and Finalizing Recognition

Y ou learned as a college student that higher education has its rules and traditions; for example, you don't receive your class schedule until your tuition is paid, and you don't receive final grades until all requirements are fulfilled.

Your research also follows its guidelines — as determined by stylebook rules for citing and recognizing sources. During your early years of college research, you'll find that documentation rules are nonnegotiable, such as intricate punctuation in source reference entries. As you progress in your research, you'll discover that a stylebook like Chicago's more than 1,100 pages doesn't specify enough of the rules.

This chapter explains ironclad rules for crediting research sources, documenting sources, identifying what does and doesn't need citing, creating lists of sources, and annotating those sources (when you need to).

Put on your research face and let the citing begin.

Recognizing the Why of Documentation: Scholarly Way or Highway

Documentation styles, which include citing and listing sources, are like a classroom full of instructors simultaneously teaching rules. Of course, they can be confusing. But as an experienced scholar, you've learned to divide and conquer and only listen to the rules for your research, the ones that apply to your sources and documenting.

Documentation styles add consistency to your paper, a valued commodity of research writing. Lack of a style is like all writers using their own alphabet.

REMEMBER

Because learning multiple documentation styles can be like studying multiple languages simultaneously, some schools adapt a style almost exclusively throughout the university. And some professors adopt their exclusive style — sometimes in contrast to the university's style. Your favorite style is the one preferred by the professor in the course you're currently writing a paper. You may also have two favorite styles, in two different courses in the same semester.

Chapter 2 offers an overview of the three popular documentation styles. The following sections dive deeper and explain citations and references of the three popular styles.

Surveying documentation styles

Learning one documentation style is less challenging than mastering three or more at the same time. But you usually don't have choices because your university, department, or professor determine the styles assigned for your research projects.

Three popular documentation styles are common in college, and you'll be required to become proficient in at least one. You may be forced to master two. Needing to familiarize yourself with three is like getting struck by lightning three times on the same beach, but it does happen.

Here's a quick look at three well known documentation styles for college students:

>> **APA (American Psychological Association):** APA's guidebook, *Manual of the American Psychological Association*, offers documentation guidelines for psychologists, scientists, and similar professionals. Their recent 7th Edition represents an increased focus on guidelines for student papers in the

humanities. APA includes exemplary sections on writing style and respectful language.

>> **MLA (Modern Language Association):** MLA's guidebook, *MLA Handbook*, focuses on guidelines for students writing papers on literature, communications, and similar fields of study. MLA's 9th Edition includes exemplary sections on citations and works cited examples.

>> **Chicago (Turabian):** *The Chicago Manual of Style* (CMOS), 17th Edition, focuses on guidelines for book publishers, and writers and editors in the humanities and social sciences. This *For Dummies* book is published in CMOS style (but the Dummies brand does have its own style). Chicago includes the immersion of Turabian, a popular style used in high school and college in the 1950s. Exemplary sections in Chicago include manuscript preparation and language conventions.

Focusing on the similarities

Fortunately for you, these three styles share formatting similarities such as margins, spacing, and font preferences.

Here are examples of language agreements by all three styles:

>> **Serial comma:** A comma follows all items in a series, including a comma before the "and." It looks like this:

> My favorite authors are Ernest Hemingway, Walter Isaacson, Malcom Gladwell, Adam Grant, and Ray Didinger.

>> **Possessives:** An apostrophe "s" ('s) forms the possessive singular of proper nouns (see Chapter 12 for a parts of speech review). Here's a sample:

> St. James's Doghouse was damaged by an impaired driver.

Other styles prefer s' like this:

> St. James'

Here are examples of formatting disagreements of all three styles:

>> **Prepositions in titles:** APA capitalizes all prepositions in titles four words or longer:

> Realtors *With* Causes

MLA and Chicago recommend lowercase for all prepositions in titles:

Realtors *with* Causes

See title case and sentence case explained in the nearby sidebar.

>> **Names of list of sources:**

APA uses the heading reference.

MLA uses the heading works cited.

Chicago uses the heading bibliography, sometimes reference.

When annotating a list of sources (see Chapter 16) and briefly describing each source, all three styles use the heading Annotated Bibliography.

WARNING

How important are the names of these headings listing sources? They can be grade changers. When professors first survey your research paper for grading, they look at your list of sources and the heading, which reveals your knowledge of the style you're required to use.

Throughout this book, I use the terms reference (APA), works cited (MLA), and bibliography (Chicago) interchangeably.

REMEMBER

Your professor's preferences — for all style and documenting guidelines — take precedence over stylebook requirements and guidelines in this book. Your professor's word is the golden rule.

HOW PROFESSORS APPROACH DOCUMENTATION STYLES

Teaching a documentation style in college is about as popular as teaching grammar to math majors. Beyond style basics, many professors create reminder sheets of specialized citation and reference entries.

Citation rules overload professors' mental storage space because they may be required to teach, for example, APA and MLA to two different classes, use Chicago for their professional publications, and use AP (Associated Press) for a journalism student they may be supervising.

Professors also use a resource that you should use: style guides from your writing center website. (Refer to the Cheat Sheet at www.dummies.com for documentation resources available online.)

Professors emphasize plagiarism prevention and focus on citations and references for common entries (books, journal articles, websites, and social media). Study the documentation models that your professors use in class and take screenshots if necessary. Refer to the models as you write your paper.

You're expected to demonstrate accuracy with citations and reference entries of basic sources. Professors won't scrutinize details such as reference punctuation unless you demonstrate eye-catching errors.

If your professor is teaching a course that focuses on a documentation style as well as research writing, you're going to feel a higher level of documentation perfection. But you're also going to have the opportunity to learn more detail.

When you have a choice of styles, choose either APA or MLA, whichever one you feel more competent with.

Surveying Citations in Three Styles: APA, MLA, and Chicago

You may wonder why there are so many different documentation styles. Is there logic behind the differences of APA, MLA, and Chicago? And why so subtle differences as those between the author and page?

Here's the thinking:

>> **APA citations focus on author-date.** This focus was established more than a half-century ago. The organization of psychologists believed that (in addition to the author) the date of a scientific document and data is more important than the page number.

>> **MLA and Chicago citations focus on author-page.** The MLA at its inception in the 1950s believed author-page should be the focus of documentation because locating a passage in literature is more important than the date of the publication. Chicago also emphasizes page focus.

In other words, for APA citations, think author-date and for MLA and Chicago citations think author-page. The following sections take a deeper dive into the ins and outs of citations for the three documentation styles.

APA citations

APA appears to be more popular in college than high school. A number of universities are requiring almost exclusive use of APA. APA follows many style guides and requires the author-date format for citations. It looks like this:

> (Smith, 2023)

When a page number is required for a quotation, or by your professor for a paraphrase or summary, the page number follows the date and looks like this:

> (Smith, 2023, pp. 47–52)

When the citation is written in a sentence that includes the name of the researcher, it looks like this:

> Smith emphasized the importance of reading saying, "If all students in grades three through twelve doubled their reading time, the education system would save billions of dollars, remediation would be significantly reduced, and dropping out of college would almost be eliminated" (2023, p. 47).

And when the sentence lacks the name of the researcher, it looks like this:

> An expert in literacy emphasized the importance of reading saying, "If all students in grades three through twelve doubled their reading time, the education system would save billions of dollars, remediation would be almost eliminated, and dropping out of college would almost be eliminated" (Smith, 2023, p. 47).

REMEMBER

The difference between the words *required* and *recommended* is that if your professor suggests it, it's required. When following a stylebook for a class project, all rules and recommendations are requirements — unless your professor overrides them.

Your eagle-eye will note the following details about APA citation style:

- » Only the last name of the author is used.
- » The author's last name is followed by a comma.
- » The abbreviation "p." is used for page number.
- » The citation is positioned inside the period.
- » The end quotation is positioned before the parenthesis.

MLA

MLA became the documentation style de jour in the mid 1950s, replacing the cumbersome footnote style of Turabian, a style that later merged with Chicago. MLA varies from APA and includes two variations of the author and page-centered format. They differences are the following:

>> When the author's name isn't mentioned in the text, the citation looks like this:

   A recent study suggested that education could save billions of dollars if students in grades three through twelve would double their reading time (Smith 47).

>> When the author is mentioned in the text, the citation includes the page number and looks like this:

   Smith suggested that education could save billions of dollars if students in grades three through twelve would double their reading time (47).

Note the following details of MLA citations:

>> When the author and page number appear, no comma separates them.

>> When the page number appears, no reference to "page" or an abbreviation is included.

Chicago citations

Chicago is the unpopular relative among documentation styles. It's the least popular documentation style among students, especially when professors require the cumbersome notes and bibliography format. Here's a look at Chicago's two citation options:

Author page

Author page duplicates MLA's citation styles. It simply requires writing in parenthesis the author of the source, followed by the page of the source. The parenthesis is usually positioned at the end of the sentence that requires the citation. It looks like this:

   (Smith 45)

Author-page is the basis format for citing any source in Chicago style.

But you know citations can't be that easy, and the details damage grades. Delving deeper, when the citation includes a quotation, or your professor requires a page number for paraphrases and summaries, the citation looks like this:

(Smith 2023, 47)

And this is what author–date (without mentioning the author's name in the sentence) look like in a sentence:

> Another researcher emphasized the importance of reading saying, "If all students in grades three through twelve doubled their reading time, the education system would save billions of dollars, remediation would almost be eliminated, and dropping out of college would almost be eliminated" (Smith 2023, 47).

If you're a detailed person, you noticed the following:

» Only the author's last name is used.

» No comma follows the author, Smith.

» Parenthesis are positioned inside the end punction mark.

Notes and bibliography

The most unpopular variation of citations is Chicago's notes and bibliography style, also called footnote style. This style requires positioning numbers (beginning with 1) at the end of the sentence requiring the footnote.

TECHNICAL STUFF

The number in the footnote is called a superscript because it's positioned slightly above the text line. You can imagine the logistics of typing superscripts on a manual typewriter. If you can't, ask your grandparents.

Citation similarities and differences

Styles are like people, each is unique, yet all share similarities and differences.

And here's what's similar in the three common styles:

» When an author or creator's name in unavailable, the citation begins with the title. It looks like this:

> The committee's report concluded that the post-Covid workplace has forever changed ("Today's Workplace," 2023).

>> When a page number isn't available, the section of the source (Chapter 8, Section 5, Part 2, and so forth) replaces the page number. It looks like this:

> Mendez added, "The challenge of managers today is not losing the synergy of the workplace office" (Part 1).

Table 8-1 shows citation style differences.

REMEMBER

Citation forms in Table 8-1 may vary according to whether or not the author's name is referenced in the text.

TABLE 8-1   Citation Differences among Documentation Styles

Characteristic	APA	MLA	Chicago
Citation emphasis	Author-Date	Author-Page	Author-Date
Author identification	Barret, J.	Barret, Jose S.	Barret, Jose S.
Multiple authors	(Barret & Seal, 2023)	(Barret, Jose, and Tony Seal)	(Barret, Jose, and Tony Seal)
	(Barret et al., 2023)	(Barret, Jose S., et al.)	(Barret, Jose S., et al.)
Citation formatting	Author-Date:	Author-Page:	Author-Page:
	(Troy, 2023, pp. 21–40)	(Troy 2023, 21–40)	(Troy 2023, 21–40)
List of sources	References	Works Cited	Bibliography
"Page" references	p. (page), pp. (page range)	No abbreviation for "page"	No abbreviation for "page"
Punctuation reminders	Commas after author and date	No comma after author	No comma after author
Use of "and" and ampersand (&)	Use ampersand (&) with more than one author	Use "and" with more than one author	Use "and" with more than one author

Identifying What Needs Documenting: Crediting Sources

When you think source, think citation. When you think citation, think reference. And while you're thinking, focus on the detail of crediting sources according to style requirements or your professor. Remember that your professor's eye is conditioned to recognize inaccurate citations more than accurate citations.

REMEMBER

Citation accuracy begins by identifying source elements as soon as your research verifies a source for your paper. This attention to detail represents a major stress reducer and time-saver compared with scrambling to identify elements when you're recording a citation during writing and building your reference page. You'll overlook this recommendation only once. This time-saver strategy represents the best time management tip in the book.

Many college students experience documentation distress during the source-crediting process of deciding what to cite and how to cite. "What" and "how" to cite a source frequently needs a "why."

Here's a list of why sources need documenting:

>> Credit authors and works from where ideas originated.

>> Demonstrate knowledge of the worldwide standards for crediting works of others.

>> Avoid plagiarism in the form of false representation of ideas.

>> Distinguish between student-author's ideas and source's ideas.

>> Provide other scholars a trail to retrieve the sources.

The following sections identify source information that requires documenting and show you models of documenting in APA, MLA, and Chicago.

Summary and paraphrase

Summaries and paraphrases are writing tools for packing pages of information into a few sentences or a paragraph.

Both techniques require citing because you're taking ideas from a source and explaining it in your words. Here's what citing a summary and paraphrase look like in three documentation styles:

>> **Summary:** Here's a summary example in APA:

Pirillo (2023) supported research that correlated high levels of vocabulary in the home with high reading levels in the classroom (p. 142).

REMEMBER

Because the author and date are included in the sentence, only the page number is enclosed within the parenthesis. And APA requires an abbreviation for "page."

STYLE OPTIONS FOR CITATION SENTENCES

In the three popular styles, you have two choices of writing your citation sentences: narrative and parenthetical. Here's a look at them in APA style:

- **Narrative-style sentences:** The author is referenced in the text, usually at the beginning of the sentence. The author tells the narrative. It looks like this:

  Graham (2023) explains the post-pandemic workplace has resulted in a new variation of the old four-day work week (p. 105).

- **Parenthetical-style sentences:** Parenthetical-style sentences lack the name of the author in the text and include the author's name in the parenthetical citation. It looks like this:

  The post-pandemic workplace has resulted in a new variation of the old four-day work week (Graham, 2023, p. 105).

>> **Paraphrase:** Here's a paraphrase sample in MLA and Chicago:

  Ellis and Topez examine social media career dreams of middle school children who said "social media stardom" offers more money than college graduates "ever dreamed of" (160).

REMEMBER

Professors vary among their preferences of including page numbers with both summaries and paraphrases. Ask their preferences.

Quotations

Keep your options open with your life and especially with your quotations. Quotations speak in three lengths, which the following sections discuss with examples of how to cite each. Chapter 6 explains how to set up and follow up quotations.

Sentence quotations

Use full sentence quotations strategically in your research. Here's a look at a sentence quote in APA:

  "Read and ask questions. Then read some more and ask more questions," suggested a reading expert on the committee (Dillard, 2023, p. 56).

Partial quotations

Partial quotations are easier to incorporate into your text. Here's a look at a partial quotation in MLA:

> Dillard explained the simplicity of educating yourself, by encouraging students to "Read and ask questions" (56).

MLA requires the page number in parenthesis when the author's name is mentioned in the sentence.

Block quotations

Use block quotes with the care of bleach-cleaning products. Misuse causes irreparable damage, such as your professor thinking you're using block quotes to reach your word length.

Here's a look at MLA guidelines for block quotes:

» Use for quotes five lines or longer.

» Indent a half-inch from the left margin.

» Introduce with a colon.

» Credit with the page number in parenthesis if the author name is mentioned.

Here's an example in Chicago:

Jackson described public schools in America post-World War II:

> The concrete building had two distinctive entrances labeled "Boys" and "Girls." The words were carved into stone as if to say, "This is how it is, and we don't plan to change." The message was as loud as a fireworks finale on the Fourth of July. The discipline continued into the classroom where corporal punishment was a regular practice. Children who told their parents of being spanked in school were frequently also punished at home (47).

Analysis and synthesize

Chapter 6 explains these two heavyweight forms of evidence. Here's an analysis sample in Chicago:

> NIL has changed the landscape of college athletics. Student-athletes have transformed into student-athlete-entrepreneurs. "Free agent" athletes are exiting the

portal with multi-million-dollar contracts. Has pay-for-play progressed to athletes-for-hire? Has NIL compromised the "student" in student-athlete? Has the emphasis of earning an education been replaced with building an empire (Balis 72)?

Here's a synthesis sample in Chicago:

NIL has changed relationships among teammates and classmates by creating economic "haves" among superstars and "have nots" among substitutes. The difference in wealth is reflected in lifestyles on campus, and economic divergence in the classroom where "fast-food workers share intellectual space with the fast and furious (Grossman 26)."

Statistical data within source content

Statistical data — similar to quotations, specific terminology, and visuals — needs content from within their source. Occasionally, sources bias their data, and source content helps identify the bias.

Here's a Chicago example of statistical data within source context:

The EPA estimated air pollution in some western major cities at 11 percent, an improvement over the past two years (EPA 2023, 76).

Terms specific to a source or field

What makes a specific term special enough that it needs documenting? Terms specific to a field need documenting when the special meaning differs from the term's traditional meaning. Here's an example in MLA:

Hollis and Thomas studied literacy from the perspective of "literacy-deprived populations" and found a high correlation between "vocabulary depth" and reading levels (Branson 56).

The two terms in quotation marks reference a meaning in the study that differs from their traditional meaning.

Photos, Internet images, and art

Did you create it? That's the question that determines the need to document visuals you take from the internet. Documenting visuals includes a brief description and date of the source. Here's an example in APA:

The photo verified the time period ("1980-style clothing," 2023).

Legal references

Here's another professor pleaser. If you stress some brain neurons, you can almost always connect legal references with your thesis or rebuttal. Remember, the law is always on your side.

APA manual includes plain-language explaining how to cite legal references. Table 8-2 shows examples of well-known Supreme Court decisions and landmark legal documents. They appear in APA citation style.

TABLE 8-2

Citations of Landmark Legal References

Supreme Court Cases	Landmark Legislature
(*Marbury v. Madison*, 1810)	(Civil Rights Act, 1991)
(*Miranda v. Arizona*, 1966)	(Lilly Ledbetter Fair Pay Act, 2009)
(*Roe v. Wade*, 1973)	(National Defense Education Act, 1958)
(*Obergefell v. Hodges*, 2015)	(Clean Air Act Amendments, 1970)
(*Brown v. Board of Education*, 1954)	(The Americans with Disabilities Act, 1990)

Controversial information

If information contradicts common knowledge or appears illogical, cite it. Your readers need the source. Here's an example in APA:

> The 1964 Alaskan earthquake was a video presentation staged by rogue journalists (Hertz, 2023, p. 147).

Personal communications

Evidence and background information for your research frequently includes email, texts, posts, interviews, and telephone conversations. These sources are labeled as personal communications and cited as shown in the following example:

> The epidemic of betting on campus was endorsed by Dr. Brogan's email that said fantasy sports was a frequent discussion topic among students before the beginning of class (Personal communication, November 17, 2023).

Here are additional common college sources needing documentation.

Sources

electronic sources	YouTube channels	conference sessions	recorded webinars
Internet sources	dissertations	public laws	book chapters
podcasts	annual reports	anthologies	lectures
Facebook page	grants	ethical codes	press releases
book reviews	TED talks	infographics	patents
software	treaties	editorials	speeches
documentaries	artifacts	reports	TV series
tweets	apps	book reviews	public laws

No-Fault Citing? Looking Closer at Citation Generators

Citation generators are like power tools — used accurately they can provide detail, refinement, and professionalism to your work. Used incorrectly, they're the potential for destruction and a bloody mess. They're style specific and dependent on the accuracy of the information you input. The following sections identify the pros and cons of citation generators and the cautions you need to take if you plan to use them.

Identifying the pros and cons

Citation generators are populating the research landscape like pixels on growth hormones. They can save you time or cost you time. They can also cost you grade points when they generate inaccurate information or formatting. Avoid blaming the error on the citation generator — professors don't buy it.

Here's a look at the pros of citation generators:

>> Save you time and stress

>> Can build your reference list

>> Is sometimes affiliated with your documentation style

>> Is frequently affiliated with library databases

>> Is becoming more efficient and reliable, and are beginning to be developed with AI

REMEMBER

For your convenience citation generators are a standard add-on with almost every library database — another reason to like your local campus library.

And here's a look at the cons of citation generators:

>> Cost you time and stress

>> Produce inaccurate results when information is entered inaccurately

>> Require input of exact information about the source, including type (journal article, website, or podcast)

>> May result in document formatting errors when used with copy and paste

>> Need detailed proofreading of results

>> May solicit you for contracted services or premium edition payment

>> Does not always include the latest edition of your documentation style

>> Require your commitment to practice time before using.

Using a generator: Necessary cautions

Finding a reliable citation generator is like trying to find good food at a college organization meeting — food that doesn't taste free. If you decide a citation generator is the best use of your time, use it with the following cautions:

>> Inaccurate input of information produces inaccurate results.

>> Misspelling source elements produces incomplete results.

>> You're responsible for accuracy of results of information generated.

>> Your professor may not endorse your use of citation generators.

>> Be suspicious of results from unreliable generators that insist on giving you what they want, rather than what you want.

>> Information generated may not be current.

Understanding Common Knowledge

Some information is common and some is commonly uncommon. You don't need to cite the former; you do need to cite the latter.

Common knowledge is information almost every educated person can easily recall, find in a general encyclopedia, and ask AI to access for you. It doesn't require citing and includes information such as the following:

>> Abraham Lincoln was the 16th President of the United States.

>> Steve Jobs created the iPhone.

>> Majoring in English prepares students for entering into the field of business.

>> College is called higher education because it requires a higher level of studying than high school.

A unique feature of common knowledge is that readers accept the information as factual without knowledge of its origin.

But some seemingly common knowledge isn't so common. You may commonly know that the Pacific Ocean is the largest and deepest of the five oceans. But what isn't commonly known is its depth of more than 35,000 feet, a little more than six miles deep. Cite it because it's specialized statistical information that details a fact.

REMEMBER

As a general rule, cite it when you doubt it's common information. And if you have that plagiarism fear that every sentence needs a cite, schedule a therapy session with your reference librarian or the writing center.

Finding Freebies from the Public Domain

You found the cookie jar of sources — free with no obligations and it's perpetually unlocked. It's called public domain. The frequently confused phrase *public domain* refers to content that isn't protected by copyright law, meaning college students such as you are entitled to use public domain materials without obtaining permission.

That means you don't need to text Shakespeare to ask permission to reference *Hamlet*. But you continue to have the obligation to attribute the author, cite the source, and include it in your references.

Types of works designated public domain and no longer protected by copyright law (in the United States) include the following:

>> Books 70 years after the author's death

>> Books whose copyright has expired, generally older than 75 years

>> Books published before 1927

>> Works published by the U.S. government or by specific state governments

>> Plays of Shakespeare

REMEMBER

Internet materials aren't exclusively public domain and must meet the preceding criteria to be labeled as such.

Finalizing Sources: List of References

The final list of sources is like one last curtain call, a full-cast show of the stars of the performance dressed in full regalia.

The list of sources that follow presented as formal entries represent samples in the three popular styles. Use examples from here and other resources to verify the correct format for the type of source. If you prefer, use models in conjunction with a citation generator.

TALE OF TWO CAPITALIZATION STYLES

Documentation style rules frequently appear inconsistently illogical. Why can't styles reach agreements?

Here's an example look at two opposite looks to capitalization in titles:

- **Title case requires capitalizing major words in titles.** This includes parts of speech such as verbs and nouns and all words four letters or longer. Excluded from capitalization are three-letter or fewer conjunctions, prepositions, and articles (a, an, and the). The first words of titles and subtitles (following the colon) are capitalized.

    Here's an example of title case capitalization: The Great Debate: Veggies or Meat on Your Pizza

    Title case, common to APA, includes the following uses:

    - Titles of books, periodicals, and reports used in text
    - Heading levels introducing a new section of research
    - Titles of figures and tables
    - Titles of movies, plays, songs, TV shows, and works of art.
    - Titles of your papers

- **Sentence case,** common to MLA and Chicago, requires lowercase letters for most words in a title. Exceptions to lowercase include first words of titles and subtitles and proper nouns.

    Here's an example of a sentence case title: The great debate: Meat or veggies on your pizza.

    The title looks so much less appetizing in sentence case.

APA requires sentence case for titles, such as when they appear in the reference section of the paper. When they appear in the text of the paper, they are written in title case. In other words, think: Title case for titles in the text of the paper. Think sentence case for titles in the list of sources in the reference.

MLA and Chicago require title case for both titles in the text and titles in the works cited and bibliography.

APA and other styles include hundreds of variations for entries within references, works cited, and bibliographies. This section includes a small sampling. Complete listings of models are available in stylebook guides and on credible style websites.

Sample APA entries: References

Create models for entries you use regularly. The list that follows shows examples of entries for APA's references page.

Book

McAnn, C.A., & DeLancy, A.J. (2023). *Successful workplace practices in the age of technology*. National Technology Commission. https://doi.net8:1420/888806203-422.

Journal article

Davis, J.L. (2023). When the workplace leaves the workplace. *Today's Workplace Journal, 8*(21), 135-158. https://doi.edu8:1420/8888349629-422.

Blog

Kutch, A.J. (2023, April 5). When reading becomes passive. *The Reading Review Blog.* http://garnetmedia.org/blog/2023/4/when/reading/becomes/passive.

Webpage on a website

Boyer, J.K., Kipp, S. J. & Shoeman, A. S. (2023). *Engineering in the new age.* https://engineering.careers/strategies/3444/4634356/EGHD3465/.

Instagram highlight

The Center for Statistical Control [@CSC] (n.d). *When numbers don't lie.* [Highlight]. Instagram. Retrieved May 1, 2023 from https://bitly.com/33SCht/.

Here's what a typical APA reference page looks like:

Sample MLA entries: Works cited

The list that follows shows examples of entries for MLA's works cited page.

Book

Herbert, John J. *Technologies for New Ages.* New York: Carson & Co. 2023. Print.

Online journal article

St. Germain, Celia. "*Writing Levels and Success Levels.*" *Digital Digest*, vol. 8, no. 6, 2023, https://doi.org/10.00000089-568.

Blog

Rydell, Penny. "Academic Winners and Losers in Pandemic Times." *Education Review*, 16 May 2023, www.theeducationreview.org/blog2023/05/12/there view/weekly.

Encyclopedia reference

Reilly, Carol. "Viruses." *Encyclopedia of Computer Bugs.* Ed. Allan E. Olsen. Vol. 1. 2023. Print.

Newspaper

Selman, Ryan. "Fear of Writing." *Aston Times* 14 January 2023: D1. Print.

Here's what a typical works cited page looks like:

Works Cited

Herbert, John J. *Technologies for New Ages*. New York: Carson & Co. 2023. Print.

Reilly, Carol. "Viruses." *Encyclopedia of Computer Bugs*. Ed. Allan E. Olsen. Vol. 1. 2023. Print.

Rydell, Penny. "Academic Winners and Losers in Pandemic Times." *Education Review*, 16 May 2023, www.theeducationreview.org/blog2023/05/12/thereview/.Weekly.

St. Germain, Celia. *"Writing Levels and Success Levels." Digital Digest*, vol. 8, no. 6, 2023, https://doi.org/10.00000089-568.

Selman, Ryan. "Fear of Writing." *Aston Times* 14 January 2023: D1. Print.

Sample Chicago entries: Bibliography

The list that follows shows examples of entries for Chicago's bibliography page. (Some professors may prefer "reference" to "bibliography.")

Book

Jennings, Carlie. *It Started Without a Cause*. Philadelphia: J.J. Curtis & Co., 2023. Print.

Book chapter

Jordan, John Paul. "Travels on a Timeframe." *In Here, There, and Everywhere*, 58–73. Tampa: Clear Press, 2023.

Journal article

Gray, G.W. "Working with our Working Memory." *Journal of Neuroscience* 85, no. 2 (2022): 138–157.

Newspaper article

Owen, J.K. "Sports' Life Lessons," *Today's Student Athlete*, November 18, 2022, sec. D.

Website

Brown, Erin. "Exploring Errors in Quadratic Equations." *Math Matters Blog.* https://mathmattersblog.com/2023/03exploring-errors-in-quadratic-equations-2023.html.

Here's what a typical bibliography page looks like:

Bibliography

Brown, Erin. "Exploring Errors in Quadratic Equations." *Math Matters Blog.* https://mathmattersblog.com/2023/03exploring-errors-in-quadratic-equations-2023.html.

Gray, G.W. "Working with our Working Memory." *Journal of Neuroscience* 85, no. 2 (2022): 138-157.

Jordan, John Paul. "Travels on a Timeframe." *In Here, There, and Everywhere*, 58-73. Tampa: Clear Press, 2023.

Annotating bibliographies

Every time I assign a research paper, I require an *annotated bibliography*, a short paragraph following the source evaluating the use of the source in the research. The annotation requires understanding the source, also important for converting sources into evidence and supporting the thesis.

The following sections explain variations of annotated bibliographies that some professors may assign and show how the assignments are formatted.

Recognizing the variations of annotated bibliographies

An annotation is usually a three-to-five-sentence paragraph. Variations for annotated bibliographies include the following:

>> **Descriptive:** Describes each source with a short summary of arguments and ideas

>> **Evaluative:** Evaluates the strength of each source and the value as supporting evidence

>> **Relevancy:** Identifies the contribution of each source as evidence supporting the argument

Formatting annotated bibliographies

Professors usually identify the formatting required for annotated bibliographies. Formatting usually includes single-spaced paragraphs positioned under the source. Here's an example in APA:

Brogan, J., & Daniels, T. (2023). *Capitalizing on a science and accounting major.* (2nd ed.) STJPress. https://doi.org/10.171000000056-084.

Brogan and Daniels examine advantages of a dual major in the sciences and accounting. They highlight the hands-on approach and attention to detail required in both fields. They predict an increase in dual majors in seemingly incongruous fields of study, such as science and accounting.

FAQs about Citing

Learning a documentation style is an ongoing process from first-year of college to last year of grad school. Here are some questions that students think about — and my answers — that students usually don't ask in class.

Do professors look up every source?

As a general rule, no. Professors prefer reading your research paper to checking your sources. But give them a reason and they'll explore your sources like a computer virus through a porous firewall. You encourage professors to search your sources when you write any of the following:

- » A direct quotation without a citation
- » An incorrect heading for the list of sources: Reference, Works Cited, and Bibliography
- » An awkward appearing citation
- » A full page of text without a citation
- » Statistical information or special terminology without a citation
- » Names of researchers and studies that lack a citation
- » Citations without references and references without citations

Can't I just "supercite?"

Just as no super-password exists, no "supercite" citation exists. You can't indiscriminately use a citation at the end of a long paragraph or page and assume it identifies some source, somewhere on the page.

Here's your college lesson for the day:

>> No lifetime pizza passes

>> No all-world ski lift passes

>> No college homework passes

>> And no supercite citations

How do I know if I have a plagiarism-police professor?

Professors don't search for plagiarism violators. They trust their students and are motivated to help them succeed. But when plagiarism comes to them in the form of a paper that shows warning signs, they fulfill their obligation to investigate it. And they have a university full of resources to help them.

Similar to looking up sources, professors don't suspect plagiarism unless you give them a reason to investigate it in your paper. Professors are always aware of plagiarism because they have a professional obligation to defend academic integrity. Professors are required to follow a process if they suspect plagiarism that usually begins with sharing their suspicions with their department chair.

If plagiarism is a major theme in your course (see Chapter 3), your professor is more likely to be very conscious of it when reading papers.

How do I start learning a documentation style?

Learning a documentation style is like learning a new language. It requires full immersion and regular use.

Here are tips to help you get started:

>> Begin with learning the style you'll be writing your first college research paper with.

- » Read journal articles in the style you're learning. You can recognize the style by the name of the sources at the end of the paper: APA (References), MLA (Works Cited), and Chicago (Bibliography).

- » Ask nerd friends for a copy of their A papers in the style you're learning and study their use of citations and formatting.

- » Learn basic citation entries (books, journal articles, websites, and social media).

- » Collect formatting models for the title page, text pages, and references.

- » Search for comparison charts of popular models.

- » Download documentation samples of the latest edition at a creditable website.

- » If you're using APA, check out my book *APA Styles & Citations For Dummies* for a companion guide.

REMEMBER

Teaching is also learning, If you explain citing and referencing sources to a group of your peers, you'll also increase your understanding of the process.

Do professors scrutinize reference errors in punctuation, italics, and formatting?

Remember that professors glance at your references when they begin the grading process. References tell them the format of setting up your reference page and the variety and quality of your sources. They're mentally checking boxes for general appearance and sources expected to appear on your topic.

If your references don't pass the eye test, they delve deeper — and examine punctuation, italics, formatting, and so forth. When they identify patterns of errors, your paper has a problem and your grade is grasping for survival.

To avoid professor scrutiny, complete the following:

- » Perfect the appearance of your references in the required style.

- » Use a variety of reliable and credible sources.

- » Review the format for entering each type of source.

- » Use a model source to duplicate the punctuation and spacing of each entry.

- » Have your sources proofread by the writing center.

Chapter 9

Classifying College Research Writing

Have you ever made plans, prepared to go out, had to cancel your plans, and ended up being disappointed? This chapter isn't like that.

This chapter is like being dressed up and having a place to go — to celebrate something. It's about owning the tools for research and finding a way to use them. And deciding which of the tools you want to use first: structures that can produce heavy-duty thinking or forms that can carry heavy research loads. This chapter shows you how to utilize your research writing skills and use them in a variety of courses.

Here I discuss forms and structures that make research writing adaptable for multi-purposes across the curriculum. I also explain research projects common to upper-levels of college and what to do if you need a proposal.

Identifying Research Categories: Assignment Structures

Research writing has the adaptability of a remote control. After you program it in your head, you can explore the world with one hand.

These sections show you the varied power of research structured to meet the needs of your assignments. You can see traditional structures for traditional assignments (persuasive, compare and contrast, and expository) and the structures that generate your brain's superpowers (analysis and synthesis, problem solving, and cause and effect).

Refresh your batteries in your remote, dig in, and score some points. These following sections explain writing structures frequently assigned by professors as research projects.

Analysis and synthesis: Difference makers

What do summa cum laude students do that non-cum laude students don't do? In addition to reading profusely and attacking assignments, they analyze and synthesize sources — two thinking skills that hang out in the cerebrum, your brain's prime intellectual real estate. Analysis and synthesis are such strong academic language that merely speaking the words in class impresses professors.

REMEMBER

Synthesis is usually reserved for assignments after students gain a few years' college experience. For example, the review of literature in major research requires a synthesis of sources. It's one of the most challenging assignments for college students.

Here's an example of a topic that can be structured as analysis or synthesis:

> Synthesize a plan for the post-Covid workplace that includes working remotely and working in an office setting.

Analysis and synthesis are two difference-makers for converting sources into evidence and improving your research grade. The mere use of the words in your writing alerts your professor that your thinking is on fire.

Analysis

Analysis is the critical examination of sources. It includes identifying the importance of information and its influence on other sources. It interprets information and reveals complications of the argument.

The process of analysis includes separating sources into smaller parts and connecting those parts to the thesis. When you analyze, you're evaluating the effectiveness of the author's sources that support the argument.

Analyzing makes meaning from evidence and is an integral part of the conclusion of your research — in addition to being used in the evidence section. It gives context to evidence.

REMEMBER

Analysis differs from paraphrase and summary by interpreting information, drawing conclusions, and discussing the significance of information. Description in paraphrase and summary isn't analysis.

Here are guidelines for writing an analysis:

>> Introduce the author, evidence, and source.

>> Summarize the evidence.

>> Explain the parts of the evidence.

>> Evaluate the importance of the evidence.

>> Explain the relevance of the evidence to the thesis.

Here's an example in Chicago of an analysis as an evaluation of admissions into college.

Almost 60 percent of students entering college neglect to earn their degrees six years after admission (Overton 87). Those appalling percentages represent not only those who leave college with shattered dreams, but also leave with an average student loan debt of $14,000. By 2020, almost 40 million Americans had some college experience but lacked degrees. The male dropout rate is slightly higher than the female rate (Collins 20).

Who's responsible for the academic and financial failures? The goal of achieving college admission begins decades before senior year in high school. Preparing for college requires working hard (an American value) to achieve the dream.

Future college students need to master literary skills needed for reading and writing. The process requires at least ten years, from third grade to twelfth grade — reading daily and writing regularly, completing homework, creating projects, researching, asking questions, and becoming educated.

Given that preparation, college is not for everyone. The trades offer successful careers for interested and motivated young adults. And they also offer entrepreneurial opportunities for those interested in building a business empire. Finland, for example, one of the top countries in the world with successful public education programs, introduces the trades into their curriculum as young as second grade.

Colleges accept too many underqualified students who lack the literacy skills to perform college-level work (Galen 54). America is the land of opportunity, but opportunities require working hard. Marginal students should be required to demonstrate college-level literacy in pre-college admission programs or in community colleges. Some underqualified college candidates should consider the trades — which need the same respect as a college degree (Schumer 78).

And why do females graduate at a higher rate than males? A number of researchers show females outperforming males at a number of grade levels. Can we conclude females show more commitment to schoolwork than males?

Synthesis

Analysis is like a fruit salad; synthesis is like a fruit smoothie blending a variety of fruit tastes into one distinctive flavor, without any one fruit overpowering the taste. *Synthesis* requires blending and interactive engagement of multiple sources.

REMEMBER

Among skills that convert sources into evidence, synthesis is like the older sibling with the Ivy League degree. It's the process of drawing insight from analysis. In other words, after identifying patterns among sources — agreement, disagreement, speculation, additional ideas, absence of ideas — synthesis makes meaning.

The purpose of synthesis is to combine all information about sources — not merely summarizing, paraphrasing, and quoting — and adding your insights. To create source synthesis, follow these five steps:

1. Separate patterns of analysis among sources.

Categorize sources such as the following: Agreement, disagreement, questioning, adding new information, avoiding information, and standing apart as an outlier.

2. Write a topic sentence or two that identifies the purpose of all sources.

Here's an example:

College students have been betting on sports since Rutgers hosted its neighbor Princeton in 1869. But handshake bets recently developed into highly sophisticated in-game betting apps that research is showing cause peer pressure to bet, mental depression and social isolation, and rapid declines in the purpose students attend college — academics.

3. Determine an organizational approach.

Identify a structure for writing the synthesis paragraphs, such as the following:

- **Thematically:** For example, betting apps, mental health issues, peer pressures, gambling addictions, or advertising exposure

- **Chronologically:** For example, development of apps, development of sports betting, or increasing trends in college gambling

- **Source authors:** Each author's individual approach to the topic

4. Draw meaning.

After reading what your sources say, formulate a "so what?" Here's an example in MLA:

Sports betting and gambling addiction may be a contributor to growing college dropout rates. Brown, Rivera, and Chen found that gambling hours, including obsessively watching games they're betting on, results in "mental obsession" during alone study time, which distracts students from study concentration. The effect of sports betting on the dropout rate may be underestimated, and the topic needs to be addressed (Williams 202).

5. Write.

Draft sentences and paragraphs with citing, following the step sequences.

Problem-solving

The world has an excess of problem-creators and a shortage of problem-solvers — that's the importance of perfecting skills of problem-solving. Good problem-solvers offer essential skills for any organization. Great problem-solvers are commonly entrepreneurs and industry leaders.

REMEMBER

Problem-solving is similar to developing research questions — if you don't ask the right question, your results will be the wrong answer. If you first don't identify the problem, you're not going to reach the solution. Solutions that don't match problems are as useless as trying to show a Golden Retriever how to enjoy water.

The following outline shows you how to structure problem-solving research writing:

» **Introduction:** Identify the problem, including a description of what sources say about it and its implication. Answer question such as:

- What does research say about its importance?

- Why is a solution necessary and why now?

- How does the problem align with the argument?

End the introduction with the thesis statement.

>> **Body:** Describe evidence that supports the problem. Refute evidence that contradicts the problem. Answer questions such as:

- What's the history of the problem?
- Who and what has been affected by the problem and to what extent?
- What solutions have experts suggested?

End the body section with an analysis of solutions to the problem.

>> **Conclusion:** Argue a solution to the problem. Answer questions such as:

- What is the importance of the solution?
- What did the research add to the discussion of the topic?
- What is the implication of the solution beyond the classroom?

Here are some topics that include multiple problems; challenge yourself to name a dozen problems related to a topic:

Topics

fair and equitable taxation	student load debt	worldwide hunger	sustainable middle-class employment
immigration	mass shootings	online dating	online bullying
mental illness and high school students	housing shortages	college plagiarism	low-cost sustainable housing
student disengagement	teacher frustration	academic-athletic balance	work-life balance
voter disenfranchisement	healthcare access	colonization of outer space	equitable public education

Here's an example of problem-solving writing in APA:

Gun violence remains a major problem across the country, especially in major cities where murders from gun violence in one city exceeded 500 murders annually. Since almost all gun violence involves teenagers, communities are approaching the problem through increasing recreational activities in an attempt to remove teenagers from the violence (Valore, 2023).

Duane and Hutson (2023) reported that 93 percent of guns used in major city violence are illegal — purchased illegally, stolen illegally, or assembled illegally (p. 84). Watson (2023) identified serious inconsistencies with background checks for purchasing guns.

Among major problems with guns and assault weapons, eliminating illegal guns should be one of the easier ones to solve — they violate the law. And if present laws lack the strength to eliminate illegal trafficking, illegal gun sales, and illegal gun possession, pass stronger gun laws. Make stronger gun laws a single-issue decision at election time.

Cause and effect

Sir Isaac Newton explained that every action has an equal and opposite reaction. His Law of Action also explains cause-and-effect writing. Actions cause reactions; causes have effects.

REMEMBER

Cause-and-effect research papers identify relationships between events (causes) and the consequences (effects) of those events. They also include analysis and implications of the consequences.

Cause-and-effect topics can focus primarily on causes, effects, or causes and effects. For example, they can focus on the causes of climate change, the effects of climate change, or a combination of both. What would Sir Isaac think about climate change?

REMEMBER

Distinguish between *affect* (a verb) meaning to cause something to happen and *effect* (a noun) meaning a result or consequence. In cause-and-effect writing, *effect* is used as a noun, the result of a cause. (See Chapter 12 for more problem pairs, similar to *affect* and *effect*.)

Professors frequently assign cause-and-effect topics because they generate college-level thinking and research. They're like putting together two and two and justifying an answer that isn't four, especially when an effect is unpredictable.

Here's a look at a few cause-and-effect topics:

>> Effects of music on exercise

>> Causes of unmanageable student loan debt

>> Effects of campus pets on stress

>> Non-economic causes of college dropouts

The complexity of cause-and-effect writing results in the use of unique language. Table 9-1 shows transitions and verbs common to cause-and-effect writing:

TABLE 9-1

Language of Writing

Transitions	Verbs
therefore	causes
consequentially	results in
as a result	influences
since	produces
because	affects

Comparison and contrast

Sometimes people like to be compared and contrasted, and sometimes they don't. But when writing and researching, comparing and contrasting is almost always a good strategy. Think about comparison and contrast as often as you think about your next long weekend.

Assignments focused on comparison and contrast include variations. They can be assigned exclusively comparing or exclusively contrasting, in addition to both. This type of research writing represents a common structure of research-writing assignment. Here's a look at some research topics:

>> Compare and contrast an autocratic style of management with a democratic style.

>> Compare and contrast the use of intelligence in the attacks on Pearl Harbor and the World Trade Center.

Expository

Curious people show a fascination with how things work. *Expository* writing explains how processes and programs work. Here's a look at examples of expository research projects at the college level:

Explain the process of the following:

>> Earning a college degree

>> Achieving financial independence

>> Understanding the message of reading a nonfiction book

>> Demonstrating responsibility as a citizen

>> Being a successful parent

>> Acting as a responsible entrepreneur

At the college level, these topics require academic evidence (see Chapter 7 for more about academic arguments). For example, arguing the steps to achieve financial independence requires economic evidence, such as referencing advice of financial advisors that may also include statistical data.

Tips for writing expository research include the following:

>> Explain the steps in the process and argue and justify their importance.

>> Support those steps with creditable evidence.

>> Document sources according to your required style.

>> Include the extended significance of the process in the conclusion (refer to Chapter 15).

REMEMBER

These tips assume following good research writing practices, such as creating a thesis and managing information (see Chapter 5), examining evidence and preparing sources (refer to Chapter 6), and citing sources and creating a reference list.

Persuasive

Persuasive research writing is the economy-class version of argumentative writing. Think of persuasive writing as serving an apprenticeship for primetime argumentative research.

The purpose of *persuasive* writing is convincing readers to take a position or to act such as support a position or endorse a product or service. Good persuasion requires good evidence. Think of evidence that persuaded you to select your college.

The following research topics can be developed persuasively:

>> The Constitution of the United States needs revising.

>> ChatGPT will be an asset to college writing.

Structuring Research-Assignment Packages: Submission Forms

You learned in middle school that H_2O is packaged in three forms: steam as gas, water as liquid, and ice as solid. Research writing appears as multiple forms. And like H_2O, you need to determine the form that best serves the writing purpose. The following sections explain writing forms and their adaptability to research writing

Reports

You've been reading reports since your first glowing report card as a quart-size academic star, and you've been writing reports since your first book report. Reports are the place settings of writing genre; they're adaptable to almost any entree or research writing requirements.

As common as reports are for informational writing assignments, they're more common as informational reading — health reports, academic reports, credit reports, employee evaluation reports, and hopefully not too many police reports or accident reports.

Reports serve several purposes, like a favorite pair of footwear that can take you everywhere. The following shows the variety of purposes that reports can fulfill.

Purposes

solve problems	establish policy	evaluate programs
disclose finances	project earnings	forecast business
manage spending	report progress	trace history
predict outcome	reveal deficiencies	change procedures
announce successes	reduce staff	compliment successes

In addition to purposes, preliminary decisions for report writing include the following:

>> **Long or short:** Can content be developed within 6 to 8 pages, or does it require 10 or more pages? What length affects readability?

>> **Internal or external:** Is the report disseminated within the organization or outside the organization, which determines tone, language, and formality? What content needs adjusting for outside audiences?

>> **Informal or formal:** Is the tone informal for a small familiar team, or formal for wider audiences?

>> **Vertical or horizontal:** Is the report horizontal across departments, or vertical within organizational hierarchy? How does vertical or horizontal influence content?

>> **Recommendation or none:** Does the report require a recommendation for action?

REMEMBER

In the workplace reports need professional appearance as hard copies or digital documents. Chapter 18 explains presentation for submitting your college assignments.

Tips for writing a report include the following:

>> Shape the report within the framework of the person who requested it.

>> Identify the question the report should answer.

>> Include tables and figures needed to clarify the report.

Essays

Essays are mini-research papers that haven't reached puberty. They include a mini-argument that hasn't yet matured into full-grown academic argument with multi-source support, a collection of citations, and a convincing rebuttal.

But what essays lack with complexity, they compensate for with economy and intense focus. Essays require an argument with three or four supporting sources. Professors sometimes assign essays because they require the skills and thinking of a research paper yet require much less grading time than research papers.

Here are tips for writing essays:

>> Choose a topic that represents a novel approach to addressing the assignment.

>> Use flashes of risky writing such as extended metaphors, outlier comparisons, and personification.

>> Connect supporting ideas with the thesis.

>> Focus on creating an engaging title, first sentence, and last sentence.

For detailed information on writing risks and essay writing, refer to my book on essays and college writing titled *College Writing For Dummies*. Also check out my other For Dummies book *APA Style & Citations For Dummies*.

Reaction papers

Reaction or response papers are like essays with a one-track mind. They focus on writing a response to an assigned reading. Reaction papers are go-to assignments for professors teaching courses such as history, philosophy, psychology, economics, and political science. Professors also assign reactions to documentaries, TED talks, lectures, plays, observations, movies, and so forth.

Reaction papers lack the formal appearance of research papers and essays, and most non-composition professors expect you to figure out a professional appearance. Use standard formatting and page appearance for your required documentation style. See Chapter 13 for formatting and Chapter 18 for preparing for submissions.

Responses also require critical reading before you begin writing and documenting with a reference page to cite your support. Frequently, you're required to engage with an additional source or two. Check with Chapter 6 for engaging with sources.

Here are tips for writing reaction papers:

>> Begin your paper with a brief summary of the source.

>> Support your thesis with regular use of "so what" and "for example."

>> Support your reactions with partial quotes from the primary source.

>> Prioritize reactions you choose to react to.

Even if you're not required to include an outside source, referencing one will impress your professor.

Structuring Research Papers across Disciplines

Skills in research writing anchor your educational investment portfolio. Building these skills improves your academic performance in courses across disciplines, and research writing is commonly required in all courses at most universities.

Seminal studies show that when you're writing and thinking about course content, you're learning that content. The following sections show you the versatility of research writing in a variety of academic disciplines.

REMEMBER

Research writing across disciplines requires use of essential writing skills common to successful research writing: identifying your audience and purpose (see Chapter 10), writing in an academic style (see Chapter 11), supporting your sources with evidence (see Chapter 6), and planning and organizing (see Chapter 14). It also requires basic research organization of an introduction, body, and conclusion (see Chapter 15).

Literature

Literature majors read, write, research, and analyze. And they live in worlds of fantasy and nonfiction. If you date a literature major, expect occasionally to enter their world of fiction.

Most literature papers include topics that analyze literature such as the following:

> How was Herman Melville influenced by Shakespeare's revenge themes?

Analysis assignments also include comparison and contrast such as the following:

> Compare and contrast Jane Austen's Elizabeth Bennet with F. Scott Fitzgerald's Daisy Jordan.

Analysis also includes motivation topics such as the following:

> What motivates J.D. Salinger's Holden Caulfield to search for his identity?

Here are tips specific to writing about literature research:

>> Include a brief summary of the literature and authors in the introduction.

>> Support the argument with partial quotes from characters.

>> Accurately punctuate titles of works (see Chapter 12).

>> Engage with experts' analysis of literary works.

>> Document references from the assigned primary sources — the literary works.

Business

Research and report writing are as common to business courses as sleep and snacks are to college students. Most business topics are information-based and written in the form of research reports. The purpose of research writing in business includes analyzing topics such as the following in the following:

Topics

profits and loses	management styles	employee relations
customer service	marketing plans	business ethics
overhead costs	business technologies	advertising
remote work	employee benefits	capital improvements

Here are tips specifically for business research writing:

>> Recognize that secondary audiences always include corporate leadership.

>> Include costs in supporting evidence.

>> Create team-building tone where appropriate.

>> Prefer discipline-specific sources as supporting evidence.

Political science

The field of politics sometimes lacks character, but it never lacks characters. Research writing in political science focuses on evidence-supported answers to why and so what. Research writing and public discourse in political science contribute to the development of healthy societies.

The purpose of research writing in political science includes analyzing and arguing topics such as the following:

>> Explain the politics of affordable healthcare.

>> Define a fair election.

>> Evaluate the role of political parties in politics.

>> Analyze the liabilities of a democratic society.

TIP

Social media generally lacks credibility as a news source and as supporting evidence. Ask your reference librarian for recommendations of unbiased news sources.

Tips for writing in political science includes the following:

>> Maintain objectivity on controversial topics.

>> Clarify discipline-specific terminology.

>> Support the argument with discipline-specific sources such as government reports and public documents.

>> Apply the argument's importance to current events.

Art history

Unlike most other disciplines, writing about art history focuses heavily on visual interpretation. Common types of research writing in art history include visual analysis and art history research.

Visual interpretation is based on identifying an observation and supporting it with description from the work itself, in addition to engaging with authoritarian opinion. Research topics in art history compare, contrast, and analyze traditional themes such as patterns of art, trends of artists, artists' contributions, and art movements.

Art history research topics include the following:

>> Compare historical portraits of da Vinci and Whistler.

>> Explain how Medieval Art influenced Renaissance Art.

>> Analyze Rembrandt's and Rubens' use of shade and light.

TIP

When you have assignment choices, choose art and artists that appeal to your tastes.

Tips for research writing specific to art history include the following:

>> Annotate (see Chapter 5) art similar to annotating text.

>> Include descriptions of the art and the artists in the introduction.

>> Engage your opinions with those of experts.

>> Document works of art as primary sources.

>> Study models of art history writing.

Education

Reports and other research assignments are as common to education courses as scissors and felt tip markers are to elementary education majors.

Writing in the field of education includes a variety of specialized research genre such as lesson plans, program evaluations, and reports in specialized areas such as special education, online learning, and technology.

Topics for educational research projects include the following:

>> Post-Covid classroom instruction

>> Health concerns in the classroom

>> School safety

>> The vanilla curriculum

Tips for educational research writing include the following:

>> Focus on discipline-specific sources such as those available from ERIC (Educational Resource Information Center).

>> Avoid being influenced by emotional involvement with some topics.

>> Clarify specialized vocabulary.

>> Choose a tone and person appropriate for topic.

Advancing Research Projects: Higher Level Learning

If you're in a position where advanced research projects are relevant to your academic life, enjoy it. Graduation day is no longer a distant dream, it's a relevant reality.

The following research projects represent your reward for your academic successes. And because of those past research successes, you have the foundation of research skills to complete projects common to superstar scholars.

Reviews of literature

How do you earn the right to be assigned the premium projects of higher-level research? You practice and perform well on the research projects assigned during the first and second years of college.

Reviews of literature are like the gift that perpetually re-gifts. Scholars perform scholarly activities and no task is as intense as writing a review of literature. Analyzing and synthesizing three times as many sources as a research paper is about as deep as it gets in higher education.

Reviews require you to analyze sources individually, in relation to each other, and in relation to the complete body of sources. It's like binging on analyzing and synthesizing sources.

At the conclusion of a synthesis of sources, you'll have the following information:

>> What's been studied on the topic

>> What's been identified as important on the topic and why it's important

>> What's controversial about the topic and the extent of those controversies

>> What experts agree and disagree on

>> What's been overlooked and neglected on the topic

Most important, reviews of literature tell you how to position your topic among other works of other researchers. Chapter 6 provides background information on reviews of literature as a resource for a collection of sources on a specific topic.

Reviews of journal articles

Journal article reviews are like the inside of a piano. Strings and hammers can appear overwhelming, but you learn to appreciate the mellow, harmonious sounds. Expect to be assigned at least one journal article review before you graduate and another one if you attend graduate school.

Journal reviews provide you an opportunity to analyze the research of professional scholars — the ones with the Persian carpets and worldwide artifacts in their office.

The purpose of reviewing journal articles includes the following:

>> Familiarize yourself with arguments of seasoned scholars.

>> Read the language of in-depth research.

>> Study the structure of peer-reviewed articles.

>> Learn the language of professional research.

Begin writing a journal article review by reading journal-reading guidelines in Chapter 5. Also annotate the article as described in Chapter 6. Be sure to follow guidelines for documenting and listing source references.

Write a journal article review with the organization of the three major parts of a research article. Here's a look at content for each part:

>> **Introduction:** Begin with a summary of the article and identification of source elements (author, title, publication, and so forth). Identify the author's argument.

>> **Body:** Evaluate the author's evidence that supports the argument: currency, authority, accuracy, writing, and relevance (as I discuss in Chapter 6). Also identify agreements, inconsistencies, gaps, and outliers.

>> **Conclusion:** Identify the extended meaning of the argument. What does the article add to information on the topic?

Here are additional tips for writing a journal article review:

>> Read the article in the sequence as I describe in Chapter 5.

>> Annotate as I mention in Chapter 6.

>> Formulate the big question that your review answers.

>> Search for models of reviews and study their structure and language.

>> Document from your journal article as a primary source.

Journal article comparison

The journal article comparison assignment is a two-for-the-price-of-one sale. It's a variation of the journal article review assignment and requires the same critical analysis skills: evaluating, analyzing, and prioritizing.

The purpose of the comparison assignment duplicates that of the article review. The comparison focuses on highlights of two journal articles.

Write an article comparison by following these three steps:

>> Follow guidelines for writing an article review as I explain in Chapter 5.

>> Identify similar characteristics in each article.

>> Conclude with an analysis of the importance of similarities in both articles.

White papers

White papers were called white because they weren't blue. Allegedly, generations ago bluebooks were the primary medium for government communications. Then along came white papers, and bluebooks were retired as artifacts of higher education.

White papers align academic research skills with product and service promotional skills of business and organizations. They're information-based academic documents written by companies and organizations for the purpose of sharing expertise.

Information in white papers includes a synthesis of research sources not readily available for readers' research. They frequently request gated content, personal contact information for generating business leads. A recent study showed a majority of white paper readers were willing to surrender contact information for contents of a white paper.

White papers require the skills of supporting an argument, similar to research writing. They also require APA or MLA documentation and compiling a reference or works cited.

REMEMBER

The length of white papers as academic assignments ranges between 1,000 and 1,500 words. White papers in the workplace range between 2,000 and 3,000 words and include charts, tables, and visuals.

Organize a white paper into these three major sections:

>> **Introduction:** A statement of the problem, thesis, and background information on the topic

>> **Body:** Identification of a problem and support of the thesis with documentation of sources in the required style

>> **Conclusion:** A solution to the problem and a revelation, such as what's so great about the solution

Examples of white paper topics include the following:

>> Climate-controlled clothing: Comfort for every body

>> The trades: The other academic fields of study

Assignment proposals

College students never know when they're going to need a proposal — for any assignment project.

Some professors assign proposals for almost every major assignment. Within a few pages, proposals reflect students' thinking and organization of the assignment. They clarify the thesis, research question, documentation, and list of sources. Proposals also reveal whether students are on track for a successful assignment.

Assignment proposals include the following:

>> Argument and research questions (see Chapter 5)

>> Availability and quality of sources (refer to Chapter 5)

>> Familiarization with required documentation style (see Chapter 8)

>> Preliminary list of references (check out Chapter 8)

>> Summary description of sources or formal literature review (see Chapter 9)

>> Plan for assignment completion (flip to Chapter 14)

Here are the parts of a research proposal that most professors accept:

>> **Title page:** A page following the required documentation style (see Chapter 13) that includes your paper's title and contact information

>> **Background:** Information describing the topic that usually includes documentation

>> **Rationale:** Justification of the importance of the topic that usually includes documentation

>> **Research questions:** Major and minor research questions that focus the project

>> **Methodology:** A plan for gathering information

>> **Review of literature:** A formal literature review if required, or a summary of sources

>> **Annotated bibliography:** Projected list of sources with a brief description of each source

>> **Completion plan:** Schedule for completing the assignment

3

Developing Essentials of Research Writing

Show respectful audience awareness by preferring people-first disability-reference language, gender-neutral pronouns, and appropriateness of race, ethnicity, and age.

Recognize purposes of assignments such as analyze, define, explain, trace, and, of course, argue.

Include style elements such as active verbs, specific nouns, sentence-length variety, sentence-structure variety, sentence-branching variety, and parallel structure.

Review fundamentals of grammar and usage including verb formations, pronoun agreement, description positioning, and confusing pronouns.

Evaluate the use of language conventions such as commas as sentence interrupters; conjunctions, colons, and semicolons as sentence separators; dashes as directional changes; and apostrophes and possessive as showing ownership.

Address documentation-style formatting such as title pages, abstracts, table of contents, heading levels, information lists, references, and major headings.

Chapter 10

Identifying Audience and Purpose

Most writing experts describe the writing process as sustained decision-making. The first two decisions successful writers make are

» Whom am I writing to?

» Why am I writing?

The decisions of audience and purpose shape content, language, tone, person, and detail. Starting an assignment without identifying audience and purpose is like starting a semester without a schedule — lack of a who, what, why, and a purpose.

Research shows that actively thinking about audience and purpose improves writing. If you're actively reading this chapter, you're thinking about audience and purpose. Here I explain audiences to address for research writing; the influence of tone, tense, and person on your audience; the importance of purpose on your writing; and the language of awareness and respect.

Figuring Out Who Your Audience Is

Your professor's first indication that your assignment's off track is language that addresses your audience. The wrong audience is as obvious as wearing shoes on the wrong feet. Here I show how to figure out your audience, address their expectations, and identify other audiences.

Gauging academic audience expectations

Write your research papers to the academic audience your professor represents, but don't write them exclusively to your professor. Let me explain. Your professor is one member of the academic audience with specific interests in teaching and research, but not the exclusive audience.

For example, your professor's academic interests may also include art history, Asian travel, historical novels, and pop culture. The broader spectrum of the academic audience may include professors with interests such as Shakespeare, international soccer, European travel, The Beatles, and Greek artifacts. Your audience includes readers with all those interests.

Picture your audience as the faculty of your university, scholars like your professor, who is one of many academicians with diverse interests. Your academic audience includes readers with all those diverse interests.

TIP

For college research writing, avoid picturing your peers as part of your academic audience. Picture writing to audience whose backgrounds exceed that of your peers.

And how are those divergent audience interests related to the academic audience you're addressing in your research paper? Academicians with varied academic backgrounds share scholarly interests such as the following:

>> **Scholarship:** They endorse research and academic argument (see Chapter 7), consistencies of documentation (refer to Chapter 8), and new thinking on a variety of academic topics.

>> **Language proficiency:** They model respectful rules of grammar and conventions and language inclusive of all people. They respect formal vocabulary, varied sentence structure, and ideas connected by transitions (see Chapter 11).

>> **Logic:** They respect logical evidence to support ideas and avoidance of logical fallacies (refer to Chapter 9).

>> **Ethical responsibility:** Scholars value accurate crediting of the research of others, clear separation of the writer's ideas from others, and the recognition of the range of opinions on an issue (see Chapter 18).

TIP

When speaking, you're unlikely to misidentify or forget your audience because they're most likely standing in front of you. For example, you're unlikely to misidentify your sibling or your professor when speaking to either of them. But you're likely to forget or misidentify your audience when writing. To sustain memory of the audience you're writing to, literally picture them and write their name at the top of your draft version.

Identifying your research audience

Because topics vary and readers' background vary, writers adjust content to readers' requirements and identify readers' requirements by answering audience questions such as the following:

>> How familiar is your audience with the topic and how much background information do they need?

>> What is the priority message you want your audience to understand?

>> What parts of the topic are your audience least and most interested in?

>> What writing structure (see Chapter 9) increases your audiences' understanding of the topic?

>> What terminology needs explaining?

>> What examples are your audience familiar with?

>> What types of sources do your audience require?

>> Will the audience accept writing that includes contractions, first person, personal experiences, and entertaining language?

REMEMBER

As Chapter 3 explains, your research audience needs consistency of your documentation style. If you're writing in APA, for example, they expect to see consistency of APA's date-emphasis style. If you're writing in MLA style, they expect to see consistent page number emphasis. Chapter 8 discusses both styles.

A point I stress in the classroom is that a major decision of inexperienced writers is what content to add, and a major of decision of experienced writers is what to cut. The former decision hinders the audience; the later decision helps the audience because it reduces unnecessary sentences and ideas.

Identifying secondary audiences

Students with near-perfect GPAs learned early in their academic careers that their grade is determined by how well they address assignment requirements, especially requirements subtly written into the assignment. Those *summa* and *magna* students focus on details that many other students overlook.

Research assignments sometimes include a secondary audience with language such as "Write a research report to the university president arguing for a sustainable source of energy on campus that may eventually reduce tuition."

Addressing such *secondary* audiences includes identifying the president by name and also addressing supporting evidence to the president.

TIP

Frequently, your professor won't tell you about secondary audiences in class but expect you to recognize this requirement in your assignment analysis (refer to Chapter 14). Professors design assignments to provide you the experiences of writing to a variety of audiences, similar to audiences you'll write to in your career.

AUDIENCE AND NON-RESEARCH-PAPER NEEDS

Different assignments are written for different academic audiences. For example, audiences who read research papers differ from audiences that read essays, reports, and assignments in your disciplines.

Here's a look at college assignments and the specific audiences they're written to:

- **Essay writing:** Your essay audience includes the academic community, but with less focus on research elements. Think of educated readers with interest in your topic. Essay readers appreciate more playful language than the serious tone of research writing. When you picture your essay audience, also include student representatives among professional scholars.

- **Report writing:** The audience for readers of reports is easily identifiable. They're members of the organization the report is written for, especially if the report is internal. If the report is external, audience considerations include avoiding information exclusive to the company. (See Chapter 9 for explanations of internal and external reports.)

- **Content assignments:** The audience for reaction papers and essays in your content courses includes the academic community with an emphasis on the subject area. For example, a reaction paper in philosophy focuses on an audience interested in philosophy and expects accuracy in philosophical content. Content is king in your subject areas.

Addressing professor-as-audience expectations

Here's more advice from Captain Obvious: Your professor assigns your grade. Addressing the academic community fulfills the assignment requirement, but fulfilling your professor's unwritten requirements earns you points for superior grades.

Professors frequently develop idiosyncrasies, personal points of focus, that they believe are relevant to successful assignments. And they're aware of these focus points when they grade. For example, if professors emphasize action verbs as I explain in Chapter 11, the absence of active verbs will eventually cost you points.

TIP

Recognize points of emphasis when your professor mentions them in class or writes them in the syllabus. They include professors' content emphasis such as the following:

>> **Research emphasis:** Using nothing older than five years, no .com websites, and only library sources

>> **Reading emphasis:** Requiring readings listed in the syllabus

>> **Formatting emphasis:** Formatting accuracy of research parts such as the title page and annotated bibliography

>> **Convention emphasis:** Avoiding overuse of exclamation marks and accurately using title punctuation

Recognizing unnamed audience expectations

Many academic affiliations are part of the audience act, including your professor's chair, department committees, and university committees. Random completed assignments are frequently submitted to committees for course and department evaluations. The purpose is quality control and upholding department and university standards.

You're expected to meet expectations of those audiences by ensuring course-content accuracy and fact-checking background information — in addition to addressing the requirement of the academic community.

Matching Tone, Tense, and Person to Your Audience

Your success as a college student depends on establishing consistency in your academic life, such as attending classes, studying, socializing, and so forth. Your writing audience needs similar consistencies with tone, tense, and person — the supporting cast for audience. Each has a say in the language and content that your audience hears. These sections explain tone, tense, and person.

Tone: Showing attitude

Tone is like the sleeping reptile in the room that you don't want to awaken; it's the attitude that your words communicate. Research writing requires consistent formal and respectful tone that avoids slang, contractions, cliches, and texting references. Let sleeping reptiles lie and keep a safe distance from disruptive tones.

When you think tone, sometimes called *voice*, think of your attitude toward your content and your audience. If someone tells you tone is in your head, believe them — it's the sound of words you hear in your head as you read.

Giving your audience what they demand — an academic tone

Your research audience demands (did you hear the tone of that verb?) a tone that's formal (see Chapter 11), serious, academic, and respectful (see the next section). Scholars don't hear anything humorous about peer-reviewed sources, annotated bibliographies, or formatted title pages. Because citations are serious business, researchers have a short memory of college fun they had on Friday nights at the local karaoke bar.

REMEMBER

You can find examples of academic tone in peer-reviewed journal articles (see Chapter 6) that you locate in your library's databases.

TIP

Additional tips for achieving an academic tone include the following:

» Avoid contractions, unlike this *For Dummies* book that encourages them.

» Avoid overwriting a formal tone with adjectives such as *esteemed, renown, elegant, profound,* and so forth. At least once in professors' career, they're described as *esteemed* — and that one time is usually when they're retiring.

» Avoid unnecessary use of the passive voice (Chapter 11 explains active and passive voice).

» Avoid wordiness in sentence structure (see Chapter 17).

» Avoid language errors (Chapter 12 offers a review).

Identifying some examples of tone to avoid

Here's an example of disrespectful (and revised respectful) tone in research writing:

» **Disrespectful tone:** Consequently, researchers *failed to understand* the implications of their findings.

  The tone of *failed to understand* communicates a weakness among researchers who don't like any reference to failure.

» **Revised respectful tone:** Consequently, researchers *underestimated* the implications of their findings.

  A much softer tone is communicated by *underestimated*. Researchers can handle that tone.

Here are examples of informal tone that you should avoid in almost all academic writing:

» **Colloquialisms:** Avoid common everyday spoken expressions such as the following:

  If you ask me . . ., they literally believe . . ., they checked up on . . ., and *don't have a clue.*

» **Cliches:** Avoid worn-out, overused expressions such as the following:

  It doesn't take a genius . . ., a prime example, and *it blew me out of the water.*

>> **Exaggerations:** Avoid hyperbole such as the following:

The dumbest thing I ever heard . . ., some professors think they're the sharpest knife in the drawer, and *that would never fly in a thousand years.*

>> **Generalizations:** Avoid sweeping generalizations such as the following:

Everyone knows that . . ., since the beginning of time . . . and *everyone knows . . . .*

REMEMBER

Texting is part of your hourly life and contains its own style and tone. Be conscious of text thinking that infiltrates your formal writing. Avoid the temptation to use texting abbreviations and emojis. Texting has its purpose, as does writing — and rarely do the two meet, especially within the pages of a research assignment.

Tense: Time frames things happen

Similar to the tone of the reptile in the room, tense should also remain silent because its shifts resound like a snare drum in your professor's ear. *Tense,* the time events happen, thrives on consistency and dislikes disruptions.

In research writing, tense errors are connected with a short leash and little patience. Unfortunately, tense use in research differs with documentation styles.

The next few sections explain how to avoid tense snafus.

Knowing the names of tenses used in research

Verb tense in research indicates the time that studies and research events happen: the *present tense* (now), the *past tense* (previously), and *future tense* (at a time yet to happen). Chapter 12 explains verb tense in detail.

Here are examples of those basic tenses:

>> **Present tense:** Whitby *agrees* with Agnew.

>> **Past tense:** Whitby *agreed* with Agnew.

>> **Future tense:** Whitby *will agree* with Agnew.

The *present perfect* tense is an additional tense used in research writing. It's formed with the verb helper *has* or *have* and the past participle of the verb and generally is used to identify an action that began in the past and continues. For a brief review of grammar specific to college writing, see my book *College Writing For Dummies* (John Wiley & Sons, Inc.).

Here's an example:

Bennett *has followed* Leon's theory on analytical accounting.

The use of the present perfect (*has followed*) indicates that Bennett followed Leon's theory in the past and continues to follow it in the present.

REMEMBER

The general rule for using tense is to use one tense consistently. For example, if you're telling a story in the past tense, keep all verbs in the past. In other words, don't let shift happen, such as in this example:

I *walked* (past tense) to the Capital Theater and the manager *recognizes* (present tense) me.

Understanding how the APA handles tense

Style guides offer recommendations for using tense with research. Here's a glance at APA's guidelines for using tense:

>> **Present tense:** APA recommends the present tense for research references such as the following:

- **Author engagement:** I *agree* (present) with Cruz and others who *support* (present) colleges' responsibility to improve retention rates.

- **Summarizing results:** Sanchez *surmises* (present) that one-on-one mentor programs *improve* (present) graduation rates.

- **Suggested research:** Topics for future research *include* (present) researching causes of increasing test scores.

>> **Present perfect tense:** APA recommends the present perfect tense for actions that began in the past and continue in the present.

Here's an example: James *has supported* (present perfect) the principles of microeconomics.

>> **Past tense:** APA recommends the past tense for research references that occurred in the past such as the following:

- **References to other researchers:** Simpson *argued* (past) that early interventions improved student writing.

- **Describing methodology:** Participants *were asked* (past) to complete a writing sample.

- **Discussing results:** Hinson's conclusion *was supported* (past) by others.

Glancing at how MLA and Chicago deal with tense

Because MLA and Chicago are more literature focused for research requirements, they offer detailed guidelines for tense use in literature.

REMEMBER

MLA and Chicago tense requirements are similar to APA, but they have a distinguishing difference for referencing other researchers. MLA and Chicago reference other researchers in the present tense.

Here's a look at MLA and Chicago recommendations for tense uses in literature:

» **Present tense:** MLA and Chicago recommend use of the present tense for the following research references:

- **References to other researchers:** Zozak and Tomlin *argue* (present) that programs reduce recidivism.

- **Description of characters' actions:** In the opening of *Pride and Prejudice*, Charles Bingley, a young wealthy gentleman, *rents* (present) a room in the house of the Bennett's, whose household *includes* (present) five unmarried daughters.

- **Plot descriptions:** The setting of Fitzgerald's *Great Gatsby is* (present) Long Island, near New York City.

Person: Gauging who's speaking

Who's the speaker and who cares? Your audience and your professor care. The *person* (speaker) used in research writing, and almost all other college writing, influences audience and tone. Here's a look at three persons used to deliver information:

First person

The *first person* delivers audience information with the pronoun *I*, as in the example:

In this book, *I* (first person) explain to you the principles of college research writing.

The first person has limited use in college research writing. Some professors prefer not to see the first person in research writing and essays because it can lack objectivity. Check with your professors on their policies for using the first person.

Second person

The *second person* delivers audience information with the pronoun *you*, as in the example:

> If *you* (second person) develop proficiency in college writing, *you* can write your way to career success.

The second person is used less often in college writing than the first person. *You* is rarely used in research writing and sometimes used in essay and other types of writing. Check with your professor on uses of the second person in your college writing.

Third person

Good things in college come in threes, especially when the "three" is the third person. The *third person* uses pronouns such as *he, she, they,* and *it*. Here's an example of third person writing:

> The major citation *styles* (third person) developed safety guidelines for people used in research studies.

The noun in the previous sample sentence (*styles*) is equivalent to the third-person pronoun *they*.

REMEMBER

The advantage of the third person, the most common in academic writing, is that it generally establishes content objectivity and is equivalent to a person on a mountain top looking down and writing a story about *they* and *them*.

Showing Awareness: General Guidelines for Respectful Language

During my consulting experiences in New Jersey schools, I'd often ask students to summarize all school rules into one rule and write it with as few words as possible.

A third grader in Winslow Township wrote a two-word rule that not only applies to elementary school, but also to people and organizations worldwide: *Show respect*.

That eight-year-old's thinking was visionary and a simple rule for everyone to follow. His rule applies beyond the classroom and offers a solution to almost any problem known to people.

Showing respect can solve problems such as discrimination, social injustice, personal differences, political indifference, racism, and war. People demonstrate respect with what they say and do. What people say with their speaking and writing has the power to change the world.

The sections that follow explain guidelines for respectful language for topics identified by APA, MLA, and Chicago. Today, APA, MLA, and Chicago base their language recommendations on their understanding of words at the time of preparing their latest editions — approximately five years ago. The guidelines in the sections that follow represent language thinking at that time — thinking that some people and groups agreed with, and some people and groups disagreed with.

Preferring people-first language

The controversy begins and language continues to evolve. Many people with disabilities prefer language that begins with the person first, such as *the person with diabetes* and *the person with paralysis*.

RAISING AUDIENCE AWARENESS: RESPECTFUL LANGUAGE

Language is a complex, growing, living tool that people use to communicate, think, and express ideas and emotions. The language of a society at any given time reflects the thinking of the people at that given time. Generations ago language reflecting thinking spoke of little respect among some groups.

For example, APA's approved technical terms describing disabilities a half century ago included language such as *crippled, deaf and dumb, idiot, mentally ill, psycho,* and *retarded* — words highly offensive by today's standards.

The disagreement over respectful language continues among universities as some schools continue to debate the meaning of language that fails to represent their beliefs, especially terms such as *slave* and *master* used to identify technology systems. Many other words with histories of disrespect continue to be challenged by people and organizations.

The lesson for respectful language includes thinking that respects all people and groups. Thinking and acting with respect produces respectful language. And be identity-appropriate language remains a moving target, ask people their preferred language of identity when possible.

But a number of people with disabilities prefer disability-first language, with an emphasis of their disability such as *the diabetic* and *the paraplegic*.

What are your options as a writer? If you feel comfortable asking, ask them their preferences. If you don't feel comfortable, prefer people-first language. If they tell you they don't like people-first, use disability-first language.

In addition, MLA recommends, "Avoid negatively judging others' experiences," such as describing people as *is afflicted with cancer, suffers from heart disease*, and *is a victim of long-term Covid*. Revise language negatively judging people, preferring people-first language, or if they prefer to disability-first language.

WARNING

Also avoid patronizing language, such as labeling people with disabilities as *warriors*, *heroes*, or *inspirational*.

REMEMBER

Don't just think of the audience you're writing to, but also think of the people you're writing to. Audience awareness is people awareness.

Using gender-neutral inclusive pronouns

When I grew up in the '50s and '60s, society — supported by pronoun conveniences — thought in terms of gender stereotypes. For examples, doctors, scientists, and CEOs were assumed males and were referenced with the pronoun *he*. Nurses, secretaries, and office support staff were assumed females and were referenced with the pronoun *she*.

Decades later, not surprisingly, programs were needed to encourage females to study in male-dominant careers of science and leadership. And in recent decades language began catching up to the beliefs that careers aren't gender specific, that any gender can fly in space, head a major multinational organization, lead a country, or perform brain surgery. And that any gender can perform duties of a nurse.

MLA recognizes the role of pronouns to take the place of people's names and that pronoun gender references often result in awkward expressions such as the following:

> When a professor prepares for class, *he or she* reviews readings assigned for class discussion.

MLA suggests that writers "minimize pronouns that exclude [genders]" and revise such sentences using plural nouns and pronouns such as the following:

> When professors prepare for class, *they* review readings assigned for class discussions.

Preferring plural nouns and pronouns also eliminates additional awkward constructions such as alternating gender pronouns and using expressions such as s/he.

In recent years, APA, MLA, and Chicago have adopted *they* as both singular and plural. Here's an example of an accepted singular noun (professor) with the singular and plural pronoun *they*:

> When a *professor* (singular) begins class, *they* (singular and plural) usually take attendance.

Gender inclusiveness was recently recognized by the University of Notre Dame when it commemorated the 50th anniversary of Title IX by adding the gender inclusive *and daughters* into its iconic fight song:

> While her loyal sons *and daughters* are marching . . .

Go Irish!

MLA highlights gender recommendations that include the following:

>> Avoid irrelevant gender references such as *NFL female official, male nurse, transgender pilot,* and *female engineer.*

>> Avoid *man* references with terms such as *humans, humanity,* and *human beings.*

>> Avoid people references with gender-specific language such as *mail-man, policeman,* and *fireman.*

>> Avoid *we* and *our* when it excludes people and groups.

You can find more information on gender inclusiveness in the section "Being inclusive with sexual orientation and gender identity" later in this chapter.

In the following sections, I regularly reference APA because that style offers detailed guidelines for the topic in which they're referenced. Usually, MLA and Chicago agree with APA but lack similar detailed guidelines in their manuals.

Respecting race and ethnicity

Language referencing race and ethnicity evolves and reflects changes, as once acceptable language becomes unacceptable. For example, long-time professional sports franchise nicknames were considered offensive and recently changed to

Washington Commanders and Cleveland Guardians. A dozen other professional sports franchises, as well as more than a dozen universities, have also abandoned offensive nicknames and mascots.

APA identifies race as "physical differences that groups and cultures consider socially significant." APA's names of races include Native American, First Nation or Alaska Native, Asian, Black or African American, and White or Caucasian.

For the purpose of not creating hierarchy, APA recommends listing races with a purposeful design such as alphabetically, population, or geographical.

Other APA recommendations related to race and ethnicity are endorsed by most style guides and include the following:

>> Avoid the outdated *minority*.

>> Prefer *Native American* to *American Indian*.

>> Avoid stereotypes associated with descriptions such as *well-mannered, intelligent,* and *behaved*.

>> Avoid *those people* and *you people*.

>> Capitalize racial and ethnic names because they're proper nouns.

>> Avoid racial stereotypes that associate race with dress, appearance, accessories, food, and so forth.

Honoring age references

Age is common to all people, but not all people are common to all ages. Consequently, some age groups are frequently referenced with biased language. APA, more than other style guide, highlights respectful language and recommends showing respect for people with the follow guidelines:

>> Use specific references to age such as the following: *infant, toddler, adolescent, 50- to 60-year-olds, the over 80 participants, nonagenarians,* and *centenarians*.

>> Avoid stereotype generalizations such as *terrible twos, mean teens,* and *the frail and elderly*.

Terms like *elderly, old-timer, geriatric, golden-ager,* and *aged* represent language displeasing to many older people. Terms like *elderly* and descriptions like *frail* misidentify many older adults who run marathons, jump from airplanes, lead countries, serve in the military, and write books. Terms acceptable to many in the over-65 crowd include *senior, senior citizen,* and *older adult*.

In 2020 APA passed a resolution recognizing age bias, stereotypes, and discrimination against older adults because it affected their mental health. APA recommended practices and education for students and psychologists to counter the negative effects of ageism. The resolution and practices are available on the APA website.

Being inclusive with sexual orientation and gender identity

Two major areas of evolving respectful language are sexual orientation and gender identity. APA identifies sexual orientation as a person's feelings and sense of identify and includes terminology such as *heterosexual, bisexual,* and *homosexual.*

APA describes gender as "inherent sense of being" male, female, or nonbinary. Gender identity — independent of sexual orientation — includes the following terminology.

Terms

agender	genderfluid	omnigender
androgynous	gender nonconforming	polygender
bigender	genderqueer	queer
cisgender	nonbinary	transgender

The language of gender terminology continues to evolve. Choose terminology that shows respect for people and ask people their preferred identity reference.

Using best-scenario socioeconomic references

APA views socioeconomic language similar to seeing the glass half full and recommends language that identifies achievements rather than lack of achievements. For example, APA prefers *earned a high school diploma* rather than *lacks a college degree.*

APA recommends avoiding language such as *the poor, the homeless, the disadvantaged, low income, the projects,* and *the inner city.*

If you look for the best in people, you'll find it.

Justifying Why: Figuring Out Your Writing Purpose

Your writing *purpose* is the reason you're writing the assignment, the why of the assignment. When you identify the why, you identify the destination of the assignment — what the reader should understand as a result of reading the assignment.

Writing without a purpose is like college without a plan. You can't reach your career destination without identifying that destination, and you can't fulfill your writing purpose until you identify that purpose. These sections explain common reasons for writing research and other college assignments.

Assignment purposes

Your writing purpose is identified in the assignment. Sometimes you need a GPS to figure it out, but frequently the purpose is spelled out. Look for key words in the assignment that identify the why of your assignment, words such as *explain*, *trace*, *develop*, *compare*, *persuade*, and so forth.

REMEMBER

Here's a look at common purposes of college writing research assignments:

>> **To argue:** As I discuss in Chapter 7, argument is the most common purpose of research writing. When you're arguing, you're generating conversations on the topic.

>> **To analyze or synthesize:** When your purpose is to analyze and synthesize, you're being asked to identify the parts of the topic and their importance, such as analyze the effects of NIL on college athletics. See Chapter 9 for more information on analysis and synthesis.

>> **To define:** The purpose of many assignments requires you to develop a definition for a term or concept, such as define immigration in today's world.

>> **To explain:** When you explain, you interpret information for the reader's understanding, as in explaining the process for deciding which countries receive foreign aid. Explaining is similar to arguing.

>> **To trace:** The purpose of tracing includes describing a topic from its inception to present day, such as tracing the history sustainable food supplies from its beginning to present day. Tracing frequently includes other purposes such as defining, explaining, analyzing, and synthesizing.

REMEMBER

Argument is inherent to almost all research papers in first- and second-year research paper assignments.

Professor-pleasing purposes

Here's inside information: Professors have a purpose for every project assigned, and that purpose includes providing you an opportunity to show your understanding of content — the content they're responsible for teaching you. See Chapter 14 for more information on professors' purposes.

Unspoken purposes

Sometimes earning good grades can be as simple as the famous movie line, or as professors say: "Show me the content." What follows are unspoken purposes that help you earn grades you can bank on.

Professor unspoken purpose

Professors have an unspoken purpose with assignments. They want you to demonstrate understanding of the content in the assignment. For example, if the assignment includes the topic of *Hamlet*, they want you to demonstrate your understanding of Shakespeare's play in the assignment.

You fulfill your professor's understanding of content by engaging with course content in your research paper. Your professor expects to see you manipulate content by explaining it, analyzing it, synthesizing it, comparing it, contrasting it, and applying it to other fields of study.

REMEMBER

As a professor grading papers, I overvalue papers that show an understanding of course content and undervalue papers that show lack of understanding content.

Readers' unspoken purpose

A comment I frequently write on student papers is "lacks reader value," referring to the writer not fulfilling the purpose of giving the audience a topic of value. For example, a research paper that argues gun violence needs to offer insightful preventative suggestions to reduce gun violence.

Writer's unspoken purpose

The writer has an audience obligation to give readers new information or new insights that justifies their reading time.

A final unspoken purpose of any assignment is earning a good grade. Nothing wrong with wanting an "A," as long as you realize that good grades are earned, not awarded.

Chapter **11**

Writing with Style

When you think of writing style, think writing personality as deep as its DNA. Your writing style is the product of the writing choices you've been making your academic life — choices that range from topic selection to revision decisions. Your writing DNA includes your reading background, writing accomplishments, and life experiences that generate ideas and argue thesis statements.

Your writing DNA also includes the writing tools you choose to construct your thoughts: word choices, sentence structures, paragraph development, and connection controls — the writing elements that connect your ideas with other scholars.

In this chapter I explain two parts of speech that energize your writing, sentence structures that speak to scholars, word choices that highlight your ideas, and paragraph constructions that develop thesis statements. I provide you with dozens of examples of sentence varieties that add music to your writing.

REMEMBER

The goal of your writing is not to sound intelligent, but to express yourself intelligently.

Silence your devices and listen for the heartbeat of your writing style.

Showing What's Happening: Verbs and Nouns

When I presented writing workshops to K-12 teachers, I ended with this reminder: Teach your students to write with action verbs and picture nouns.

If you as a college student remember only two of the eight parts of speech, remember verbs and nouns, action words and name words. These two parts of speech are the air and water of your academic writing life and your writing afterlife, although some professors argue they're more important than that.

Nobel Prize author Ernest Hemingway was one of the first legendary writers to advocate for action verbs and picture nouns. He allegedly suggested beginning writers use more verbs and nouns than adjectives and adverbs.

Here I delve into more specifics explaining how to choose verbs that activate your sentences and choose nouns that elicit vivid images of topics you're writing about.

Keeping your verbs active

The power of action verbs connects directly to the brain, and science today verifies Hemingway's importance of action verbs. Brain-scanning machines show that active verbs such as *achieved*, *defended*, *delivered*, and *earned* activate or "light up" the brain.

Here's an example: Picture the verb *got* as in "got a degree." What image do you see in your brain? You don't picture anything specific in your brain — and neither does your reader when you write *got*.

Now picture *earn*, as in "earn your degree." Your brain is bursting with studying you've done, papers you've written, presentations you've prepared — hours of intellectual activity that earns a college degree. The writer-reader connection requires you, the writer, to create an idea that you translate into a verb that communicates that same idea to the reader.

Here's an example of a vague verb revised to an active verb:

> **Vague verb:** They *went* from Toledo to Chicago.
>
> **Revised active verb:** They *drove* from Toledo to Chicago.

In the vague example, *went* communicates an image of general travel. In the revised example, *drove* clarifies the specific image of travel. You immediately visualize a four-lane highway with fast-moving traffic and crowded rest stops. Table 11-1 shows some vague verbs revised to active verbs.

TABLE 11-1

Vague Verbs Revised to Active Verbs

Vague Verbs	Revised Active Verbs
Fixed errors	*Revised* errors
Did their assignments	*Completed* their assignments
Get there by 8:00	*Arrive* by 8:00

Differentiating active and passive verbs

The heart and soul of sentences, verbs identify who is doing what, and how well they're doing it. They speak softly or loudly — and thrive on making a scene. They're happiest when they're lighting up your brain, and they dislike being disconnected from other sentence parts.

Verbs speak in one of two voices:

>> **Active:** When verbs are active, the subject performs the action and receives the emphasis of the sentence. Here's an active voice example:

> The administrators *assembled* (active voice) the study participants to begin the experiment.

> The *administrators* receive the emphasis of the sentence and performs the action of assembling the study participants.

>> **Passive:** When verbs are passive, the subject receives the action and the doer of the action is deemphasized. Here's a passive voice example:

> The study participants *were assembled* (passive voice) by the administrators to begin the experiment.

> The receiver of the action (participants) is emphasized, and the doer of the action (administrators) is deemphasized.

REMEMBER

Your high school English teacher may have referred to the doer of the action as the *subject*, the verb as the *predicate*, and the receiver of the action as the *direct object*.

Knowing when to use active voice

As a college student, write almost exclusively in the active voice. It's the natural pattern that people speak and write. It's also the pattern identifying how people read and listen. Readers and listeners are focused on the topic you're talking about and what happened.

Active voice is also the pattern in which people think. They generally think of ideas and people — and then think of their actions and implications. The active voice emphasizes that the doer of the action is more important than the receiver of the action. Here's an active voice example:

> The conductor *convened* the orchestra for a final performance.

In the passive voice, the receiver of the action (orchestra) receives the emphasis. Here's a passive voice example:

> The orchestra *was convened* by the conductor.

REMEMBER

In research writing, write thesis statements in the active voice and generally use the active voice to write the introduction, most of the body sentences, and the conclusion.

Here are examples of active voice verbs commonly found in each of those research sections:

>> **Introduction:** Psychologists *are studying* relationship effects of sober dating.

>> **Body:** A body of research *supports* the damaging psychological effects of binge-drinking dating.

>> **Conclusion:** Researchers *agree* that long-term effects of binge-drinking dating on future relationships need to be studied.

Recognizing when to use passive voice

The passive voice has its uses, but it's like occasionally driving over the speed limit. You need to know when to use it and how to use it safely. Misuse can easily damage your writing. APA says that "many writers overuse the passive voice." Don't be one of those excessive users.

Here's a look at when and how to use the passive voice:

>> **Irrelevant and insignificant subjects:** The doer of the action lacks importance. Here's an example:

A category 5 hurricane *was identified* in the south Atlantic Ocean.

The origin of the hurricane lacks importance. What's important is that the hurricane was identified and people in the path receive warnings.

>> **Unidentified subjects:** The subject is intentionally unidentified. Here's an example:

Errors *were made* with the software installation.

The writer chooses not to dime out the culprit who incorrectly installed the software.

The expressions *dimed out* and *culprit* represent slang and informal language unacceptable for use in research writing. *For Dummies* sometimes tolerates playfulness in its tone.

>> **Unknown subjects:** Grammar, like life, has many unknowns, and occasionally the subject of the sentence is unknown. Here's an example of a sentence where the writer doesn't know who performed the action.

Paintings in Egyptian tombs *are dated* more than two thousand years ago.

The artist is unknown, but the art is worth bucket-listing.

>> **Methods section of research:** The passive voice is frequently used in research to explain methods of collecting information. Here's an example:

Information on psychological effects of sports betting *was collected* from national data centers on gambling.

The psychological information in the sentence communicates more importance to the reader to the reader than who collected the data.

Avoid using the passive voice to disclose weaknesses in your research, such as neglecting to identify who conducted the study in this example: A study *was conducted* to analyze the effects of students' studying while sleep-deprived.

Furthermore, avoid using the passive voice when it causes complicated and wordy sentences such as the following:

>> **Wordy passive voice:** Early flying machines and flying wings *were experimented* with by Eilmer of Milmsbury and Leonardo da Vinci hundreds of years before the Wright brothers historic flight in 1903.

>> **Revised with active voice:** Before the Wright brothers' historic flight in 1903, Eilmer of Milmsbury and Leonardo da Vinci *experimented* with flying machines and flying wings.

Using show-don't-tell verbs

Like many people who value an active day, verbs thrive on activity. They prefer to show you action, rather than tell you what happened.

Here are samples of *telling* verbs revised as *showing* verbs:

Telling verb: The researcher *was displeased* over the results of the study.

Showing verb: The researcher *refuted* the results of the study.

Telling verb: The class *was* happy when the awards *were announced*.

Showing verb: The class *cheered* the awards announcement.

A variation of inactive *telling verbs* includes a collection of verbs called linking verbs that merely connect the subject with the noun or adjective that follows the linking verb. Linking verbs include *am, is, are, was, were, be, been, seems,* and *appears.*

Here are linking verb examples and their revisions:

Linking verb: The research assignment *seemed* difficult for first-year students.

Revised: The research assignment *exceeded* skills of first-year students.

Linking verb: Some college seniors *are* apprehensive about leaving college.

Revised: Some college seniors *fear* leaving college.

As a general rule, avoid almost all linking verbs by revising them as active verbs.

Disclosing hidden verbs

Verbs not only enjoy activity, but they also prefer full disclosure from being hidden in wordy expressions. Table 11-2 shows examples of wordy verb expressions fully disclosed as active verbs.

TABLE 11-2

Disclosed Hidden Verbs

Wordy Verb Expressions	Action Verbs
reached disagreement on	disagreed
settled on arbitration	arbitrated
came to a conclusion	concluded
set a requirement	required
offered a suggestion	suggested

Chapter 17 explains additional strategies for clear and concise writing.

Utilizing specific nouns

In addition to verbs, Hemingway emphasized the importance of nouns for beginning writers. More specifically, specific nouns that readers can envision with pixel-perfect images. Specific nouns, like active verbs, activate brain-imaging machines.

Here's an example: Picture, as if you were reading, the noun *person*. Then picture the noun *athlete*; then picture *football player*; and finally picture *Tom Brady*.

Reflect what just happened in your brain. The noun *person* recalled your thinking about one of hundreds of people you know. *Athlete* narrowed your thinking to people who are athletic, and *football player* narrowed your thinking to athletes who play football.

And Tom Brady appeared in your brain as if he were face-timing you. You most likely envisioned him wearing one of his team uniforms with an emboldened 12.

Your brain may not score specific images like TB12, but that's an example of the image you want your readers to recall when you write nouns. Table 11-3 shows you the continuum of noun images that range from general to specific.

WARNING

Avoid vague nouns such as *thing, way, factor, case,* and *stuff*.

TABLE 11-3

General to Specific Nouns

General	Less General	Specific
seat	bench	pew
entertainment	play	*Our Town*
author	novelist	Toni Morrison
athlete	basketball player	Caitlin Clark
light	ceiling light	chandelier

Varying Sentence Patterns: Mashing Words

Music has been identified as the universal language, appealing to people worldwide. It moves people spiritually, physically, and emotionally. The patterns of sentences create the music of language. Studies have shown that music can heal people, and parents know that the sound of language can sooth children.

Good writing moves readers similarly and causes readers to laugh, smile, nod, and cry. And sometimes good writing by students moves professors to draw an A-frame house on students' papers.

These sections explain patterns of sentence structures, sometimes musical, that complement meaning, improve writing style, and can raise your writing level an octave or higher.

Focusing on sentence length

Sentences with similar rhythms are like music with the same endless percussion beat: da dum, da dum, da dum. Varying sentence length alters sentence rhythm, adding variety to your writing and establishing reader interest.

Avoid patterns of predictable sentences that have the feeling of an elevator that stops at every floor.

Steering clear of sentence length problems

Long sentences, approximately 35 to 55 words, are sometimes as interesting as waiting at a railroad crossing for the passing of a hundred-car freight train. But their purpose in research writing includes explaining complex information.

Lengthy sentences can be intimidating to some readers, but not to professors when they contain complex research ideas. With the exception of occasional long sentences in the body section of your research, prefer a sentence-length range between 21 and 34 words.

REMEMBER

APA doesn't designate sentence length, but their guidelines apply to professional researchers more than college students. Almost all college writing programs encourage sentence variety with varied sentence length, guidelines preferred by almost all college professors.

Creating length variation

Vary long sentences and short sentences to create surprise and drama in your writing. Here's an example of lengthy sentences sandwiching a five-word sentence and a three-word sentence:

> Unlike personal loans for vacations and expensive transportation, students apply for student loans for the purpose of investing in themselves and the financial security of their families, and in many cases snapping a decades-long line of poverty (37 words). But loan costs are unreasonable (5 words). In addition to loan repayments, students are required to repay high interest rates, high service changes, and begin repaying as soon as the loans are secured and while they are in college (32 words). Here's a solution (3 words): Cap reasonable amounts students can borrow with colleges offering scholarships for students in good academic standing, and also lower borrowing rates to 2 percent, beginning when students graduate (28 words).

Patterns of long sentences are tools of professional researchers and used for research paper writing. Long sentences frequently appear in the body section and conclusion of research papers where evidence and implications are developed. Think of longer sentences as approximately 35 words or longer, with an oversupply of words such as *since, therefore, who, that,* and *which* clauses — and excessive punctuation of semicolons, colons, and commas.

Avoid confusing longer sentences with boring and uninviting sentences. Correlate sentence length with sentence complexity, such as the following 50-plus word sentence appropriate for a research paper conclusion, and addressing a topic that interests readers of this book:

> A student's decision to apply for financial aid requires projection of economic conditions at the time of anticipated graduation and degree-earning potential in the major field of study — high-risk factors that if predicted incorrectly or if the student's degree-earning abilities are overestimated could result in lifetime consequences of financial instability.

TIP

Avoid confusing long sentences with wordy sentences. Chapter 17 explains reducing wordiness from sentences with the goal of saying more with fewer words.

Branching variety

Sentences, like most trees, fully express themselves when they branch out. But unlike trees, sentences branch in three directions, each adding to writing variety. The following sections peel back the bark and explain how sentences branch.

To the right

Right-branching sentences (sentences that detail information following the subject and verb) are a fundamental structure of sentence writing and sentence variety. Brain-friendly, right-branching elements add importance to the subject and verb and serve as placeholders for a variety of additional sentence elements, including the following:

» Bulleted or numbered lists

» Series of items

» Numbered steps

» Explanation following a colon or dash

Here's the recipe for right-branching sentences. Begin with a simple subject-verb sentence, and blend in ingredients such as a prepositional phrase, an appositive, and a dependent clause.

Here's what a right-branching sentence looks like:

Researching (subject) *begins* (verb) in the library, the academic center of your campus (appositive), where research librarians can help you with the fundamentals of searching databases (dependent clause).

In the sample sentence, the subject and verb are followed by the right-branching elements "in the library . . . searching databases."

To the left

Left-branching sentences are like waiting in traffic for a light to turn green. The sentence remains in neutral until the subject and verb are identified. Here's an example:

To encourage students to think before answering the question about the journal article, the *professor* (subject) *waited* (verb) five seconds before calling on a student.

In the sample sentence, the subject and verb are preceded by the left-branching "To encourage . . . journal article."

Limit your use of left-branching elements because they delay readers' understanding of the subject and verb and the sentence's main idea. Left-branching forces readers to think: "Get to the point." Used strategically, left branching can build drama before getting to the point, assuming the reader still cares about the point.

Lock left-branching sentences in your writer's toolbox and use them sparingly. They're common in historical documents such as the *Declaration of Independence*: *When in the course of human events . . .* and proclamations by local governments that begin with *Whereas . . .*

In the middle

Middle-branching sentences can serve as a breath of fresh words tucked between the subject and verb — as long as the breath doesn't require CPR.

Here's an example of a middle-branching sentence:

> The *professor* (subject), thinking about the disappointing research projects that were just returned to students at the beginning of class, mentally *regrouped* and *started* (compound verbs) lecturing.

In the example sentence, the middle-branching element (thinking about the disappointing research projects that were just returned to students at the beginning of class) is positioned between the subject and verb.

Going for grammatical variety

Sentence variety begins with grammatical constructions called *form* and *purpose*. These two variations offer flexibility to express thoughts simply or intricately and assertively or subtly.

Sentence forms

Sentence variety by form includes the following:

>> **Simple:** Simple sentences express one complete thought (one independent clause) with at least one subject and one verb. Here's an example:

> *Covid* (subject) *changed* (verb) the structure of the workplace.

An *independent clause* includes a subject and verb that expresses a complete thought. The previous example (*Covid changed . . .*) is an independent clause.

>> **Compound:** Compound sentences contain two or more independent clauses, connected by a conjunction, comma, or semicolon. Take a look at this example:

> *Casey argues that success requires a work ethic and intelligence* (independent clause), and *Ruiz disagrees* (independent clause).

The two independent clauses are connected by the conjunction *and*.

Compound sentences are connected with *coordinating conjunctions* (see Chapter 12), words that connect equal constructions such as independent clauses. Common coordinating conjunctions include *and, but,* for, and *or*.

>> **Complex:** Complex sentences contain one independent clause and at least one dependent clause. Here's an example:

> *Because most colleges are expensive* (dependent clause), *most students work to help support themselves* (independent clause).

A *dependent clause*, also called a *subordinate clause*, begins with a *subordinate conjunction* and depends on the independent cause for its meaning. Subordinate conjunctions include *although, because, before, once, since, until, when,* and *while*.

Adopt the complex sentence as your go-to sentence for college writing. Its structure allows one main idea (one independent clause) and at least one subordinate idea (one dependent clause), allowing the flexibility to make a statement and then offer an analysis of that statement. The complex sentence adapts itself to the ideal average sentence word-range between 25 to 30 words.

>> **Compound-complex:** Compound-complex sentences consist of two or more independent clauses and one dependent clause. For example:

> *Carlson found that exercise improves GPA* (independent clause) *when the exercise is aerobic* (dependent clause), *and Grossman's research supported her findings* (independent clause).

Compound-complex sentences are used to express complex ideas and are usually found in the body section of research papers.

The length of compound-complex sentences generally exceeds the average length of a sentence (22–34 words). Complex sentences are effective tools for college students to use in research writing.

Sentences purposes

The following classifications identify the variety of sentence purposes:

>> **Declarative:** A declarative sentence states a fact and includes a subject and verb. Here's an example:

> *Successful writing* (subject) *results* (verb) from successful reading.

Declarative sentences are the building blocks of writing a sentence and expressing an idea. When you're challenged to express a complex thought, return to the principles of a declarative sentence: Who or what do you want to make a statement about (subject) and what action (verb) did the subject perform?

» **Interrogative:** An interrogative sentence asks a question, such as the following:

How close was Leonardo daVinci to creating a flying machine?

Interrogative sentences represent a form of sentence variety, in addition to focusing readers to think of the answer to the question.

» **Imperative:** Imperative sentences are known as command sentences. They also give advice. Here's an example:

Use the active voice almost exclusively in academic writing — with the exception of research papers.

Imperative sentences are commonly used in persuasive writing.

» **Exclamatory:** Exclamatory sentences show surprise or emotion, such as the following:

The results were unexpected!

Exclamatory sentences are seldom used in research writing but serve a limited purpose in essay writing, reports, and reaction papers. Think of them as spicy hot seasoning on your food. What you think is too little may be too much.

Striving for structural variety

Language structure has the variety of student personalities on a college campus. The variety of English language structures — beyond basic subject–verb–object sentence pattern — allows almost unlimited combinations of words and phrases to express ideas.

Here's a look at a few examples of structural sentence variety:

» **Prepositional phrase-subject-verb-compound object:** *At the beginning of class* (prepositional phrase), *some professors* (subject) *announce* (verb) *assignment reminders and upcoming readings (compound* object).

» **Dependent clause-subject-verb-prepositional phrase:** *Although research is time consuming* (dependent clause), *the skills (subject) to acquire new knowledge apply* (verb) *across the curriculum* (prepositional phrase).

>> **Compound gerund-subject-verb-direct object-dependent clause:**
Researching and reading (compound gerunds) *represent* (verb) *two skills* (direct object) *that college students need to practice regularly* (dependent clause).

>> **Subject-appositive-verb-prepositional phrase-dependent clause:** *Library databases* (subject), *the key to successful research* (appositive), *are underutilized* (verb) *by college students* (prepositional phrase) *who lack research experience* (dependent clause).

Here's a brief review of grammar terminology used in the previous sentence variety examples:

>> **Prepositional phrase:** A small grouping of words that begin with a preposition, include a noun or pronoun, and are used as an adjective or adverb. Common prepositions include *at, to, from, after, in, above, into, at, until,* and *with.* For example: Class met *in the library.*

>> **Gerund:** A gerund is a verb form that ends in *ing* and is used as a noun. Here are examples: *writing, reading, thinking, researching, celebrating,* and *coordinating.*

>> **Appositive:** An appositive is a noun next to another noun that explains the first noun. For example: Professor Stanley, *winner of the achievement award,* is scheduled to lecture in Wilson Hall.

>> **Object:** A direct object, used in the sentence variety examples, is the receiver of the action and usually follows the verb. For example: The study results showed *correlation* among researchers.

Varying Word Patterns: Letter Power

Here's more advice from Captain Obvious: Writing in an academic style requires the use of academic words. Each content area contains terminology specific to its discipline.

Your word choices create the style and structure of your sentences, with an emphasis of active verbs and specific nouns explained earlier in this chapter. These sections show you academic terminology in a variety of academic areas.

Recognizing research words

Word choices are like the foods you put into your digestive system. Healthy food (and exercise) is the foundation of a healthy you. With unhealthy food, your nutrition needs major revision.

Verbs and nouns represent healthy word choices, especially for your research paper writing which requires a strong diet of academic language. Here's a look at academic words regularly used in research writing.

>> **Verbs:** clarify, highlight, analyze, synthesize, collaborate, identify, conclude, advance, contemplate, prevail, substantiate, confirm, underline, implement, surmise, approximate, diffuse, disseminate, advance, qualify, argue, attribute, generate, administer, append, amend, commemorate, draft, facilitate, migrate, minimize, investigate, fund, and envision

>> **Nouns:** surveys, questions, results, conclusions, evaluations, antithesis, assessments, consensus, theories, investigations, evidence, conclusions, illustrations, acquisition, acknowledgement, ambiguities, concept, fluctuations, and resolution

>> **Adjectives:** robust, rigorous, compelling, dynamic, accessible, accurately, adjacent, arbitrary, and analytical

>> **Transitional words:** consequentially, therefore, resulting in, as a result of, and whereby

Utilizing sensory words

Since we learn through the senses, audience meaning is enhanced by sensory words whose meanings shortcut to the brain and remain in storage for decades. Here's an example: Recall childhood memories of sounds and smells. Can you recall sensory words from your playground or favorite video games? Can you recall cooking smells of your favorite cookies?

Unlike the brain's rapid-response to sensory words, non-sensory words are wired directly to your brain's text processing center and require longer developing time. Research also shows that sensory words are commonly used in business and improve sales. Check out sensory words used in advertising and on food menus.

Use sensory words as appropriate in your college writing, including your research paper writing. Here's a list of words that appeal to the senses:

>> **Sight:** branching, colossal, disheveled, massive, delicate, robust, and exotic

>> **Sound:** crushing, crashing, monotonous, muffled, deafening, and piercing

» **Touch:** palatable, dense, fragile, shrunken, and slippery

» **Taste:** raw, refreshing, hearty, mild, and fresh

» **Smell:** antiseptic, reeking, acrid, and stagnant

TIP

Sensory words are also commonly used in email such as the following: *I have a mountain (sight) of work for this afternoon. I can squeeze (touch) time tomorrow. Would you like to share a crusty (taste) pizza for lunch?*

Including content words

In your classes you're surrounded with academic words from course content. Here's some examples:

» **Health and nutrition:** calories, cholesterol, protein, and vitamins

» **Math:** coordinates, perpendicular, mean, radius, cone, and parallel

» **Political science:** alliance, impunity, lobby, advocate, compromise, and legislature

» **Philosophy:** logic, ethics, moral, pathos, aesthetics, and catharsis

» **Literature:** characterization, plot, narrative, soliloquy, protagonist, and theme

Identifying cautious words

Because academic language discusses complex issues, words of caution are sometimes required to qualify absolutes and ensure accuracy. For example, when rules lack absolute certainty, they may require qualifiers. Here's an example:

The results of the study indicated that *excessive* sports betting *usually* results in declining grades.

The qualifier *excessive* identifies a high-level of sports betting, and the qualifier *usually* explains that declining grades is likely to occur. Other common qualifying words include the following:

» appears

» can

» could

» generally

» ideally

» likely

» may

» possibly

» sometimes

» usually

Building Better Paragraphs: Idea Placeholders

Paragraphs are like your respiratory system, circulatory system, immune system, digestive system — that's enough systems to know that you don't have much life in your writing without them.

The building blocks of major ideas, paragraphs support your thesis, develop your argument, and answer your research questions. Without good paragraphs your paper is on life support.

REMEMBER

Paragraphs usually consist of five or six sentences and are longer for research papers. If you don't have at least one indentation in a page or printed text, your paragraph is too long. Paragraphs for essays, reaction papers, and reports are shorter than research paper paragraphs. These sections look at the major elements of paragraph building.

Topic sentences

Topic sentences are the packaging for paragraphs and identify the one main idea developed in the paragraph. Located in the body section of research papers, topic sentences introduce pieces of evidence.

Some topic sentences are positioned as transitional sentences and include key words such as *also*, *added to*, *additionally*, and *another*. Here's an example of a transitional topic sentence:

> Chiminez *also* provides evidence supporting the belief that college loans contribute to unreasonable lifetime debt after graduation.

And here's an example of a traditional topic sentence:

> Stockton's study titled "Loans of Destitution" supports the belief that college loans contribute to unreasonable lifetime debt after graduation.

Supporting evidence

Supporting evidence is located in the middle sentences of the paragraph. Types of evidence used in research includes expert testimony, statistics, studies, and quotations. Paragraphs are stronger when they include evidence from several sources.

Here's an example of supporting evidence that includes multiple sources:

> *Murdock and others* argue that the post-Covid workplace "cannot include the flexibility that employees expect."

Concluding sentences

The purpose of concluding sentences includes summarizing the paragraph and identifying the importance of the piece of evidence. Here's an example:

> The research of Murdock and the findings of Summers and others support the belief that multitasking lacks brain-friendly processing. Therefore, students' belief in its effectiveness is a false premise and ineffective study strategy.

Connecting sentences

The purpose of connecting sentences is to align evidence to the thesis and identifying the "so what" of the evidence. Here's an example of language connecting evidence to the thesis:

> The argument that multitasking improves study habits lacks support by current researchers and represents a detrimental study practice for students who believe in its effectiveness.

Balancing Elements: Parallel Structure

Parallel structure is the grammatical principle that similar ideas require similar grammatical structures. The principle helps the writer express complex ideas logically and helps the reader comprehend complex ideas clearly. Lack of parallel structure is like having each of your devices operating with a different platform.

Here's an example of unparallel structure:

> First-year college students face many challenges including adapting to a higher level of academics, for the first time accept responsibility for acting like an adult, and to build a new social life in an unfamiliar environment.

The reader comprehends *adapting to a higher level of academics*. But the next challenge beginning with *for the first time*, confusing the reader because it's not parallel with *adapting to a higher level* ...

Here's an example of the previous sentence written parallel:

First-year college students face many challenges including adapting to a higher level of academics, accepting responsibility to act like an adult, and socializing in an unfamiliar environment.

The sentence was revised parallel by beginning all challenges with –ing gerunds: *adapting*, *accepting*, and *socializing*.

Parallel structure uses in research writing include the following:

» **Items in a list:**

The job-searching process includes the following:

- Creating a resume
- Searching for companies
- Writing a cover letter
- Preparing for an interview

» **Items with conjunctions such as *and*:**

Many college students enjoy a quiet walk-through campus *and* a quick workout on the treadmill.

In this example, the conjunction *and* connects parallel items that begin with a noun and verb (*quiet walk* and *quick workout*).

» **Items in a series:**

My favorite sports authors include Ed Gebhart, Harry Chaykum, Ray Didinger, Stan Hochman, Bill Lyon, *and* Red Smith.

The serial comma, the comma following *Bill Lyon*, is required by APA, MLA, and Chicago.

REMEMBER

Organizing Writing: Transitions and Flow

Think of *transitions* as the organizational structure of a piece of writing, like a book's spine that secures all pages between the covers. Writing organization begins with the beginning and end, the opening and closing of the piece of writing. What remains after the beginning and end is the middle.

Here's a look at organizational structure of a piece of research writing:

>> **Opening:** Includes the title, first sentence, opening, thesis, and introduction to the topic; in research frequently includes the headings "Introduction" and "Statement of the Problem"

>> **Closing:** Includes application of the thesis to broader audiences and in research sometimes includes the heading "Discussion"

>> **Body:** Excludes information in the opening and closing and contains evidence that supports the thesis

Within the organizational structure, transitions establish relationships between sentences and paragraphs using words such as: *similarly, however, yet, finally, specifically, such as, consequently, therefore,* and *furthermore.*

Theses flow with a logical organization such as least important to most important, chronological, or sequentially.

TIP

Evaluate your flow of information with a reverse outline. Identify each paragraph topic in a few words and evaluate the logical flow of those paragraph topics.

IN THIS CHAPTER

» Diving deeper into verbs and nouns

» Solving problem pairs and trios

» Singling out attention-seeking words

» Capitalizing the tall and short of it

Chapter **12**

Reviewing Fundamentals: Grammar and Conventions

Grammar and conventions are the least favorite kids on the playground, but their teachers require everyone to play with them — hoping that they develop into best buds.

Your college professors, lacking the patience of elementary teachers, expect near-perfection with grammar and conventions. Committing a repeated violation is considered a capital offense because of higher expectations in college.

In this chapter I highlight verbs and noun variations that improve writing clarity, pronoun rules that avoid disagreement, and description positioning that aligns ideas in your head with those on paper. I also review punctuation and spelling rules that avoid reader distractions.

These grammar and usage rules can't earn you points, but they can prevent your losing you points that can bankrupt your grading budget.

Following Rules of Language: Grammar and Usage

How important is grammar and usage in your life? A recent study showed that misuse of grammar can be a dating deal-breaker among college students, and they wouldn't date peers who use double negatives, incorrect pronouns, and faulty sentences. Faulty writing can also ruin your writing grade. For help with basic grammar issues, see Geraldine Woods' *Basic English Grammar For Dummies* (John Wiley & Sons). But if you enjoy the humor of grammar, read Lynne Truss' *Eats, Shoots & Leaves: The Zero Tolerance Approach to Punctuation* (Profile Books).

The following sections aren't meant to entertain you, but rather I include them to inform you of grammar basic to your research writing.

Considering verb variations: Parting ways

Think of verbs as a three-part performance:

>> **Present part:** Used for the present tense

>> **Past part:** Used for past tense

>> **Past participle:** Used with helping verbs to form additional tenses

These sections review verb forms necessary for understanding verb tense formations.

Principal parts of regular verbs

Identification of the correct verb part is determined by their classification of being *regular* or *irregular*. It's not complicated. Let me explain.

Most verbs are *regular*, meaning they form the past and past participle by adding *d* or *ed* to the present part: Table 12-1 shows examples.

In other words, the past tense of a regular verb is formed by adding d or ed to the past part as in the examples: They *researched*. They *revised*.

Principal parts of irregular verbs

Regular verbs are hard-wired in your daily speaking and writing. No problem. The *irregular verbs* are the problem, especially the past participle of irregulars because they require a helping verb such as *have* or *had*.

Principal Parts of Regular Verbs

TABLE 12-1

Present	Past	Past Participle
research	researched	(have, has, had) researched
revise	revised	(have, has, had) revised
contact	contacted	(have, has, had) contacted
notify	notified	(have, has, had) notified
support	supported	(have, has, had)

In other words, when you speak or write a verb such as *gone*, an auxiliary verb is required with it. The problem with learning the past participle forms of irregular verbs is that they require memorization. But you'll learn those forms by ear as you hear them used correctly in the college environment.

Table 12-2 shows principal parts of common irregular verbs.

Principal Parts of Irregular Verbs

TABLE 12-2

Present	Past	Past Participle
do	did	(have, has, had) done
be/are	was/were	(have, has, had) been
begin	began	(have, has, had) begun
come	came	(have, has, had) come
run	ran	(have, has, had) run
choose	chose	(have, has, had) chosen

In other words, the past tense of an irregular verb is formed with the past part of the verb, as in the examples: They *began*. They *chose*.

REMEMBER

Past participles of regular and irregular verbs cohabitate with auxiliary verbs such as *have*, *has*, or *had*. Helping or auxiliary verbs are verb forms necessary to express some tenses. Helping verbs include *are*, *is*, *am*, *be*, *been*, *can*, *do*, *does*, *have*, *has*, *must*, and *should*. Main verbs with helping verbs look like this: *is* considering, *will be* revising, *has been* anticipating, and *should* research.

Ensuring pronouns agree: Compatibility

Pronouns and their elements like to agree, but like people, they have their bad days and require an attitude change to be agreeable. When relationships are good, pronouns agree with their *antecedent* (the noun or pronoun they replace) in these four ways:

>> **Person:** First (I, we), second person (you) and third person (they)

>> **Number:** Singular (refers to one) or plural (refers to two or more)

>> **Gender:** Female, male, and nonbinary

>> **Case:** Subject, object, and possessive

Look at this example showing how pronouns and antecedents agree:

> *She* and *David* drove to Boston to visit *their* older brother.

The pronoun *their* (third person, plural, male and female, possessive) agrees with its antecedent (*she* and *David* are equivalent to *they*).

Additional rules for number agreement (singular and plural) include the following (with their compatible examples):

>> **Singular nouns connected by *and* require a plural antecedent.** *Philosophy* and *psychology* (plural) have *their* (plural) unique challenges.

>> ***Both, few, many,* and *several* require plural antecedents.** *Few* (plural) college courses lack *their* (plural) required readings.

>> **Compound subjects joined by *or* or *nor* require an antecedent agreeing with the subject closer to the verb.** *Wi-Fi* (singular) or *routers* (plural) have *their* (plural) regular problems.

>> **Course names require singular pronouns.** *Mathematics* (singular) *has* (singular) *its* (singular) unique vocabulary.

REMEMBER

The plural pronoun *they*, inclusive of all people, has been adopted as both singular and plural by all major style guides. Here's an example: The *dentist* performed *their* implant surgery.

Positioning description: Location, location

Professors don't accept student misspelling excuses such as you left out only one letter. Neither do they accept misplacing description of adjectives that produce often illogical sentences, such as: Isabelle rode the horse with a smile.

REMEMBER

Positioning descriptive elements in a sentence is as important as correct order of letters in spelling. Accurate positioning of description is important to professors and should be important to you.

The following guidelines (with their compatible examples) help you with positioning description:

>> **Immediately before or after the word it describes:**

> **Misplaced:** The researchers talked about improving math performance *at the conference in Hawaii*.

> **Revised:** *At the conference in Hawaii*, the researchers talked about improving math performance.

The description *at the conference in Hawaii* is inaccurately positioned after *performance*, but it requires positioning closer to *researchers*, the word it describes. In the revision, *at the conference* is positioned before the word it describes *researcher*.

>> **Following introductory participle phrases (–*ing* or –*ed* phrases used as adjectives) with the subject of the sentence:**

> **Misplaced:** *According to Cahill and others*, mentoring must be implemented by schools to solve problems.

> **Revised:** *According to Cahill and others*, schools must implement mentoring to solve problems.

I revised the example by repositioning the subject *(schools)* after the introductory participle phrase *(According to Cahill and others)*.

>> **Logically position awkward adverbs:**

> **Misplaced:** People who are honest are *usually* truthful.

> **Revised:** Honest people are *usually* truthful.

> **Misplaced:** I *almost* revised half the research paper.

> **Revised:** I revised *almost* half the research paper.

> **Misplaced:** I *only* submitted half the report.

> **Revised:** I submitted *only* half the report.

Using conjunctions: Connecting here to there

Conjunctions escalate your writing from first-year college to graduate school. They transform simple sentences to compound and complex sentences — and from simple ideas to complex ideas. Three variations of conjunctions are available for your writing flexibility, which I discuss here.

Coordinating

Coordinating conjunctions connect equivalent elements, shown here with their accompanying examples:

> » **And:** Some successful students research in the library, *and* some research remotely.
>
> » **But:** Library databases are your best sources, *but* some students prefer to struggle with Internet sources.
>
> » **Or:** Research in the library, *or* research at home — but meet with a reference librarian before beginning your research.

Correlative

Correlative conjunctions are used in pairs. They connect equal elements and represent a good tool for sentence variety:

> » **Both . . . and:** *Both* working in the library *and* working remotely are successful strategies.
>
> » **Either . . . or:** *Either* carefully analyze the research assignment *or* suffer the consequences.
>
> » **Not only . . . but also:** *Not only* meet with your professor, *but also* meet with the writing center.

Subordinating

Build a relationship with *subordinating conjunctions* because they're used to create complex sentences, your go-to sentences to express complex ideas (see the following examples):

Conjunctions

after	because	in order that	since	whenever
although	before	just as	so that	whether
as if	even if	once	unless	who
as soon as	even though	provided that	until	which

Study examples of the following sentences using subordinating conjunctions:

>> **Even though:** *Even though* your library invests in academically vetted, peer-reviewed databases, some students prefer beginning their research online.

>> **When:** *When* your research frustrates you, remind yourself of the big picture of why you're doing the work.

>> **Since:** *Since* current resources are required on almost every topic, learn date selection features on database parameters.

>> **Whenever:** *Whenever* you're challenged to express your idea, redirect your thinking to identify the subject you're talking about and the action it performs.

Solving relating pronoun problems

College writers and many graduate-level writers frequently confuse some pairs of related pronouns. Here's a look into problem-pair pronouns:

>> **That, which:** *That* introduces clauses essential to sentence meaning. *Which* introduces clauses nonessential to sentence meaning. Nonessential clauses are marked off with commas. Here are examples:

- The field of study *that* offers flexibility in business is a management major.

- A management degree, *which* offers flexibility of careers, is popular with many college business students.

>> **Who, that:** *Who* refers to people; *that* refers to ideas, objects, and organizations. For example:

- The professor *who* appeared as a guest lecturer also answered questions about artificial intelligence.

- Students are expected to use databases *that* are peer-reviewed and vetted by academic committees.

>> **Who, whom:** *Who* is a subject pronoun; *whom* is an object pronoun. For example:

- *Who* answered that difficult question in class?

- For *whom* did you go to the bookstore?

>> **Who's, whose:** *Who's* is a contraction for *who is; whose* is a possessive pronoun. Here are two examples:

- *Who's* responsible for the weather balloon that flew over the country?

- *Whose* backpack was left in the classroom?

Creating Sentence Cadence: Punctuation

Punctuation has been a challenge for students since the invention of the printing press between the 9th and 14th centuries — as well as the accompanying rules of punctuation — that became the standard of authors who wrote the thickest grammar books.

Some early punctuation rules were written in fast-drying concrete and some were written in sand at the water's edge. Many rules originated by printers who identified appropriate stops and pauses when text was read aloud.

Regardless of the uncertain origin of punctuation and its rules, college students are expected to understand basics of punctuation rules that I explain in the following sections. Think of punctuation as the assistive devices that control smooth flowing sentences. These sections highlight APA, MLA, and Chicago punctuation commonly used in research and other college writing.

Commas: Taking short breaths

Commas are short breaths in the middle of sentences, like riding the local train into a major city. Each stop allows a brief opportunity to regroup and check out what's ahead.

The following comma rules with the accompanying examples are highlighted by major style guides and identified as points of emphasis for college writers.

>> **Following an introductory dependent clause:** *Since some college students experience high levels of stress post-Covid,* researchers are beginning long-term studies of student stress and pandemics.

Omission of this comma following an opening introductory clause has been identified as the most common comma error among business writers in North America. It's also a common error among college writers.

>> **Following a four-word or longer prepositional phrase:** *At the start of new semesters,* many students create a calendar of assignment due dates.

>> **Preceding a conjunction in a compound sentence:** Some college students embrace the excitement of research, *and* they develop research skills that complement their careers.

>> **Following items in a series that precede "and":** My favorite authors include *Adam Grant, Walter Isaacson, Malcom Gladwell,* and *Ray Didinger.*

>> **Separating adjectives that independently describe the same word:** Kiehl's robust, seminal study was recognized at the national conference.

>> **Separating aside comments:** Matson's study, *for example,* included populations neglected in previous studies.

>> **Separating dates and locations:** Leonardo da Vinci was born April 15, 1452.

When the date and year appear in the middle of a sentence, a comma follows the year, as in this example: Leonardo da Vinci was born April 15, 1452, and died May 2, 1519.

>> **Separating an appositive from the main sentence idea:** Da Vinci, *arguably the most creative person who ever lived,* frequently missed deadlines working on commissioned artwork.

Colons and semicolons: Taking deeper breaths

Colons and semicolons identify reader stops longer than a comma's half-stop and shorter than a period's full-stop. The following sections explain uses of colons and semicolons.

Colons

Think of the colon as a marker indicating information that requires major processing.

Colon uses common to your everyday life include displaying time (11:13 a.m.) and separating hours, minutes, and seconds (4:23:03).

Two colon rules emphasized by MLA are the following:

>> **Introduce a list of related items.** Use a colon to introduce a list and after words such as "as follows" and "the following." Here's an example:

> Guidelines for writing successful research papers include the following:
> * Analyze the assignment.
> * Identify the purpose of the assignment.
> * Create a thesis statement and research questions.
> * Research evidence using library databases.
> * Write a first draft beginning with the body section.

Note that items are written parallel (see Chapter 11) with each item beginning with an action verb. Each item begins with a capital letter because it begins a sentence, and each item ends with end punctuation because it's a sentence.

>> **Elaborate a previous sentence or clause.** Because many research sentences are longer than the average of 25 to 30 words, colons are frequently used to extend sentences such as the following:

> Here's a piece of evidence-supported advice for ensuring college success: Attend class; complete assignments; and socialize.

Semicolons

Semicolons are like commas on steroids. They're like super separators who clarify boundaries for complex groups of related words, phrases, and clauses that are separated by commas.

Here's an example:

> Research writing success requires aligning an assignment topic that includes a course reference, extended application, and required reading; researching library databases, academic search engines, and artifact collections; and writing and revising drafts, completing a reference section, and having a draft reviewed by the writing center.

The sample sentence contains three series that explain requirements of research writing success:

> aligning an assignment topic . . . reading;
>
> researching library . . . collections;
>
> writing and revising . . . center.

The semicolons separating these long series contain commas that clarify the smaller series within the semicolon series. The example sentence is also an example of a *serial semicolon*, a semicolon positioned before the final series item.

Dashes and slashes: Interrupting politely

Two marks of punctuation visually on different paths are dashes and slashes. Dashes can be rude interruptions, but their use isn't as confusing as slashes, either/or message.

If your curiosity includes the backslash (\), it's not a mark of punctuation. It's used exclusively in computing.

Dashes

Dashes are like weather, adaptable to sudden changes. They appear in two sizes with conflicting purposes. Here's the explanation:

>> **En dash (–):** The highly compatible *en dash* happily joins equal elements such as points in competitive events and page numbers identified for future reference. Here's a sample sentence containing uses of both:

   The Eagles defeated the 49ers 31–7; see pages 21–22.

>> **Em dash (—):** The bolder and twice as long *em dash* creates scenes in the middle of populated sentences — like this bold interruption — before returning to the main sentence thought. If you missed that example, here's another one:

   The role of public education—precarious before the pandemic—faces unprecedented challenges afterward.

REMEMBER

The em dash lacks spaces before and after (—) in Chicago style and also in APA and MLA. The AP (Associated Press) style guide for journalism and news writing requires spaces before and after (—). (*For Dummies* books also use a space before and after.) As always with style variations, ask professors if they have preferences.

Slashes

Slashes are experiencing an identity crisis with APA identifying them with aliases such as *virgule, solidus,* and *shill.* Interesting.

Uses of slashes (/) (with the accompanying examples) include the following:

>> **Identify options.** The professor's style guide includes the unusual options of APA and/or MLA, but not Chicago.

Avoid all-inclusive sentences such as the following: New all-purpose footwear is designed for walking/jogging/running/mountain climbing/skateboarding and fishing.

The sentence looks like a URL and the slash uses are as useless as the shoes. And who ever heard of shoes for fishing?

Because slashes challenge reader understanding, use them sparingly, about as infrequently as you drop a course. You wouldn't like your professor telling you your research paper grade is A/F.

>> **Separate fractions.** The professor required submitting ¾ of the research paper two weeks before deadline.

>> **Abbreviate dates.** 1/14/23.

>> **Separate lines of poetry.** Once upon a midnight dreary, while I pondered weak and weary, / Over many a quaint and curious volume of forgotten lore. . . .

Ellipsis, parentheses, and brackets: Separating silently

Ellipses, parentheses, and brackets — the silent minority of punctuation — enter a sentence with a whisper and exit with a whimper. They deserve an Emmy Award for performances in research. These sections explain.

Ellipsis

Ellipsis can be annoying. Sometimes they never know when to shut down. They go on, and on, and on . . . . But looking at ellipses as a minimalist, it's one all-purpose abbreviation.

Here are examples (with accompanying examples) of their major uses:

>> **Extension of similar content:** The professor again explained to first-year students the importance of attending class . . .

>> **Omission in a quotation:** McGee says, "Gun violence is a major issue . . . in major cities."

>> **Omission of a sentence:** The oceans are underdeveloped as alternate sources of energy . . . Venture capitalists are exploring opportunities.

Sentence-ending ellipsis include the fourth dot for end punctuation: Many students disagree that college is the best years of their lives . . . .

Parentheses

Parentheses (an opening and closing performance) are the placeholders of research. Their uses include the following scenarios (with accompanying examples):

➤ **Citations:** A study of first-year college students shows that better college adjustments are made by students who spent at least a week away from home in the past year *(Gilbert, 2017)*.

➤ **Numbers and letters in lists:** The university required research papers include *(1)* introduction, *(2)* body, *(3)* conclusion, and *(4)* reference.

➤ **Reference to related material:** Most companies have policies against shopping online during company hours. *(Refer to company manuals.)*

➤ **Explanation of an abbreviation:** Please refer to the Student Assistance Form *(SAF)*.

Brackets

The purpose of brackets is to add important information [more important than parentheses] to quotations and sentences. Uses of brackets [with accompanying examples] include the following:

➤ **Further explanation in a quotation:** Smith argued that sugary drinks were not as unhealthy as reported. *[Smith's study was funded by the soft drink industry.]*

➤ **Editorial content:** They *[college seniors]* were declared "career ready."

➤ **Information within parentheses:** (Journalism, p. 34-26 *[vol. 2]*)

➤ **Expletives:** The asteroid was *[expletive]* huge!

➤ **[sic] "as written":** Allison has less *[sic]* credits than Isabelle.

Seeking Attention: Italicizing

Some words need special attention or conventions to function. When common words are attired with unique characters, fonts, and adornments, they signify meaning beyond their common usage.

Many of these word designations communicate meaning common to research. The following sections explain words with special conventions.

Italics: Making unique appearances

Italics, a cool-looking cursive font that first appeared in Italy, has been used in the English language to designate special meaning to words since the 1500s. Common uses of italics include identifying major creative works such as titles of books, pieces of art, court decisions, periodicals, movies, poems, plays, newspapers, and web pages.

Italics tell you as a reader that the italicized word stands out in its class. Examples look like the following: *Hamlet*, *Challenger*, *The New Yorker*, *The Lion King*, *The Magic Flute*, *Marbury v. Madison*, and *Titanic*.

When titles are italicized, punctuation that is part of the title is also italicized as in this example: *Who's Afraid of Virginia Wolf?*

When handwriting, designate italics by underlining. It looks like this: The causes of the sinking of the <u>Titanic</u> continue to be investigated.

TIP

Don't italicize words to emphasize them. Many professors view italics for emphasis as a sign of weak writing. Choose specific nouns and verbs to emphasize meaning (see Chapter 11).

WARNING

Take a look at additional uses of italics frequently used in college writing.

>> **Key terms:** APA emphasizes italics for key terms, such as words that require follow-up meaning in a sentence. Here's an example: The significance of a *black hole* has not been clearly defined by scientists.

>> **Words used as *words*:** When you're using a word or phrase in a context other than its designated meaning, italicize the word as in this example: Two words frequently misused are *farther* and *further*.

Numbers: Figuring out uses

Your attention to detail includes accurately writing numbers, and it's more complex than 1, 2, 3 . . . . Here's a look at guidelines for numbers (accompanied by examples) that most styles agree with:

>> **Spell the words for numbers from zero to nine; use figures for 10 and above.** Herzog's study included *seven* books and *12* periodicals. Chicago style requires words for numbers under 100, and figures when numbers are used with a unit of measurement (5G, 150 pounds). (FYI: *For Dummies* books spell out ten.)

>> **Form number plurals by adding "s" or "es."** Groups of *fours* and *sixes* were eliminated from the study.

>> **Prefer figures to represent dates, ages, scores, and sums of money.** A *$100* fuel surcharge was added to all passengers on the flight.

>> **Avoid beginning a sentence or heading with a numerical figure, including beginning with the year.** *1066* was the year of the Norman Conquest, the war that changed the English Language. **Prefer:** The Norman Conquest occurred in *1066*, a war that changed the English Language.

>> **Prefer words to express fractions.** If it's blueberry pie, I can easily eat *one-quarter* of it — if I work out immediately afterward.

APA highlights these additional guidelines for using numbers:

>> If presenting three or fewer numbers, consider a sentence.

>> If presenting four to 20 numbers, consider a table.

>> If presenting more than 20 numbers, consider a figure.

REMEMBER

Each style guide has its unique formatting features consistent with its philosophy as described in Chapter 2. Verify all style features with their respective manuals and websites.

Quotation marks: Calling out words

Quotation marks speak for words that need attention because they're words from experts. Guidelines for quotation marks that are commonly used in research include the following (the examples are italicized):

>> **Researchers' exact words:** Brogan and Miles agree on the following: "Changing majors can be an asset to most careers."

>> **Researchers' partial words:** Brogan and Miles agree that taking on another major can result in "an asset to most careers."

>> **Titles of book chapters:** Iacone's *Fundamentals of Accounting* includes a chapter titled "Taxpayers and Creative Accounting."

>> **Minor works of art such as newspaper stories, minor poems and short stories, and commercials:** His writing career began with the publication of his first poem titled "Writing from Afar."

MLA additionally suggests quotation marks for "provisional meaning" of words such as: Many experts argue that meanings of words are processed in the brain's "mission control center."

A quotation within a quotation is identified with single quotation marks as in this example: Professor Nearing said, "My favorite Shakespeare line is 'Brevity is the soul of wit'." See examples of block quotation in Chapter 6.

REMEMBER

Quotation marks, punctuation, and quoted content test your attention to detail, and errors can result in plagiarism allegations, as explained in Chapter 3. Proofread for accuracy and have your drafts reviewed by the writing center. If you ask your professors to edit your work, they'll most likely say, "I'm not your copyeditor."

Perfecting Appearance: Spelling

If you want to avoid being judged by appearance, never impersonate a spelling word. You've heard the expression books shouldn't be judged by their appearance, but they are, especially by the appearance of their spelling.

Your goal for spelling is near-perfection and a plan to avoid repeating your errors on subsequent assignments.

The following sections identify guidelines for spelling that you may have never considered spelling errors — capitalization, plurals, abbreviations, possessives, and hyphenation. They represent potential misspellings beyond letter sequence, which is easily identifiable and correctable.

REMEMBER

These rules and examples are representative of APA, MLA, and Chicago, as well as rules and conventions you've been taught and learned through your reading. If you have questions on rules in this or any chapter, consult the manual for the style you're assigned and ask your professor for guidance. Your writing center can also help you.

Capitalization: Avoiding capital offenses

If you lived about 1,300 years ago, you couldn't have erred in capitalization because all letters were capitals. But at that time, an ambitious young printer (with excessive student loan debt) designed a plan to reduce ink cost by 50 percent. She reduced the size of letters by 50 percent.

Because the new letters were smaller, she stored them in the smaller drawer cases below the upper cases — and she called the letters lowercase. But unfortunately, her descendants today continue to pay off her student loans.

Familiar capitalization rules

Here's a quick review of familiar rules for capitalization. Table 12-3 shows the rule with an example.

TABLE 12-3 **Capitalization Rules and Examples**

Rule	Example	Rule	Example
historical events	Prohibition	holidays	New Year's Day
time periods	Stone Age	continents	Europe
government bodies	Parliament	scientific terminology	Newton's First Law
famous events	Constitutional Convention	professional teams	Philadelphia Phillies
adjective from proper noun	Canadian geese	academic degrees	MFA
musical notes	F sharp	academic grade	A

Remember not to capitalize the following: seasons (summer), numbered centuries (16th century), alternate uses of proper nouns (french fries, irish potatoes), and compass directions (north).

Capitalization highlights from major styles

Familiar rules for capitalization (with accompanying examples), representative of major styles, include the following:

>> **Major words in titles of books, articles, and songs:** *Catcher in the Rye*; *Take Me Home, Country Roads*; *and On the Waterfront*

>> **Names of semesters and courses:** She enrolled in Writing As Managers in the Spring 2023 semester

>> **Religious denominations:** Methodists, Presbyterians

>> **Titles preceding names:** President Farish, Governor Stanton

>> **Titles of organizations:** American Kennel Club, National Council of Teachers of English

>> **Nouns followed by a number or letter that are parts of a whole:** Section C; Row 5; Part 2; Figure 12-2; Room 131; and Error 404

Possessives and apostrophes: Owning up

Possessives and apostrophes highlight spelling errors made by college students. Their correct use requires knowledge beyond spelling the word.

The major style guides recommend rules for spelling possessives that apply to your research writing and general college writing. The following sections explain.

Singular and plural possessives

Here's a look at rules (accompanied by examples) for spelling possessives used in your college writing:

>> **To form a possessive singular:** Write the singular form (*database*) and add *'s* (*database's*). The *database's* advantage is that it includes support.

>> **To form a possessive plural:** Start by writing the plural form (*databases*).

- **If the plural ends in *s*:** Add an apostrophe (*databases'*). *Databases'* purchases included a consortium of universities.

- **If the plural doesn't end in *s*:** Add *'s* (*children's*). *Children's* participation in research studies includes planned rest time.

Rules for forming possessives are as basic as emailing attachments. Table 12-4 looks at examples.

TABLE 12-4 ## Forming Possessives

Singular	Possessive Singular	Plural	Possessive Plural
man	man's	men	men's
woman	woman's	women	women's
child	child's	children	children's
citation	citation's	citations	citations'
girl	girl's	girls	girls'

Hyphenation: Identifying connections

The hyphen represents one of the most versatile conventions in the English language. Nearly retired by the invention of word-wrap, the hyphen connects related words and clarifies meaning. It serves in the mathematics department as a symbol (4–2=2) and connector of fractions (*three-quarters*).

It also works in the compound word industry (*self-service*) assisting compound words who haven't grown into single independent words (*homework*). APA and MLA refer compound disputes to *Merriam-Webster*.

Hyphenation guidelines (accompanied by examples) agreed on by major style guides include the following:

>> **Related adjectives acting as one:** The *award-winning* professor began the lecture.

>> **Numbers from twenty-one through ninety-nine:** The age of *twenty-one* is a milestone celebration for many college students.

>> **Clarity of meaning:** The university constructed *four-student* dorm rooms.

>> **Base-formation compounds with *pre*:** The day included *pre-admission* testing.

>> ***Self-* and *ex-* prefixes:** Many college students are described as *self-starters*.

MLA highlights additional uses of hyphens:

>> **Compound adjectives that begin with a qualifying adverb:** *well-prepared students, best-fitting device*

>> **Noun-number combinations:** *third-century* artifact, *three-week* vacation

>> **Compound adjective formed from a preposition:** *on-campus* lecturers, *in-house* training, *in-depth* analysis

>> **Adjectives separated from a compound:** *five-* and *ten-dollar* items, *pre-* and *post-college* experiences

MLA also identifies when not to hyphenate:

>> **Adjectives that include an *-ly* adverb:** thoughtfully organized research paper

>> **Compound adjectives that begin with *too, very*, or *much*:** much aligned program, very detailed program

Abbreviations: Keeping it brief

Use abbreviations sparingly — about as infrequently as you call your ex.

Here are guidelines (with accompanying examples) for spelling abbreviations:

>> **Use periods for some abbreviations.** J.F.K., a.m., Ms., and Jr.

>> **Don't use periods for other abbreviations.** APA, IQ, PhD, and MSW

>> **Form plurals of most abbreviations by adding s (with no apostrophe).**
URLs, DOIs, and PhDs

Spelling strategies: Finding what's wrong

Accept your responsibility to learn to spell because you're an educated person.
It's an easier skill to learn than writing, and here are some tips to help you:

>> Keep a list of words you frequently misspell.

>> Learn a few spelling rules, such as "*i* comes before *e* except after *c*."

>> When your word processor identifies a misspelled word, correct it. Be careful
though because spellcheckers don't catch all spelling errors, especially if the
error creates a different word, such as from and form.

>> Challenge yourself to learn to spell weirdly spelled words.

>> Collect spelling oddities such as *nth* (lacks a vowel), *facetious* (vowels in
sequence), and *almost* (letters in alphabetical sequence).

Search online for commonly misspelled words such as the "most misspelled
words in English" and you'll find lists (see the following):

Examples

separate	consensus	bureaucracy	entrepreneur
definitely	unnecessary	supersede	particularly
maneuver	acceptable	questionnaire	liquefy
embarrass	broccoli	connoisseur	conscience
occurrence	referred	a lot	parallel

Chapter **13**

Focusing on Appearance: Formatting

ormatting your research paper is like buying a luxury gift, then learning that the recipient is more interested in the packaging than the purchase. Welcome to the world of style guide formatting, the world where appearance may be more important than substance, especially if the appearance contains formatting contrary to your required style.

Each style guide has its logic for its formatting, a logic most college students won't understand. Understandable or not, students are required to follow their style guidelines.

In this chapter I identify text formatting for major documentation styles, illustrate page layout requirements that please professors, and show heading levels that distinguish major from minor content. I also identify formatting errors common to college research papers. Consistency is the key; let the formatting begin.

The research formatting in this chapter focuses on APA style and shows differences between APA, and MLA and Chicago.

REMEMBER

Because each style has its unique features and logic, verify your style features with respective manuals and websites. Then verify your verifications with your professor's preferences.

Formatting Text Appearance: Letter Perfect

Words matter. They matter when they're spelled correctly and when they're formatted accurately. Word accuracy in research includes adhering to guidelines for their required style.

Your words are seen before they're heard. And when they're seen without required formatting, they tell a message without consistency.

The following sections examine text formatting guidelines for letter-perfect accuracy with your research writing. They explain consistency of font, spacing, capitalization, and headings.

General text-formatting guidelines

Your professors have high expectations for your research paper formatting. They expect attention-to-detail and style consistent with your documentation requirements. They know that errors in text-consistency can soon result in a tsunami of faults than can sweep your grade out to "C."

Here's a look at general text-formatting guidelines that apply to almost all documentation styles:

>> **Font and typeface:** Prefer 12-point Times New Roman, acceptable to almost all professors. Style guides list font options, and professors are amenable to options for visual accommodations.

>> **Paper:** If printing, use standard 8½ x 11 white paper. Some professors prefer printing on one side for ease of reading and grading; some professors prefer double-side printing for conservation of resources. All professors expect the courtesy of crisp printing.

>> **Line spacing:** APA and MLA require exclusive double-space lines throughout the project, including headings, text, quotations, and work cited. Chicago line spacing is explained in the next section.

>> **Punctuation spacing:** Almost all style guides require one space following internal and end punctuation. This *For Dummies* book is an example of that spacing.

>> **Margins:** One-inch margins on all four sides are standard and acceptable for all styles. They're also a default for most word processing programs.

>> **Justification:** Almost all styles required left-side justification and the absence of right-side justification. This *For Dummies* book is an example of left-side-only justification.

>> **Indentations:** Each new paragraph requires half-inch indentation. Prefaces require no indentation. See Chapter 16 for more information on prefaces and other optional sections.

>> **Page numbering:** Number pages in the upper-right corner, beginning with one (1) on the title page. Some professors prefer excluding a page number on the title page.

>> **Running heads:** APA's 7th Edition deleted running heads as a requirement for student papers but continue to require them for professional papers.

>> **Title capitalization:** Capitalize first words of titles and first words of subtitles. Follow style guidelines for other capitalization in titles.

Remember that your professor's preferences are the final word for research paper guidelines. In other words, listen first to the person who assigns your grade.

Text formatting unique to MLA and Chicago

Documentation styles are a test of your attention to detail. In addition to the general guidelines of almost all style guidelines that I discuss in the previous section, the following formatting is exclusive to MLA and Chicago:

>> **Running heads:** Both styles require running heads positioned in the upper-right corner, a half inch from the top of the page. The running head includes the student's last name and page number.

>> **Hyphenation:** MLA recommends turning off word wrap, the automatic hyphenation feature.

>> **Page numbering:** Chicago offers a bottom-center option for page numbering.

>> **Title capitalization:** MLA and Chicago require capitalization of all major words, including proper nouns and words longer than four letters.

TIP

When style guidelines offer you options, prefer options consistent with other formats.

>> **Title page:** Neither MLA nor Chicago requires a title page.

>> **Contact information:** MLA and Chicago require contact information on the first page positioned in the upper left corner. Refer to the section "MLA first page of text" later in this chapter for an example.

>> **Line spacing:** Block quotations and annotated bibliographies are single spaced in Chicago. (See Chapter 6 for more information.)

>> **Date variations:** MLA requires a date format that looks like this: 12 June 2024.

Formatting Pages: First Impressions

Page appearance of your research paper is like screen appearance on your phone. You have expectations of where to see features such as time, unlock, weather, notices, and so forth.

Readers of your documentation style have similar expectations for page appearance of your research paper. Your readers, and your professor, expect page formatting consistent with style requirements for features such as text appearance, spacing, page layout, and headings and subheadings.

These sections discuss elements of page formatting common to most major styles. Verify formatting with your required documentation style and your professor.

Formatting title pages

Title pages are the new kid on the block with APA and aren't required by MLA and Chicago. APA's recent 7th Edition recognized that student writers need guidelines — in addition to research professionals for whom the style guide was originally created.

MLA and Chicago take a different approach than APA toward title pages. Rather than a separate page like APA, they require title-page information on the first page of text. Be sure to distinguish this major difference in first page appearance between APA, MLA, and Chicago.

Also recognize how strongly your professor emphasizes details of the required documentation style. For example, if your course includes teaching a documentation style in addition to research skills, your professor will expect letter-perfect attention to details such as accurate first pages.

Many first-year research writing courses also include learning a documentation style as part of course goals. Professors of upper-level research courses frequently relax documentation details such as type of title page, heading style, and some spacing requirements — and place more emphasis on research content. Read the professor's tone in the classroom toward such details. If you have doubts, ask.

Formatting title page elements

Your research paper title page (or MLA or Chicago's first page) is like your first appearance for a job interview. Before you speak, your nonverbal expressions communicate confidence, organization, and trust.

Your title page is similarly judged by appearance, accuracy, and fulfilling requirements. You want your professors reading your title page similar to going through airport security — quickly and assuredly without incident.

Recognizing APA title page elements

The elements of APA's title page (see Figure 13-1) include the following:

>> **Title:** A summary of the paper's topic and focus written with approximately 12 to 16 words and usually including a subtitle

>> **Author:** Your name as it appears on your course registration

>> **Affiliation:** The name of the department that teaches your course and your school's name

>> **Course identification:** Your official course name, number, and section number

>> **Professor's name:** Your professor's name and title as it appears on your course registration

All spelling errors aren't created equal. Prioritize accurate spelling of your professor's name and title. Misspelling professors' names on assignments shows serious lack of attention to detail. Be sure to accurately identify professors' titles. If you're not sure of an academic title, address them as "professor."

>> **Assignment due date:** The assignment due date, written in standard business format: February 2, 2023 (Remember that MLA date format is written as 2 February 2023.)

>> **Page numbering:** The number "1" located in the upper-right

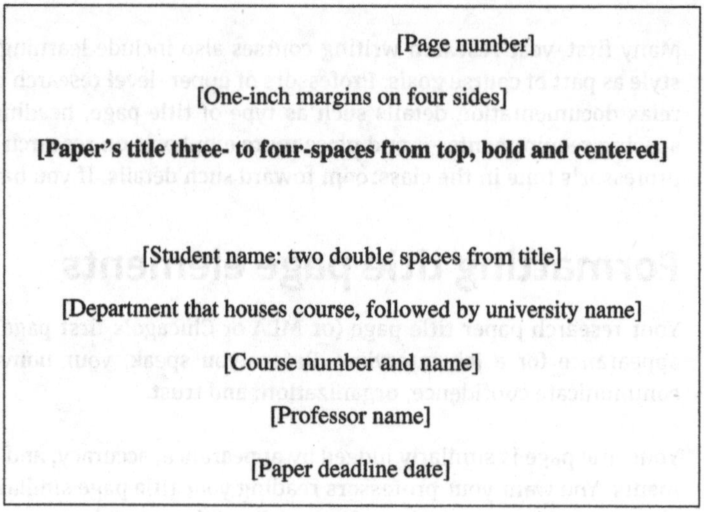

FIGURE 13-1:
APA title page
template.

© John Wiley & Sons, Inc.

Creating research titles: With subtitles

The focus point of your title page is your title (and subtitle) — your professor's first interaction with the content of your paper. Your professor's first impression of your title is one of two reactions: "has potential to excel" or "potentially another boring student research paper." You want your professor to think the former.

Titles that attract your professor's interest and engage your readers are created like this:

>> Review keyword searching terms and additional terms you added during searching.

>> Condense keywords into specific nouns and action words ending in –ing.

>> Identify keywords that answer the major research question and that identify the purpose of the assignment.

>> Consider your response to a friend's asking you what your paper's about.

>> Talk your title aloud to yourself and listen to terms you use.

>> Play with your keywords as if they were parts of a puzzle.

>> Follow the title with a colon and subtitle that narrows the topic.

Here's a sample of titles and subtitles for research papers:

>> Technology Improves Student Learning: Especially Middle School Students

>> Free Access to Higher Education: Awarded or Earned

>> Equalizing Campaign Financing: Leveling the Playing Field

>> Affordable Healthcare: Win, Win, Win

Subtitles narrow the focus of the topic. For example, these topics are narrowed with a student population such as "Especially Middle School Students" and conditions of access such as "Awarded or Earned" and "Leveling the Playing Field."

REMEMBER

Avoid titles too long, too vague, too broad, and too emotional such as

>> An Overview of . . .

>> The Importance of . . .

>> A Complete Guide to . . .

>> Why We Need to Know About . . .

>> A Manual for . . .

>> An Investigation of . . .

TIP

Write the title with the same size font and typeface as the remainder of the paper.

Avoiding title catastrophes

Titles follow capitalization rules of their style guides and are centered and usually bolded. Refer to Chapter 8 for an explanation of title case and sentence case capitalization.

Here's how to avoid attracting unnecessary professor attention to your title:

>> Don't italicize, underline, or set off with quotation marks.

>> Don't type in all caps.

>> Don't enlarge font size.

>> Don't use end punctuation unless it's part of the title.

Figure 13-2 shows an example of APA's recently designed title page for student papers and a title page accepted by most professors.

```
                                    1


              NIL: Game Changer or Game Closer


                         Shaunna S. Roberts

        Department of Sports and Recreation, Talbert University

                    DSR 1306-2: Sports and Finances

                         Professor O'Connor

                         February 2, 2024

         [The remaining three-quarters page remains blank.]
```

FIGURE 13-2:
Example of APA
title page.

Figure 13-3 shows an example of an acceptable Chicago's title page — if your professor requires one. Check with your professor for variations of the title page.

```
        Archelogy: What the Past Reveals About the Present

          [Position title about one-quarter from top of page]




                         Alexia J. Carrins

          Department of Archeology, P.M.C. Colleges

        ARC 1301-2 Archeology: Archeological Applications

                         Professor Evans

                         March 22, 2024
```

FIGURE 13-3:
Acceptable
Chicago
title page.

Formatting the first text page

Your first page of text is like the opening curtain on a performance. Accurate formatting before the first line of text will avoid a curtain malfunction and distract your professor from focusing on content. These sections show first pages of APA and MLA.

APA first page of text

Following APA's title page (and a hard page break), the title is repeated on page 2 where the text of the paper begins. Note again the title is centered and bolded. Figure 13-4 shows the top few inches of APA's page 2.

```
                                                                    2

                    NIL: Game Changer or Game Closer

        Begin your paper on this line with each new paragraph indented and

    double spaced for the remainder of the page. Indent new paragraphs.
```

MLA first page of text

MLA and Chicago don't require a title page, but they do require title-page information on the first-page of text. Figure 13-5 shows the top few inches of MLA's first page that includes contact information.

Chicago first page of text

Chicago's first page of text includes contact information. Page numbering begins in the upper-right corner. Figure 13-6 shows an example.

Formatting heading levels

An extended piece of writing without headings and subheadings is like driving without road markings — no lines, signs, or traffic lights. Reading such text is similar to driving in a demolition derby.

The major road signs throughout your research are headings and subheadings, which guide readers smoothly from title to conclusion. Subheadings identify additional levels of content.

Assanti 1

Christian L. Assanti

Professor Streb

English 137

12 March 2024

Internet Access: A Public Resource

Begin your paper on this line with each new paragraph indented and

double spaced for the remainder of the page. Note the date format and

running head that includes the student's last name.

FIGURE 13-5: Top of MLA first page.

© John Wiley & Sons, Inc.

1

Christian L. Assanti

Professor Streb

English 137

March 12, 2024

Internet Access: A Public Resource

Begin your first line of text here. Continued with double-spaced lines

and indent each new paragraph.

FIGURE 13-6: Top of Chicago first page.

© John Wiley & Sons, Inc.

APA recommends five levels for organizing text, with level 1 representing major headings such as titles, abstract, body, conclusion, and references. Rarely does a first- or second-year college student exceed three levels of headings (see Figure 13-7 for APA's five heading levels).

Designed similar to an outline, each heading requires two or more subheadings. A heading may have no subheadings, but not one subheading. Those headings and subheading guidelines are followed in this *For Dummies* book.

Level 1	**Centered, Bold, Title Case Heading**
	New paragraphs begin here, indented and double spaced from the heading.
Level 2	**Flush Left, Bold, Title Case Heading**
	New paragraphs begin here, indented and double spaced from the heading.
Level 3	***Flush Left, Bold Italic, Title Case Heading***
	New paragraphs begin here, indented and double spaced from the heading.
Level 4	**Indented, Bold, Title Case, End Punctuation**
	Double-spaced text begins here on the same line immediately after the period.
Level 5	***Indented, Bold, Italic, Title Case, End Punctuation***
	Double-spaced text begins here on the same line immediately after the period.

FIGURE 13-7: APA's five levels of headings.

Listing similar information

When content gets complex, get graphic — as with graphic organizers listing similar information. More than other documentation styles, APA emphasizes organizational visuals of page content such as bullets, letters, numbers, and steps. The following sections detail visual organization of page text.

Creating bulleted lists

Bulleted lists are the most commonly used graphics for presenting large quantities of similar information. Graphic organizers are brain-friendly because the brain thrives on similarly organized visual information.

The advantages of bulleted lists include the following:

>> Increases readability by highlighting complex ideas

>> Illustrates similar ideas in concise formatting

>> Visually highlights and focuses multi-related ideas

>> Transitions readers through a series of ideas

>> Offers reader-friendly strategies compared with long, multi-series sentences with complex information

You just read an example of an organized list of similar content. As a reader I guided you through a list of advantages of bulleted lists, each reason beginning with verbs structured parallel (*increases, illustrates,* (visually) *highlights, transitions,* and *offers*). See Chapter 11 for more information on parallel structure.

TIP

Bulleted lists and other graphic organizers appear infrequently in professional research writing such as scholarly journals, but they appear frequently in college research assignments. They're encouraged by APA, but not as strongly supported by MLA and Chicago.

Creating sequential lists of similar information

Additional graphic organizers include lettered lists, numbered lists, and steps in a process. Unlike bullets, the latter organizers require sequential positioning.

For example, the use of steps as seen in examples in this book require positioning step 1 before step 2 and so forth. Letters and numbers usually require similar sequencing. Think of sequential steps required to write a research paper, steps to install software updates, and steps to change a major.

Using graphic organizers in research

Graphic organizers such as bullets help show your professor you understand complex information.

Their uses in research writing include the following:

>> Display comparable elements of research information.

>> Demonstrate correlation of research ideas.

>> Illustrate visual connections of research elements.

>> Provide background for comparing and similar applications.

Punctuating lists

Documentation styles determine the punctuation of organized lists, but always check with your professor. Here are general guidelines for punctuating lists:

>> If listed items are complete sentences, punctuate as sentences.

>> Don't punctuate ends of fragment items using commas or other punctuation.

>> If listed items aren't sentences, don't capitalize the first word and don't end punctuate.

>> If the complete list of items is a sentence, position end punctuation at the end of the last item.

REMEMBER

Punctuation of lists varies with documentation styles. For example, *For Dummies* has its own style for bulleted lists that differs from Chicago.

Dealing with figures and tables

Figures and tables are research tools for showcasing large quantities of data, including maps, photographs, and illustrations. You can find examples in Chicago style throughout this book.

Photographs are also considered figures and may support some research topics. If you screenshot photos online, credit sources. Photos can easily be dragged into a text box that you can create with Word's "insert" heading. Documentation styles explain their guidelines for citing figures and tables and listing them into references.

General formatting guidelines for figures and tables include the following:

>> Position figures and tables immediately after their first reference.

>> Include a figure number for each figure.

>> Include a title or caption of each figure.

>> Cite figures and tables taken from a source.

Formatting Research Sections: Big Picture

Although I can't overemphasize the details of formatting, big picture formatting attracts your professor's attention — especially formatting of major headings of your paper. The following sections explain formatting of major sections of your research projects.

TIP

For simplicity of organizing major sections of research, many professors frequently instruct students to write research papers with three level 1 major headings: introduction, body, and conclusion. Professors then recommend use of level 2 headings under those three major headings. Refer to Figure 13-8 for a sample.

FIGURE 13-8:
Example of
headings as an
outline.

© John Wiley & Sons, Inc.

Introduction

The first heading that begins your research paper is the title, a level 1 heading that APA requires bolded and centered. Don't use the heading "introduction" unless your professor tells you to.

Figure 13-8 also shows level 2 headings that frequently appear in the introduction section: statement of the problem, review of literature, and limitations of the study.

A methodology heading is frequently required following the introduction. Methodology is explained in Chapter 16 as an optional section.

Body

The word "body" doesn't appear as a level 1 heading, but the body section frequently includes subheadings (level 2 and sometimes level 3). For example, the level 2 heading of NIL may include body section subheadings such as *analysis* and *results*. Chapter 15 details writing the body section of a research paper.

Conclusion

The word "conclusion" appears as a level 1 heading in the last section of the paper. Subheadings of conclusion frequently include *discussion* and *need for additional research*. Chapter 15 explains writing the conclusion section of the paper.

Formatting lists of sources

Accurate formatting of your list of sources shows your understanding of formatting styles. Source lists (references, works cited, and bibliography) are part of the big-picture organization that many professors frequently glance at to assess your understanding of the required style.

General formatting for sources

Formatting sources requires academic intensity unlike most other academic projects. Many students work on source lists in short time-blocks and work from models.

Here's a list of general guidelines for entering most sources:

>> Enter each source item using hanging indentations — the first line positioned flush left and successive lines indented one half inch. See Chapter 8 for examples.

>> Alphabetize entries by authors' last names.

>> If a source lacks an author, list and alphabetize beginning with the last name of the sponsoring organization (exclude "a," "an," and "the").

>> Refer to style guidelines for listing multiple authors' names because they vary.

>> Capitalize the first word of title and subtitle and proper nouns titles for books, chapters, articles, and webpages.

>> See style guides for capitalizing scholarly journal articles.

APA guidelines for sources

APA's list of sources is formatted with the title "References," a level 1 heading bolded and centered. Entries under APA references are double spaced throughout. See Chapter 8 for a sample reference section.

MLA guidelines for sources

MLA lists sources under the heading "Works Cited," centered and usually bolded. Entries under works cited are double spaced similar to APA. Chapter 8 includes a sample works cited section.

Chicago guidelines for sources

Chicago's list of sources differs from APA and MLA. Chicago's list of sources is titled "Bibliography," centered and usually bolded. Spacing of items differs from APA and MLA. Chicago entries are single spaced. Spacing between items is double spaced. See Chapter 8 for a sample bibliography section.

Formatting section sequences

Most people start their day with a consistent sequence of events that includes wake-up time and morning beverage time. When your sequence is interrupted — especially your morning beverage — your day heads downhill.

Your research also includes a sequence of sections from your title page to your list of resources. And when one of those sequences is interrupted or omitted, your grade heads downhill.

REMEMBER

Here's the sequence of major content sections that many professors require and that most will accept:

>> **Title page:** First page or first page of text that includes contact information

>> **Abstract:** Usually required for papers eight pages or longer

>> **Table of contents:** Sometimes required, but good to include for papers eight pages or longer (see Chapter 16 for more information on writing a table of contents)

>> **Body of research:** Major evidence section of research paper (see Chapter 6 for more information)

>> **Lists of sources:** Reference, works cited, or bibliography (see Chapter 8 for more information)

>> **End notes:** Sometimes required by your professor, especially with Chicago style (see Chapter 8 for more information)

>> **Figures and tables:** Sometimes required by your professor (refer to the section "Dealing with figures and tables" earlier in this chapter)

>> **Appendixes:** Usually optional and a good tool for supplementary information (refer to Chapter 16)

Avoiding Common Formatting Errors

Accurate formatting tells your professors you care about the rules of scholarship; careless and inaccurate formatting tells your professors scholarship lacks importance in your research.

I once heard someone say: How you do anything is how you do everything. Let your professors know you value formatting by following guidelines for accuracy. The following sections identify formatting issues common to college students.

Merging documentation styles

If you're in the unfortunate position of simultaneously writing research papers in two different documentation styles, focus on the formatting of each style, especially first pages, headings, citations, and lists of sources. To improve formatting accuracy, work with models of required styles.

Professors have trained eyes for recognizing inaccuracies of major headings, such as the title and reference headings. After professors teach a documentation style for a few semesters, they become familiar with student errors common to the documentation style. For example, a lack of hanging indentations is a common formatting error in almost all major documentation styles.

Other formatting issues common to headings include lack of centering, lack of required bolding, and indiscriminately italicizing and underlining. Always refer to models of formatting common to your required style.

Varying font sizes

Set it and forget it — 12-point Times New Roman. It's the most consistent formatting requirement across documentation styles. Use it consistently from the first page to the last page.

REMEMBER

Your research paper isn't a test of your layout skills and use of ornamental fonts in headings. Professors don't award style points for artistic fonts. Incorrect fonts are easily recognizable by your professor and distract from the content of your paper. If you want to be 100 percent sure of a formatting guideline, don't vary from 12-point Times New Roman — from starting line to finish line.

Introducing justification issues

Another hands-off formatting zone is margin justification. Your documentation style formatting includes only left-side justification, meaning all lines of text begin the same distance from the left margin. Almost all your college writing is formatted with left-side justification, one inch from the left edge of the paper.

Don't engage right-side justification, where ends of all lines of text align stacked. This book is an example of left-side alignment and a ragged right-side alignment.

Creating optical illusions

Really? Here's a list of what some students will do to create an illusion of longer research papers:

>> Increase margins to one-and-a-quarter inches

>> Increase font size to 14 points

>> Increase spacing between lines

Some students perform these formatting adjustments for the purpose of increasing their paper by a few lines or paragraphs. And they think professors don't notice an enlarged line of type.

Falsifying the appearance of a paper is a form of plagiarism (see Chapter 3) and a strategy for sabotaging a grade. And students don't think professors notice. Really?

Writing Research Papers

4

Plan and organize your research writing by outlining your content, reviewing your documentation style, identifying campus support services, assembling feedback teams, committing to a completion schedule, and planning back-up contingencies.

Prepare for writing your first draft by establishing a writing ritual, identifying an inspirational writing location, exorcizing stress and delays, assuming a growth mindset, and generating preliminary ideas.

Apply ethics and objectivity to your research writing by balancing evidence that supports the argument, writing with respectful and fair language, and coordinating objective and subjective language.

Supplement required research paper sections with optional headings such as a title page that shows a professional appearance, a table of contents that highlights major topics, introduction subheadings that state the problem and review literature, middle subheadings that pinpoint minor content topics, and conclusion subheadings identifying implications and topics needing further study.

Model the revising process of legendary writers following a plan that includes implementing feedback to evaluate the structure and organization, applying sentence-improvement strategies such as selecting action verbs and specific nouns, eliminating unnecessary and overused words, and editing issues common to college writers.

Capitalize on the 60 minutes before submitting your paper by check-listing for parts and pages positioned accurately, integrating elements of an academic writing style, accurately formatting major sections, including all required deliverables, and finally asking if anything's missing.

Chapter **14**

Planning and Organizing Research Writing

I magine a research paper submitted to a professor that contains pages out of sequence and headings omitted from major sections, printed with a cartridge that's had its final word.

How do you avoid research papers like this that professors use as an example of what not to submit? You begin planning and organizing as soon as you're assigned the paper, and you adapt the mindset that you'll work hard to complete a successful paper.

In this chapter I explain planning and organization required to complete a successful research project, such as performing preliminary writing requirements, analyzing assignment deliverables, developing a growth mindset, and populating content in major sections of your research paper.

As you plan and organize, remember the words of Eleanor Roosevelt, "It takes as much energy to wish as it does to plan."

Early-Bird Planning: Preliminary Priorities

You've heard the expression that the early bird gets the worm. If the early bird is writing a research paper, it not only gets the worm, but it also earns the grade.

Planning for a research paper begins for many students as soon as they receive the assignment. A body of research shows a correlation between beginning writing projects early and earning good grades.

The following sections explain planning that precedes writing the first draft such as creating an outline of your research paper's content, familiarizing yourself with your documentation style, choosing an assignment framework, identifying available writing support, assembling feedback teams, and designing a time-management plan.

Outlining: Making your blueprint

Think of your outline as the blueprint for constructing your project. It establishes the foundation for each of the following:

>> Identifying the paper's direction from opening to closing — in other words, your outline is your road map

>> Creating a framework for answering research questions

>> Structuring evidence that supports the argument

>> Providing a prompt for developing content

>> Establishing a path for fulfilling the paper's purpose

Fortunately for you as a student, research projects include a built-in outline structure: an introduction, body, and conclusion. Each of those three structural parts contains subheadings that resemble the outline in Figure 14-1:

TECHNICAL STUFF

For Dummies authors begin new books by creating the table of contents, an outline of major topics in their books. After a *For Dummies* editor, an expert on structural organization, offers feedback for revising, the final outline serves a road map for writing. Book writing doesn't begin until the outline is finalized. Minor sections in outlines frequently change as topics write themselves into their final resting place. Similarly, begin your research paper with a sequential outline of major headings within the paper's introduction, body, and conclusion.

```
Introduction
    Engaging opening (see Chapter 15)
    Description of argument (see Chapter 7)
    Importance of argument (see Chapter 5)
    Limitations of the study (see Chapter 16)
    Thesis statement (see Chapter 5)
Body
    Evidence #1 supporting argument (see Chapter 6)
    Evidence #2 supporting argument
    Evidence #3 supporting argument
    Evidence #4 supporting argument
    Evidence connection to thesis
    Evidence rebuttal (see Chapter 7)
Conclusion
    Summary of evidence (see Chapter 15)
    Importance of evidence
    Application of evidence
    New insights from evidence and research
    Suggestions for new research
```

FIGURE 14-1:
Sample outline
structure.

© John Wiley & Sons, Inc.

Mastering your documentation style

Mastering your required documentation style is like learning passwords required to organize your online life. You'll frequently ask why, but you'll be happy to know what.

Early in the planning process, familiarize yourself with the required documentation style. If you worked with the style previously, focus on areas that showed deficiencies in previous assignments.

Soon after being assigned the research paper, review fundamentals of your required style that includes the following:

>> Page layout, section organization, and levels of headings (see Chapter 13)

>> Citation and reference formatting (see Chapter 8)

>> Paraphrasing, summarizing, and quoting (see Chapter 6)

>> Plagiarism prevention (see Chapter 3)

Also review elements of academic writing style that include the following:

>> Bias-free language (see Chapter 10)

>> Clear and concise expression (see Chapter 17)

>> Language proficiency (see Chapter 12)

>> Appropriate audience and tone (see Chapter 10)

>> Action verbs and specific nouns (see Chapter 11)

Framing your assignment type

The framework for your assignment is like the structure that supports a building. Your goal is to design a structure that supports the major sections of your research.

REMEMBER

The framework of your paper may be determined by the assignment with language such as "define," "compare and contrast," "explain the causes and effects of," and "analyze."

Frequently — and designed intentionally by your professor — the structure is your decision to choose a framework that successfully develops your topic.

Here's a look at common structures that develop college research topics:

>> **Analyzing and synthesizing:** Identifies parts of an issue and relationships of those parts and relationships of parts to the whole

>> **Problem-solving:** Emphasizes a solution to a problem

>> **Showing cause and effect:** Describes causal relationships

>> **Comparing and contrasting:** Identifies what's similar and dissimilar about an issue

>> **Persuading:** Convinces reader to act or support an issue

Chapter 9 shows these structures in detail, explains how they're created, and illustrates model language. I explain the importance of these writing purposes in analyzing assignments in the section "Answering the Asks: Analyzing Assignments" later in this chapter.

Recognizing available support

Professors look at students' ability to initiate academic support as an asset; students frequently view their need for help as a liability. No one knows everything, and if they want to learn new ideas, they'll need help from someone — frequently a someone who dedicated their life to helping you.

Colleges recognize that academic support is integral to the learning process and provide help as part of your tuition services. Colleges also recognize that almost every student needs academic support in pursuit of their degrees.

TIP

As you begin your research process and recognize your need for help, utilize the following forms of academic support that are available on most campuses:

>> **Professors:** Check with your professor early in the research process, ensuring that you're progressing in the right direction. A visit during office hours can provide you an evaluation of your topic and research questions.

>> **Writing center:** Use the writing center to receive feedback for your outline, thesis, and writing structure.

>> **Library:** In addition to library resources and research specialists, most libraries also provide audio and video equipment for your research projects. Chapter 5 explains full services of most college libraries.

>> **Academic support services:** If you need a refresher of study skills such as notetaking or outlining for your research, the academic support center found on most campuses can help you.

TIP

Your laptop is your indispensable tool for writing and researching. Keep it healthy by promptly downloading university updates. Also, most university technology centers service a slow or infected computer as part of your tuition services. And in some cases, they may have the capability to provide you a loaner computer while your laptop is being serviced. Technology services also usually provide digital repositories such as cloud storage.

Assembling peer feedback teams

Completing a research paper may not take a village, but it does require a support team of students. Also, many peers in your class will be looking for similar support that includes the following:

>> **Feedback reviewers:** Receiving peer feedback may be a requirement, but it's also beneficial to receive feedback from a student who is writing the same

assignment. See Chapter 17 for detailed information about peer feedback and its role in the revising process.

>> **Proofreaders:** Think of proofreading as editing for spelling, grammar, and punctuation also mentioned in Chapter 17.

>> **Documentation reviewers:** Solicit a reader or two to review your research specifically for documentation errors.

REMEMBER

The writing center also offers this same feedback. However, performing this review with your peers includes the benefit of seeing peers' language for your same assignment. It's a double-learning opportunity to receive feedback on your paper and see papers written by your peers. Feedback can also be performed by a small team of students who meet and read each other's papers. Be sure feedback collaboration is permissible by your professor and not a plagiarism violation. See Chapter 3 for a review of plagiarism.

Managing time

You know the drill. Every book about writing and college tells you how to manage time and schedule academic activities.

Rather than thinking about time management as slotting your day from morning classes to midnight study, think of managing your academic life by accepting responsibility to complete quality work within the hours you commit to your schoolwork.

Here's a look at guiding principles for completing your schoolwork within your available study hours.

Committing to the project

You decided to enroll in college as a path to your career. Commitment controls your academic success or failure; it's your relentless determination to educate yourself and earn a college degree. Commit yourself to finding a way, using available resources, to graduate and fulfill your dream.

Believing in yourself

Believe in yourself and your ability to build on past successes. College requirements become more and more demanding, but your academic experiences and accomplishments are also increasing. Recognize your academic strengths and continue to improve your liabilities. You're building confidence and a history of successes as you complete courses and semesters.

Prioritizing tasks

The best management of your time is prioritizing your work based on what needs to be accomplished short term and long term. Priority tasks include reading, writing, preparing for tests, and planning for future responsibilities. Also dedicate a few minutes daily to evaluate your planning and thinking about your future.

Establishing successful habits

Past successes build future successes. Develop successful habits through repetition of what works. Learn your circadian rhythm, the time of day you're most productive. Studying is a daily routine. Understand your study patterns well enough to recognize that some days won't be as productive as other days but also realize that other days will be more productive.

Setting realistic expectations

Form realistic academic expectations. You're unlikely to earn an A on every project and in every course. You'll experience academic setbacks — everyone does. Develop the mindset to learn from your failures and apply those lessons to new projects. Find ways to move forward.

Developing flexibility

Develop a routine that includes the flexibility of allowing controllable diversions. Learn to not only say "no" to distractions, but also to say "yes." You can say "yes" because you control your schedule, rather than your schedule controlling you.

Practicing self-care

Include fun and activity in your daily schedule. Prioritize a social life at school by participating in organizations that offer relaxation and reduce stress. Also learn to study socially by occasionally meeting in peer groups to discuss class projects and ideas for assignments. Commit to a form of exercise three or four times weekly.

Envisioning success

Efficient management of time requires designing a workable system of organization that results in effective use of time. Envision your academic life daily, weekly, monthly, and by semester. Successfully prepare simultaneously for the next class and the next semester. Avoid thinking of graduation as a dream; think of it as a plan.

Answering the Asks: Analyzing Assignments

Completing writing assignments is like playing a puzzle game with your professors. They creatively design a task that resembles what you may be required to do in another setting such as solving a problem in the workplace.

They don't tell you how to solve problems step-by-step. They start the problem with limited directions and require you to finish solving it by completing the project. You get to fill in the missing parts and learn through the process, and professors are pleased when you pleasantly surprise them.

These sections explain how to figure out what professors want, and then deliver what they didn't expect.

TIP

Be sure to write what you're expected to answer, not what you can find the most information for.

Adapting an assignment mindset

What's the biggest obstacle that prevents students' completing successful major projects? It's a fixed mindset and the belief that the project is too difficult, that it's not their strength, and that they can't complete it successfully.

What's the biggest asset that contributes to students' completing successful major projects? It's a growth mindset and the belief that they can succeed if they work hard, that they can access support when they need it, and that success requires their best effort.

The difference between mindsets is similar to the difference between a successful student and an unsuccessful student — and the difference between celebration and consternation.

The following sections examine the value of a growth mindset while planning and writing an academic project such as a research paper. Table 14-1 looks at differences between mindsets.

Committing to time requirements

Research papers require time — your precious time that may result in a temporary limitation of your social and social media lives. Major projects also require a growth mindset and the determination that you'll commit the time and locate resources that will result in successful projects.

TABLE 14-1   Growth Mindsets versus Fixed Mindsets

Growth Mindset	Fixed Mindset
Believes effort results in accomplishment	Believes accomplishment results from having innate talent
Values feedback as part of the process to succeed	Views feedback as criticism of work efforts
Views failures as opportunities to improve	Views failures as lacking innate talent to succeed

TIP

A traditional first- and second-year college research paper — the experience of in-depth analysis of a topic your professor designates as high priority — generally requires a time commitment between two and four weeks and a major focus of your study budget hours. To use your time effectively, review the section "Managing time" earlier in this chapter.

Immersing yourself as a reader and researcher

Research papers require concentrated college reading and researching skills (see Chapter 5) — they're not child's play. Familiarize yourself with reading academic journal articles (check out Chapter 6) and similar research studies.

Focus on annotating (also discussed in Chapter 6) as you read, record specific notes, and look for implications. Generally, read and research for patterns and outlier ideas. Your paper will also include your personal reactions to ideas you read.

Read and research with a growth mindset and the confidence that you can extract information you need and that support is available for what you need help with. Your reading and researching skills are integral to the success of your paper.

Immersing yourself as a writer

Your writing success is based on your reading and researching success. Writing is another commitment that requires a growth mindset and confidence that you can achieve writing proficiency.

Research shows that writing is a process that includes feedback and revising (see Chapter 17). Most successful students utilize university resources for feedback on their writing. Research also shows that feedback from professors and writing centers results in higher writing grades. They also save you time.

Furthermore research reports that students' lack of planning prevents them from utilizing feedback. They don't complete writing drafts within a time frame to have them reviewed. Students who plan ahead stay ahead.

Unconfusing yourself

Professors don't try to intentionally confuse you. But sometimes a disconnect occurs between what they assume you can understand and what you can figure out.

Professors also expect you to know when you need support and that resources to help you are available. In addition to writing resources available on your campus (see Chapter 20), visit prominent college websites available online and explained in the section "Writing resources" later in this chapter.

ASKING QUESTIONS AND CLARIFICATIONS

Students understand that asking questions is integral to the teaching and learning process. But what some students sometimes don't understand is that sometimes how questions are asked can undermine what is asked — especially questions for clarification during a class discussion.

Avoid asking questions that include a tone of embarrassing your professor, such as the following:

- But you just contradicted what you said earlier by saying . . .
- But the syllabus says that . . .
- Now that has me all confused . . .

Frame questions in a tone that doesn't question your professor's ability to explain content and shows that you accept some responsibility for misunderstanding, such as possibly not completing required readings.

Here are examples of how to politely frame questions and ask for clarification:

- That's an interesting concept, could you give an example of that?
- I want to get a better understanding of that, could you explain a little bit more?
- I'm a little unsure of that, could you go into more detail?
- Am I correct interpreting what you're saying as . . .?
- So then what you're saying is . . .

Some questions should never be asked because they show what you didn't do, such as read the syllabus. Here are examples of questions that don't need to be asked because the information is easily available to you:

- When's the next test?
- Is anything due next Tuesday?

And some questions should never be asked:

- Is the title page included in the page count?
- How many cuts am I allowed before it affects my grade?
- How can I get an A in this course?

And a question professors never want to hear after a missed a class: Did I miss anything important Tuesday? To which professors may respond with: "No you didn't. Tuesday was another day we didn't do anything important."

Interrogating your assignment

Your assignment sheet is like a treasure hunt for you to discover what your professor wants. Some requirements are clear, such as due dates; some requirements aren't as clear, such as "synthesize" (see Chapter 9).

Identifying your professor's requirements is like an additional research project that begins with formulating and answering questions about the assignment. These sections analyze these questions.

Why is this project assigned now?

Position the assignment in context of the course. For example: Is it a department requirement for all first-year students that also requires learning a specific documentation style, or is it a course-ending project that's similar to a final examination? The former tells you to focus on accuracy of documentation style. The latter tells you to focus on course content that you're required to show an understanding of.

What's the significance of the assignment title?

The title tells you the broad topic of the assignment. For example, it may be a thematic title such as overcoming adversity that most likely tells you to respond to your research question with psychological evidence. If the title is content focused, such as 18th-century romantic authors, that most likely tells you to respond with examples of 18th-century romantic authors and their literature.

What does the assignment reveal about professor expectations?

Professors reveal expectations with language such as "management majors are expected to fully understand the role of small business in a large economy," "first-year students are expected to master proficiency in APA's documentation style," and "writing arts majors are expected to write clear, concise prose with near-perfection use of conventions of language." More specifics on what professors want is detailed in the section "Professors' expectation for your research" later in this chapter.

What does the assignment reveal about the type of evidence required?

The type of evidence required for research is generally indicated by the type of evidence specific to your academic discipline. For example, evidence for historical topics includes historical documents, historical events, and artifacts. Evidence for art history topics includes experts' interpretations and historical pieces of art. For more information on preparing evidence, see Chapter 6.

What does the assignment say not to do?

Professors who teach research assignments for a number of semesters become familiar with patterns of issues that they recommend students avoid. The language of what not to do in your paper appears as follows:

>> "Do not use sources from popular news magazines such as *Time* and *Newsweek*."

>> "Avoid overuse of block quotations."

>> "Do not merge formatting styles for citations."

>> "Limit use of the passive voice."

>> "Do not think of contracting your paper from an online source."

>> "Do not use patterns of long wordy sentences."

TIP

Be sure to write what your professor expects you to answer, not what you can find the most information about.

Identifying what, why, and when

As soon as you're assigned a research project, perform a quick read through (without taking notes) to form an overview of the requirements. Then begin another reading annotating information (see Chapter 6), circling and underlining requirements, listing questions, and creating to-do lists.

The following sections identify topics to help you analyze assignments.

Identifying deliverables

Deliverables identify parts of the assignments you're required to submit, or "deliver" to your professor. Create this to-do list beginning with your second reading of the assignment. The accuracy of this assignment list has a major influence on your grade. You can't earn credit for what you neglect to submit.

Deliverables commonly required by college professors include the following:

>> **Ten-page research paper:** A ten-page requirement means submitting between 10 and 12 pages, the length your professor estimates is required to complete the assignment. Most professors calculate page length as pages between the introduction and conclusion, excluding pages for front matter before the introduction and back matter after the conclusion.

>> **Annotated bibliography:** Annotated bibliographies are frequently required (see Chapter 6 and 16) because they help show your understanding of sources.

>> **APA documentation style:** If you're more familiar with an alternate documentation style and your professor includes wording such as "APA documentation style preferred," check with your professor about using another documentation style. Remember than another style risks your professor not remembering during grading.

>> **One section reviewed by professor:** If the writing process is emphasized in your course, your professor may offer you the opportunity to submit a short section of your paper for early review before the deadline. Take advantage of such opportunities. Your professor will remember your initiative and organization to submit a section for review. Chapter 17 explains the revising process.

>> **One-page diary of a research session:** The purpose of requiring a diary entry is that they require reflection, and research shows that quality reflection usually results in quality revision. Label diary entries and include the date of the reflection.

>> **Portal posting:** If you're required to post your paper on a portal or class site, a PDF format is usually required. Include this converted format in your early planning, especially if you're uncomfortable with the conversion format. Also include this requirement on one of your to-do lists.

TECHNICAL STUFF

Your assignment deadline date identifies the date your assignment is required to be in the hands of your professor in a readable format (print or electronic). It doesn't mean handing your professor a thumb drive or saying it's on your computer and your computer crashed. You're also responsible that an emailed attachment opens.

Identifying audience

You'd never begin a conversation without knowing whom you're speaking to. Nor should you begin a research paper without an awareness of the audience you're writing to.

REMEMBER

Fortunately for you as a college writer, research paper audiences rarely vary as they do for other college writing assignments. Unless specified otherwise, your research paper audience is the academic research community as explained in Chapter 10.

Answering the major ask

The research paper assignment puzzle includes discovering the piece that identifies your writing purpose — the key writing task you're required to address.

Fulfilling the purpose sets in motion a series of supporting requirements that include the following:

>> Determining the assignment topic

>> Creating the thesis

>> Developing research questions

>> Researching evidence

Verbs that identify the assignment purpose, what you're asked to develop with the topic, include the following: analyze, argue, compare, define, evaluate, and explain. These verbs identifying writing purposes are explained in detail in Chapter 10. These purpose verbs also determine the structure or framing of your assignment, which I explain in the section "Framing your assignment type" earlier in this chapter.

REMEMBER

As Chapter 7 discusses, argument is inherent in almost every college writing assignment. You're convincing your reader and professor the importance of the topic.

Professors' research expectations

Students sometimes complain that their professors expect too much and their student expectations too high. Students should complain when their professors expect too little — and students deliver it.

Here's what most professors are expecting from student research:

» **Innovative approaches:** Professors value unique approaches to assignments. They usually can't define "innovative," but they know it when they read it. Innovation appears in your topic selection or conclusion, where you offer insightful applications on your topic. See Chapter 15 for an explanation of writing the conclusion. The academic community highly values original thought, and it's how you impress your professor.

» **Research competency:** As a scholar-in-training, you impress your professor with research competency such as citing with professional accuracy, integrating peer-reviewed sources, and precisely formatted references — in addition to a well-structured argument. Scholars display characteristics of scholarship.

» **Literacy proficiency:** Reading and writing are the basic skills of higher education. You can't survive college without them and you're unlikely to have been accepted into college without them. When professors grade papers, it's difficult for them to see beyond poor writing, especially when colleges invest heavily in writing support. See Chapter 11 for more information on elements of academic writing.

» **Course content integration:** Your courses are content driven and that's what professors are passionate about teaching. Although documentation styles, formatting, and peer-reviewed sources may appear to be the focus of your research papers, professors' focus remains the content. Captain Obvious would remind you that a psychology paper should be about psychology, a business paper should be about business, and so forth.

» **Initiative:** College students are expected to figure things out, such as synthesizing complex ideas, locating reliable and appropriate sources, formatting according to your documentation style, and locating support you need. Your professor is always available, but in reality, they prefer you help yourself as much as you can.

Coordinating rubric requirements

When professors provide rubrics for assignments, they're further explaining the assignment, telling you parts that contain higher point values and require more attention than parts with lower point values.

Grading rubrics prioritize assignment requirements with statements such as the following:

>> Include at least three peer-reviewed sources.

>> Support your argument with at least four pieces of reliable evidence.

>> Ensure there are no more than two minor citation errors to make that A.

>> Reference at least one example of course content in the conclusion.

The value of rubrics includes the following:

>> Provides additional detail defining professor expectations

>> Models language for discussing your paper with your professor

>> Points out focus areas for peer feedback

>> Represents another resource for you to figure out what's expected

Populating Pieces: Major Sections of Assignments

You've probably heard of plug-and-play technology. But you don't hear about the planning that precedes plug and play — software that that allows one device to talk with another.

Developing content for your major research sections requires preparation of the "software" that develops into your "hardware" — notes from your research that you develop into the major content sections. Writing from notes is easier than writing from a blank screen.

Theses sections identify ideas for developing the major sections of your paper.

Introducing the problem

Professors value papers that create an engaging opening impression. The secret to a successful research paper is a strong introduction, a strong evidence section, and a strong conclusion.

Content for the introduction includes the topic, thesis, and the major research questions (see Chapter 5 for discussion on all three). The development of those major elements comes from background materials you read about for creating your title, first sentence, and your opening paragraph (refer to Chapter 15).

Information for the introduction includes facts about the importance of the topic. As you research and read about your topic, identify ideas that could develop into those opening elements.

Body-building evidence and rebuttal

A strong mind produces a strong body of evidence to support your paper and the counter-evidence that refutes your argument. Chapter 6 explains evidence and how to prepare it.

The major content of the body section is the evidence you research to support your argument. That's why Chapter 5 emphasizes the importance of meeting with a reference librarian and beginning your search with your library's databases.

Library sources provide instant credibility with your professor and almost eliminate unreliable sources. It's win, win, win — your professor, your paper, and your grade. Chapter 15 details writing the body section.

Developing a conclusion

Avoid thinking of your conclusion as your farewell to the topic. If you do, also say farewell to a good grade. The conclusion is a grand opening to your intellectual analysis of the topic.

As you write the body section (or as you go back to studying the body section), create a to-do list of the implications of the topic and your thoughts about those implications.

Think of the conclusion as the big-picture of your topic, such as considering the connection of ideas you learned to your academic life. Chapter 15 offers specific information for writing the conclusion.

Calling for Backup: Priorities and Contingencies

The unexpected happens — in life and in college academics. Some disruptive elements can be planned for, others can't. Fortunately, you can plan for technology malfunctions and for back up resources that are crucial to your research.

These sections offer contingencies for unexpected events that college students frequently face during the research writing process.

Technology

Your academic life has been enhanced by technologies, which are almost always reliable. But failures aren't exempt from inconveniences such as power outages or local network crashes. And technology seems to fail when you need it the most, in the middle of the night while working on a paper due the next morning.

Fortunately, technology isn't health, and you can plan contingencies such as the following:

» **Laptop and word processing:** Expect malfunctions and plan for it. Familiarize yourself with back-up laptops and printing, such as campus computer labs and compassionate friends. Some campuses designate one lab for 24-hour availability. Find out if your campus has one and bring cookies to share with friends who will also be there.

» **Printing:** Plan for printing backup such as computer labs, a friend's printer, and nearby business retail centers if the outage is campus wide. And you may need to bring your own paper.

» **File backup:** You learned early in your college career that professors don't accept the excuse that your computer crashed or you lost your file. Learn storage available to you as a college student. Additional storage includes cloud storage, email, and auxiliary hard drives. Back up and back up your backups. They can avoid an academic crisis.

TIP

When technology crashes, don't expect a class extension of your deadline. Most students meet deadlines under extreme circumstances. Professors are reluctant to delay deadlines because it conflicts with the next due assignment.

Writing resources

Frequently during your writing, you need factual information or a writing clarification such as a citation formatting or thesis example. And you frequently need that information when your people resources and campus services are recharging.

Here's a list of back-up resources I frequently recommend to my students for writing information or clarification:

>> **Purdue OWL (Online Writing Lab):** One of the most inclusive resources for anything writing related — https://owl.purdue.edu.

>> **Amherst College:** A user-friendly website with easily identifiable writing handouts, it also includes links to other college writing resources — www.amherst.edu/academiclife/support/writingcenter/resourcesforwriters.

>> **North Carolina:** Includes a unique opening page with alphabetized links to more than a hundred writing topics — https://writingcenter.unc.edu.

>> **Harvard College:** In addition to writing handouts, it includes a collection of handouts on study skills; don't expect anything less than the best, it's Harvard, the oldest institution of higher learning in the United States — https://writingcenter.fas.harvard.edu.

>> **Boston College:** Another strong user-friendly and inclusive writing resource — and alma mater of three grandchildren — www.bc.edu/bc-web/schools/mcas/departments/english/undergrad/bc-writing-center.html.

Documentation resources

You can't have too many resources for downloadable handouts explaining documentation styles. Because of the complexity of documentation styles, you'll have questions when your major sources of information are unavailable and you'll need quick answers. Here's a list of on-demand contingencies that can answer your documentation questions:

>> **Style manuals and websites:** Print manuals are budget busters, but copies are usually available in your library.

>> **Citation generators:** Use them with caution as explained in Chapter 8.

>> **Online writing centers:** The college websites in the previous section contain excellent documentation handouts.

Chapter **15**

Creating Draft One

Where, when, and how you write may not be a priority for you, but they're high priorities for your brain that thrives on stimulation, circadian rhythms, organization, and inspiration.

Your brain also stores a lifetime of experiences — including recent ones from your research — awaiting you to recall them for your speaking and writing. Draft one, one of two or three, is within you and this chapter helps you capture it on screen.

Here I explain writing rituals that prompt your brain and help overcome anxiety. I guide you through writing a first draft in five easy-to-follow steps, and help you ensure ethics and objectivity in your writing.

Listen to those voices of your research paper within you, and you can produce your first draft.

Awakening Inspiration: Rituals and Environment

Musicians do it; athletes do it; professors do it; astronauts do it; and writers do it too. They begin their writing with rituals, a series of sequential routines to stoke their neurons and fire up their brain. Rituals ready the brain for writing and seamlessly transitions into writing your first sentence and paragraph.

These sections explain how to awaken your writing senses, reduce stress, and prepare your brain for writing.

Warming writing senses

Your academic control center, your brain, doesn't awake from sleep and run a marathon. It needs a warm-up period, another purpose of writing rituals. After warming up, you're ready for marathon writing.

Your goal for awakening writing senses includes preparation for creating ideas into a meaningful form of written communication. In other words, you're ready to write your research paper.

The following sections explain the importance of writing preparation that opens the flow of ideas.

Writing rituals

Think of rituals as the brain's way of readying you for intellectual engagement. They prepare your brain to transform 26 letters into an original research project. Almost all writers begin with some form of ritual, including the simple act of sitting in a chair or sprawling on a lawn to begin writing.

You can easily imagine writers through the ages preceding writing with a ritual such as positioning themselves with a window view overlooking pyramid construction. Table 15-1 shows readiness rituals of writers you may recognize.

Rituals of these legendary writers included traditions common to many writers today: writing during the early part of the day, isolating themselves in a distraction-free location (with devices muted), and committing themselves to developing a daily writing habit. Many of them also walked frequently during breaks from their writing.

Your purposes for establishing a writing ritual include the following:

>> Create a comfort zone and familiarization preceding drafting.

>> Reduce anxieties and awaken the creative brain.

>> Establish discipline for the creative process.

>> Create a transition into drafting the first sentence and paragraph.

>> Discover a time and setting conducive to productive writing.

TABLE 15-1	**Rituals of Famous Writers**
Writer	Ritual
Lewis Carroll	Wrote in purple ink
Charles Dickens	Slept facing north to replenish his creativity
Hilary Mantel	Wrote in long hand and on the computer
Haruki Murakami	Ran and exercised before his 4 a.m. writing session
Barack Obama	Wrote first drafts by hand on yellow legal pads and preferred writing when his family was asleep
Dr. Seuss	Wore a collection of hats to ignite his writing
John Steinbeck	Wrote his drafts in pencil, one of exactly two-dozen pencils he positioned perfectly sharpened at his desk
Leo Tolstoy	Wrote every day to avoid losing the writing habit
Edith Wharton	Read her working texts from novels to house guests
Virginia Woolf	Wrote standing up

Writing locations

Your writing senses are also awakened by where you write. Discover your location inspiration from among the following:

- » Quiet isolated settings indoors or outdoors
- » People-populated locations where you see everything but hear nothing
- » Outdoor views of nature and water
- » Library cubicles surrounded by books
- » Unoccupied classrooms that provide academic ambience

Some students supplement their writing location with low, slow, background music, such as an instrumental playlist that excludes distracting lyrics. You're a serious writer when your playlist includes music for writing.

TIP

Discuss writing rituals with your friends, especially friends who have scored high on their writing assignments. It's also a good topic to bring up in class with a question such as: What does research say about the correlation between writing rituals and writing success?

Time frames

As a college student, my primetime for writing was late night to 1:00 a.m. In recent decades my circadian rhythm switched from writing during darkness to writing from early morning to noon. Discover the ideal "write" time for you.

Try writing something during that time almost every day. Your options of what to write include the following:

>> *Freewriting* (an unstructured free flow of written ideas that reflects the brain's thinking on the topic; see the section "Generating ideas: Prewriting" later in this chapter for an example)

>> A to Z lists

>> Notes (see Chapter 6)

>> Course to-do lists

>> Formal writing projects (see Chapter 9)

TIP

An effective writing strategy includes writing one-sentence summaries of what you learned in your recent classes.

The advantages of writing in the morning, especially before classes include the following:

>> Working memory is clutter-free from events of the day.

>> You aren't required to follow a dress code.

>> You're unlikely to be distracted by people.

>> You're unlikely to be thinking about a TikTok post.

>> Most people are more productive then.

REMEMBER

A number of studies show that writing reduces stress.

Exorcizing excuses: Stress and delays

If you're looking for an excuse not to begin a writing session, you'll always find one. But as you develop patterns of regular writing sessions, the excuses will escape you. The creative brain doesn't turn on and off like an ice cream dispenser. It sometimes defaults to other interests such as social media and social activities.

The following sections explain how to reduce stress and detour delays in your writing production.

De-stressing and defeating delays

Humans tire and need rest for almost one-third of their day. A tired brain is an unproductive brain and also a reminder to you that academic success requires rest, exercise, and healthy eating habits.

When stress and exhaustion overpowers your commitment, take a break and recharge your power supply. Stress frequently results from too many academic requirements due in too short a time frame — controllable by better planning. Planning and starting assignments early (see Chapter 14) contributes to reducing stress. Planning includes preparing drafts of assignment sections with enough time to have them reviewed by your professor and the writing center.

REMEMBER

Many professors recognize that early submitted assignments, such as those submitted a day before the deadline, usually represent the best assignments in the class.

TIP

If your academic stress or personal stress overpowers you, help is available for you at the student health center. Visit in person or call; they're staffed with trained professionals to help you. They can get you back on track, and it's a resource used by many college students.

Detouring delays

All writers experience delays in their writing production — periods of time when word flow dams up and sentences fail to stick to the screen. Here's what many successful college writers do to when word flow slows:

>> Review flow of information for a section you're working on.

>> Revise (see Chapter 17) a section of completed text.

>> Review formatting for citations and references.

>> Create a title page.

>> Review logic in your evidence section.

>> List applications of your topic beyond the classroom.

>> Create a to-do list.

Promise yourself a reward after working another hour — or find yourself a puppy looking for a playdate.

Adults experience fatigue and resulting stress; you're the judge of balancing rest, stress, and your commitment to your academics. You have options for addressing stress and fatigue, including the following:

>> Take a half-hour nap. It worked in your first few years of grade school.

>> Take a half-hour break, with or without exercise.

>> Continue less-demanding parts of your writing project such as formatting.

Preventing perfectionism

A fixed mindset (unlike the growth mindset in Chapter 14) believes that assignments such as research papers require perfect completion in one draft and that sentences and paragraphs require perfection before moving forward.

The need to achieve perfection paralyzes progress of most students. Work hard to complete assignments the best you can, and access support when you need help. Be proud to be a nerd, but don't try to be a perfect nerd. Research shows that success results from average intelligence combined with above-average work habits.

Writing the First Draft: The How-To

The most difficult part of every assignment is starting, taking that first step. Congratulations, you've successfully started your assignment. Your first step for your first draft is a few pages forward. Your first completed draft will be a visible sign that you completed more than half your research paper. You'll feel as good as creating a short list of your remaining courses until graduation.

When you've completed draft one — in addition to progressing from a blank screen — you'll have accomplished the following:

>> Transposed notes into words, sentences, ideas, and major sections of your research paper

>> Prepared a foundation for revising and writing a second draft

>> Demonstrated commitment to your research writing

>> Practiced thinking in a growth mindset and applied your best effort

>> Produced a blueprint for completing the project

The following sections explain how to continue the warm-up process and complete that first draft.

Generating ideas: Prewriting

Your research has been completed; your notes have been recorded; and your ideas are awaiting the big reveal. You're ready for prewriting, gathering information that's stored in your short-term memory. It's like information on the tip of your tongue speaking to you.

Here are a few classroom-tested strategies, commonly used by college students, to generate ideas for developing your first draft:

>> **Freewrite:** This multipurpose idea generator is surprisingly effective, and you won't believe it until you try it. It's better than a free app and you're not required to surrender contact information. It's simply writing with a pen and paper for ten consecutive minutes. The act of writing with a pen in your hand shortcuts information from your brain to the paper. Here's an example of freewriting on the topic sports betting and college students:

> Sports-betting among college students is formation of the perfect storm for students: providing the excitement needed to develop addiction, stealing time from their academics, and contributing to developing mental health issues. It's like recent trends on campuses of giving free beach towels to students who sign up for credit cards. Each free beach towel gets you deeper and deeper into debt. And colleges are taking millions of dollars from sports-betting companies to advertise their betting on campus. It's like college providing the alcohol for college parties and then arresting students for drinking. The atmosphere provides students with everything they need for creating an addiction: athletic excitement, competition, user-friendly betting technology, and wall-to-wall sporting events to bet on. Students don't need another distraction from their academics and another diversion from the real reason they're in college — graduate.

>> **A-Z generator:** This technique works because the brain likes a little prompt. It works like this: Record an implication of sports-betting beginning with each letter of the alphabet. It looks like this:

> **A**nother encouragement to drink and lose money

> **B**etting creates a brain dependency that needs to be satisfied

> **C**ampus creates an atmosphere conducive to gambling

> **D**efenses aren't available for students to manage gambling.

>> **Visualization:** Draw a stick figure of your argument. Include balloons on the heads of figures. Or draw balloons representing people arguing over your topic.

>> **"What if" it:** Ask your topic questions that begin with "What if." Here are examples on the topic of sports betting in college: What if it became a major? What if it has already reached the addictive level among students? What if it contributes to the college attrition rate? What if funds from student loans were used for betting? What if it resulted in additional sports-fixing scandals similar to basketball in the '60s?

>> **Interrogation:** Ask your topic questions such as the following: What are the demographics of students who do not bet? How much betting is affiliated with campus teams? What are reasons for students not to bet? How serious is the sports-betting problem on your campus? How does sports betting affect couples' relationship? At what stage does sports betting become an addiction?

Creating the first draft in five easy steps

Completing the first draft of your research paper doesn't assure you a position in the graduation procession, but it moves you closer to successfully completing a major course requirement. Your goal for draft one is to write the general structure for the research project: introduction, body, and conclusion.

These steps explain how to complete that first draft.

Step 1: Prepare yourself and your research

Preparation includes your commitment to your writing as explained in Chapter 14, in addition to identifying your ideal writing location and time.

Additional preparation includes the following:

>> Gather your assignment, to-do lists, notes, laptop, assignment model in your required style, and references to your documentation style.

>> Review your argument (see Chapter 7), thesis, and major questions (see Chapter 5).

>> Establish time frames for completing the first draft (approximately two to three hours).

>> Mentally separate yourself from your devices and distractions.

>> Focus on developing your thesis and answering your research questions.

Write with the goal of completing sentence and paragraph structure and avoid obsessing with details.

Step 2: Review your notes and outline

Review your notes and outline, categorizing information for the introduction, body, and conclusion.

Identify major concepts from your notes and readings such as the following:

>> Reasons why . . .

>> Causes of . . .

>> Effects of . . . on . . .

>> Importance of . . .

>> Wider implications of . . . include . . .

Continue to categorize and re-organize notes into major sections, primarily background information for the introduction and evidence for the body.

Step 3: Write the evidence paragraphs first

Begin writing your paper in the middle or body section with your researched evidence that supports your thesis. If you lack body content to write, you need more research.

Here's a list of tips for writing the evidence paragraphs:

>> Begin writing the evidence sentences by introducing the piece of evidence with the author, source, and summary or paraphrase of the evidence as in this example:

> Stewart's "Today's Gambling Addictions" argues that today's college campuses are "petri dishes for growing addiction" because of the "energy of students, propensity for risk, and availability of disposable cash" (2022, p. 146).

>> Complete citations as you write.

>> Explain the connection of the evidence to the thesis as in this example:

> Stewart describes a college atmosphere that perpetuates financial risk-taking that may lead to gambling addiction.

See additional sample language for writing evidence in the section "Body" later in this chapter. Chapter 6 details more information on evidence.

TECHNICAL STUFF

For Dummies authors similarly begin writing with the major content section, Part 2. After the major content sections of the book are written, they begin Part 1, Chapter 1. At that point they know what they're introducing.

Step 4: Write the conclusion second

One of the reasons why you're in college is that you're inquisitive; you regularly ask why (and many college students ask why not). Your research readers share your curiosity. After you explain "what" in the evidence paragraphs, readers instinctively think "why." Why is the argument important and why should readers care about it?

Begin the conclusion with a brief summary of the evidence. Follow the summary with a synthesis (see Chapter 9) of evidence. Also reference the introduction in the conclusion — a frequently used writing strategy to connect the beginning and end of your message.

Consider answers to the following questions for writing the conclusion paragraphs:

>> What's the big-picture importance of the argument?

>> What are logical conclusions resulting from the argument?

>> What's the importance of your evidence?

>> What's your takeaway message about your research?

>> What new topics does the research raise?

Avoid presenting new research in the conclusion. The section "Conclusion" later in this chapter models language common to the conclusion.

Step 5: Write the introduction last

Finally, write what the reader reads first, the importance of the topic. The purpose of the introduction is to familiarize readers with the topic, its importance, and why they should care about it.

The first sentence and opening of the introduction are designed to engage the reader in the topic.

Include the following information in the introduction:

>> An overview of the argument

>> Recent research on the topic

>> Positioning of this research among other research on the topic

>> Research questions

>> Explanation of how the paper will develop

>> Thesis (positioned near the end of the introduction)

Check out the later section "Introduction" later in this chapter for some model language from introductions.

Thinking critically

The roots of critical thinking date back to Socrates more than 2,000 years ago and the belief that logic should by supported by evidence and that reasoning should be examined. Thinking critically means that you reflect on information, examine individual components, and question validity. When you think of critical thinking, think of questioning your ideas with why and why not.

Apply critical thinking to your research by evaluating answers to questions on the following topics of your research:

>> **Argument:** What is the argument and what isn't the argument? What value does the argument offer value to the academic community? Does the argument include an issue that reasonable people disagree with? Does a body of evidence support the argument? Does some evidence refute the argument? What's missing from the research and what's significant about the omission? To whom is the argument important and why?

>> **Evidence:** Is reliable evidence available (see Chapter 6)? How will your research position itself among other's research? Is the application of evidence logical?

>> **Conclusion:** Are conclusions logical? Do conclusions flow from the thesis? Do conclusions apply to extended audiences?

>> **Logic:** Does the research follow thinking of what reasonable people would consider logic? Are logical fallacies avoided (see Chapter 7)?

Modeling Major Sections: Introduction, Body, and Conclusion

You've heard the expression that seeing is believing, but in research writing (and almost all other academic writing) seeing also models the structure of the completed assignment, especially the language of the assignment. Your best preparation tool for writing a research paper is a model provided by your professor.

If models aren't provided, they're available from the documentation resources identified in Chapter 14. Remember that online models, unlike professor models, don't represent requirements of your professor. These sections offer model excerpts for writing the major sections of research papers.

Introduction

Invest writing time in your first sentence and opening. Here's a look at a sample first sentence and opening:

> Whether student loans should be paid by the federal government is not the only elephant in the classroom. The issue of exorbitant college tuition also remains. Costs of college continue to rise like a weather balloon caught in the jet stream. What Carson describes as a trillion-dollar student-loan debt in 2021 is approaching a trillion and a half in early 2023 (p. 245).

The introduction excerpt that follows developed from this thesis statement:

> The purpose of this research paper is to argue that college loan costs should be minimal, college tuition costs should be reduced, and students should be required to maintain at least a "B" average to qualify for loans.

Here's a look at sample introduction language following the opening:

> Half of students who graduated from a four-year public university in 2021 were also accompanied with student loan debt averaging $22,000. Students over fifty years of age who graduated more than two decades ago have been repaying student loans for more than twenty-five years — about the same number of years that graduates in the 70s paid off a thirty-year home mortgage (Hargrave, 2020).
>
> How did student loan debt rise so high and tuition rise so fast from a time when cost at a four-year public institution averaged slightly over $1,500 a year in the 60s? And at a time when the G.I. Bill paid college costs for members of the military returning to civilian life. In addition, students who graduated in the 1980s benefited

from interest-free student loans while they were in college — unlike most loans today that require repayment immediately upon receiving them. Morris (2022) also points out that in the past decade, new car loans were one-third the cost of student loans.

The Higher Education Act created the Guaranteed Student Loan Program modeled after the home mortgage program and eventually merged private banking into the education lending industry. And since the purpose of business is to make money, the costs of loan services soared.

The increase in student costs coincided with tax cuts and reduced federal spending resulting in higher tuition costs and increased student loans. Simultaneously, colleges offered the amenities of a five-star country club.

In addition to lower interest loans needed, student loans today need a student responsibility component. Kirsten (2022) suggests "minimal" cost loans with qualifications including maintaining at least a "B" GPA or pay a higher loan rate. Paul and others disagreed with Kirsten's suggestion (2022).

Additional research on the topic shows that in the past decade college tuition rose three times the cost of living (Duane, 2022) and interest on student loans tripled compared with those in the 80s and 90s.

Body

The focus of the body section is presenting evidence that supports the argument. Here's a look at sample evidence found in body paragraphs that argue the dangers of sports betting in college:

Parsons (2022) explains that college is a fertile environment for promoting high-risk behavior such as sports betting and other forms of gambling. Research by "College Betters Anonymous" shows that colleges successfully cultivate gambling addiction with data such as the following:

- College students' at-risk gambling rates are three times higher than non-college adults.

- More than three-quarters of college students experienced gambling loses in the past year that they described as "moderate or worse."

- Students who bet on sports are 75 percent more likely [than non-sports betters] to participate in card-playing gambling "at least fifteen hours weekly."

- Almost 10 percent of college students have been identified as experiencing "moderate to serious" gambling addiction.

- At least 35 percent of college students reported missing at least one class because of a gambling issue.

- Students with athletic experience are more than four times more likely to participate in gambling than non-athletes.

Sports betting conflicts with the mission of college and poses a threat — at least equal to drinking — to students by encouraging risky financial behavior, creating an environment conducive to gambling addiction, and compromising available study hours (Quarez, 2022). The potentially addictive environment is encouraged by universities who accept millions of dollars from sports betting companies to advertise on campus (Mattson, 2021).

Locke (2022) reported that almost one-quarter of college students bet on sports in addition to weekly participation in gambling by playing cards. She also found a correlation between gambling more than twenty-five hours per week and lower GPA's. Rockman (2022) found that gambling was more widespread in schools with a "high athletic profile" (p. 213).

Conclusion

The conclusion develops the importance of the argument. Here's an example of language common to the conclusion of a research paper:

The college mission includes developing habits of academic discipline, solving problems, and participating in community service activities. Weekly patterns of risky financial behavior and other potentially addictive behavior conflict with academic values (Franklin, 2023). In addition, colleges' advertising sports betting companies promotes that potentially-addictive behavior. Students' risk of heavy financial losses also contributes potentially addictive behavior such as criminal activity (Schwartz, 2022).

Study of sports betting and other forms of campus betting needs to be prioritized because of its direct application to academics. Gambling consumes students' study time, adds another stress to their lives, and affects mental health — in additional to financial loses.

Sports betting in college increases the need for additional research such as the following:

- College culture that encourages gambling, and the relationship between gambling and grades

- Demographics of students who identify as at-risk gamblers

- Relationships between campus gambling and student loan debt

- Successful remediation for helping gambling addiction

UNDERSTANDING THE VALUE OF STUDYING MODEL PAPERS

At the introduction of teaching writing assignments, I was assured to be asked a question by a student who will usually earn an A in the assignment. That question is: Do you have any models of the assignment to provide us with? I would never think of teaching a writing assignment without a model, a best practice endorsed by leading writing experts.

Students who earn exceptional grades on writing assignments have learned the value of studying an assignment that models exceptional writing — especially professors' models that show requirements professors are looking for.

The major asset of a professor model is that it demonstrates examples of a title page and other major section headings. It also shows examples of source entries in the list of references and optional parts acceptable for students to include in their papers.

Here are examples of questions to ask to analyze professor models:

- **Structure:** How the model is organized into major parts? What writing features are common to the opening and closing? What subheadings are included in each section? How extensive is the literature review section?

- **Supporting evidence:** What type of evidence supports the argument (see Chapter 5)? How extensive is the use or peer-review sources? Is social media referenced as a source? How are evidence sentences structured? How current is evidence?

- **Writing style:** Does the model include an emphasis of action verbs and specific nouns? Does it include combinations of sentence lengths? Are sentences concise and revised for wordiness? Is word choice formal and inclusive of academic vocabulary? Are cliches generally avoided?

- **Formatting:** Is formatting in the model representative of the style required? Does the model include variations of style recommendations? Does the model include optional style section such as an abstract, annotated bibliography, or appendix?

Honoring Olden Rules:
Ethics and Objectivity

Ethics and objectivity should be as simple as people respecting people. But unfortunately, they aren't that simple and writers need care expressing their ideas. College writers today face the challenge of expressing themselves in a society that has blurred lines between right and wrong, ethical and unethical, and objective and subjective. These sections help define those distinctions.

Ethics and college writing

Ethics is generally defined as what most people consider the right thing to do. In other words, ethics is what's inherently right or wrong in a given situation. Writers' ethical responsibilities to their readers includes a fair and honest representation of information. For college writers, many ethical violations are considered plagiarism (detailed in Chapter 3) such as summarizing without crediting a source.

Ethical and objective responsibilities of college writers include the following:

>> Show a balance of evidence that supports an argument (see Chapter 6).

>> Identify or exclude authors who benefit from positions they take.

>> Use language that's respectful, courteous, and fair (see Chapter 10).

>> Learn to accurately paraphrase, summarize, and use a quotation (see Chapter 6).

>> Record notes accurately and cite sources responsibly (see Chapter 8).

The foundation of academic research is built on trust that information is accurate, fair, and ethical. Unethical research compromises integrity of all research.

Consider the following examples of unethical behavior:

>> Not participating in a team project and receiving the same grade as participants

>> Writing a slanderous online evaluation of a professor

>> Falsifying the volume number of a reference because you can't locate it

>> Adding a source reference from a friend who said she didn't need it

What's considered ethical isn't always obvious and frequently results in an ethical dilemma. Many businesses and organizations create guidelines to determine what's ethical, and most universities establish codes of academic integrity to define ethical behavior (see Chapter 3).

Using objective language

When writing to your research audience, you're entitled to your opinion, an ethical opinion supported by facts. But you're not entitled to your facts when they're inaccurate, biased, and lack objectivity.

Here's a look at guidelines for objectively presenting information to your research audience:

» Avoid unnecessary and excessive use of first person "I." Prefer objective third person references to "they and it."

» Give information rather than judgment:

Judgment: Eating excessive red meat is unhealthy.

Information: The National Heart Association says that eating red meat three times weekly contributes to dying five years earlier than non-meat eaters.

» Use exact numbers when available:

Students who visit the writing center at least five times a semester earn better grades than student who don't visit them.

» Avoid intensifiers such as *very, critically, excessively, drastically perfectly*, and *deadly*.

Intensifiers: College students who participate in sports betting *excessively* experience *drastically* lower grades.

Revised: College students who participate in sports betting ten hours or more weekly experience a one-point GPA drop.

» Avoid informal presentation of information:

Informal: I am pretty sure over exercising isn't good for you, and no wonder students fall asleep in class.

Revised: Excessive exercise causes fatigue.

» Avoid unobjective language that appeals to emotions:

Unobjective: Some schools offer horrible educational experiences for children.

Objective: Some schools neglect to meet the needs of their students.

Balancing objectivity with subjectivity

Writers express their opinions by balancing objectivity with subjectivity. The latter represents writing based on opinion, interpretations, and feelings. Subjective writing frequently begins with "I believe," "I feel," and "I think."

Subjective writing has its place in research writing — primarily in the conclusion where you interpret your research and its implication beyond the classroom. Here's an example:

> New developments in artificial intelligence (AI) offer opportunities to improve college writing instruction. For example, most experts in AI argue that all writing should be reviewed before reaching its audience. That reviewing represents opportunities for revising and feedback — two major components of process writing, the writing endorsed by instructional experts.
>
> From my experience as a college professor specializing in writing courses, I believe that assignments can be designed to significantly reduce, or eliminate, use of artificial intelligence. This opinion is supported by Ballinger and others (2023). Dickerson and Cher (2023) suggest designing assignments that require reference to a specific book, for example, or reference a course discussion. These strategies and others are currently being tested by artificial intelligence with Stanton taking the role as lead researcher (2023).

Objectivity in the previous excerpt includes factual information referencing researchers: Ballinger, Dickerson, Cher, and Stanton. Subjective elements in the excerpt are represented by use of the first person: "my experience and I believe."

Chapter **16**

Identifying Required and Optional Headings

I f you're the type of person who thrives on options, this chapter offers you more choices than an ice cream bar with 101 flavors.

You achieved your independence as a college student. Your self-sufficiency making academic decisions will be tested as you reach the three-way intersection of professor requirements, style requirements, and assignment options. This chapter helps you avoid a catastrophe as you cross that intersection.

Here I guide you through the maze of requirements and options for major divisions of your research project. I explain the advantage of choosing a title page as an option, inserting a table of contents, and embellishing an ending with options.

Finalizing Required Front Headings: Attention Grab

Your options of headings to insert into your paper is as simple as 1, 2, 3.

» Your professor requires it — you include it.

» Your documentation style requires it, and your professor agrees — you also include it.

» You decide you need it, and your professor approves your decision — you also include it.

The front of your research is filled with requirements. If your professor, for example, determines you need a title page, it's a requirement. If your documentation style requires an abstract, it's a requirement. If you determine your paper needs a table of contents, it's a requirement. In other words, keep a to-do list of requirements questions to ask about them in class.

The following sections identify headings of your research paper that many professors will require — and also accept as optional.

Title page

APA's 7th Edition stipulated requiring a title page (also called a cover page) for student papers. MLA and Chicago don't require a title page, but they accept one, assuming your professor approves.

If you're using a documentation style other than APA, ask your professor the question: Do you require a title page and do you have a design preference? The answer you want to hear is: "A title page is optional."

If the answer is "A title page is required," you're either following your professor's design, APA's design, or the generic design explained in this section (see Figure 16-1). This figure shows a generic title page but remember that you need professor approval if you're using MLA or Chicago.

TIP

When you have the option of using a title page, use one. The advantages of title pages include the following:

» Adds a professional appearance to your paper

» Appears on almost all-important documents

> **FIGURE 16-1:**
> A generic title
> page for a
> research paper.

Sports Gambling in College: A Losing Bet
Stephanie Wright
Sports Psychology 302
Professor O'Brian
March 3, 2024

© *John Wiley & Sons, Inc.*

>> Identifies you to your professor as the author

>> Highlights the research title to your professor, which immediately engages your professor with your topic

>> Avoids beginning your paper with a text-dense page

Here's a layout of a generic title page most professors accept:

>> **Paper title:** One quarter from top of page, centered, and bolded

>> **Student name:** Double-spaced below the title

>> **Course name:** Double-spaced below the student name

>> **Professor's name:** Double-spaced below the course name

>> **Due date:** Double-spaced below the course name

REMEMBER

If you're required to use APA style, follow their guidelines for a title page. Chapter 13 explains title pages requirements for specific documentation styles and provides samples.

Table of contents

As a professor who has read thousands of research papers, I value a table of contents that identifies locations of topics included in the paper. The contents page also says the complexity of the paper requires a list of topics to identify its organization. It also adds to the professional appearance of your paper.

A research paper without a table of contents is like a website without a homepage. And remember that a professor is unlikely to tell students not to include a contents page, allowing the opportunity for you to include it and strengthen your paper's organization.

Use these guidelines to create a contents page:

>> Center and bold "Table of Contents" [without quotation marks] at the top of the page.

>> Position content headings numerically.

>> Indent subheadings.

>> Capitalize keywords in content entries.

>> Align page numbers flush right.

>> List only the page number that begins the content.

Figure 16-2 shows a table of contents that most professors will accept.

Table of Contents

© John Wiley & Sons, Inc.

FIGURE 16-2: A sample table of contents for your research paper.

Introduction

You're aware that documentation style rules don't always follow logic. For example, the introduction begins the paper but doesn't begin with the word "introduction." It begins by repeating the title of the paper. See Chapter 13 for an example.

TIP

The introduction section of research papers commonly includes subheadings that most professors like to see in your introduction but are unlikely to tell you to include them. Take the initiative and include subheadings in your introduction, showing your professor you value those topics in your paper.

Include the following subheadings in your paper:

>> Statement of the problem

>> Review of previous research

>> Research questions (see Chapter 5)

>> Limitations of the study

These subheadings add organization to your paper and show your professor the location and detail of the content. The following sections delve deeper.

TIP

Unless your professor tells you not to use subheadings, include them to highlight information.

Statement of the problem

A *statement of the problem* is standard content to include in your introduction. The information is required with or without a subheading.

The purpose of the subheading includes identifying the issue the paper addresses. For example, if the paper is arguing the need for reasonable college tuition, you'd explain the problem with language such as the following:

Increasing college tuition costs has reduced educational opportunities for many students who earned the right to qualify academically but lack financial resources. In addition, many students who choose to attend these higher-tuition schools cause a financial burden on themselves and their families by taking on additional student loan debt.

TIP

Create subheadings consistently and use parallel structure (see Chapter 11). Microsoft Word and Google Docs contain a style feature for consistent formatting of headings.

WARNING

When you choose subheadings in your introduction (or any other part of your paper), develop each topic with at least four paragraphs. A subheading with little information under it tells your professor you have little information on the topic.

Review of previous research

This subheading includes background information on the topic and how your research aligns with other research on the topic. If you're not required to write a formal review of literature, this review extends approximately a page and a quarter.

If you're required to write a formal literature review, this subheading extends two to three pages. See Chapter 9 for more information on writing a formal review of literature.

If you're not required to write a formal review, prefer language such as the following:

> McMaster's says, The post-Covid workplace "continues to search for its sweet-spot" (2023, p. 243). She further explains that employees have acclimated to their homework environment and that "increased production at home" supports the argument to continue working from home (p. 287). Sullivan suggests, "The value of working from home has not been validated by long-term studies," and added, "It's too soon to invest in a major restructuring of the workplace" (2023, p. 104).

> The purpose of this research is to examine a topic that remains unexplored: the finances of office buildings left unoccupied and partially occupied since Covid and answers the question: How are building costs affecting company budgets? It's a decision that Sharky says, "may result in decisions that businesses never even considered" (2023, p. 127).

Limitations of the study

The limitations subheading shows your responsibility and ethical values as a researcher by disclosing weaknesses in the research. Limitations are common to almost every piece of research, and readers of research recognize that fact.

REMEMBER

As a novice undergraduate researcher, insert your limitations toward the end of the introduction. Common limitations of undergraduate research include the following:

>> **Access:** Some topics may require detailed information only available through organizations that most students don't have access to.

>> **Sample size:** A study that provides evidence may include a limited sample size that reduces validity of the study. For example, a study of left-handedness

of college students may be limited by a reduced left-handed population of college students.

>> **Currency:** The study of many technology trends may be limited by current availability of information reaching library databases.

>> **Time constraints:** The time frame of professional researchers may range between nine months and a year. College students frequently have weeks and some supporting research may not be available within that timeframe.

WARNING

Professional researchers with complex limitations of their study frequently position limitations in the conclusion (discussion) section of their paper where they can convert limitations into assets of the study.

Language common to introducing limitations of the study includes the following:

>> However, the research includes the following limitations . . .

>> Common to a majority of research, the study's limitations include . . .

>> The study viewed through the limitation of . . . nonetheless shows . . .

>> As with most studies, the limitations . . .

>> As with most college students, time frame constrictions resulted in . . .

Determining Optional Front Headings: Ready Reserves

When you're completing most college assignments, such as a reaction to your assigned reading, you don't want options. You want to know the exact requirements and then complete them the best you can.

But research papers include as many options as a college meal plan. Choosing some options can improve your paper and your grade — and are as comforting as choosing a steady diet of pizza.

This section explains research options commonly used in the front of your research paper. It also recommends which options to utilize. The one option you don't have is choices that conflict with your professor's requirements. Remember that professors' requirements rule.

The following sections explain research heading options that usually improve your grade.

REMEMBER

Some options here are sometimes required by professors in first-year research papers to give you experience with them for your future use. For example, a methods section in a first-year paper is likely to include only sources you researched. But in advanced research papers, methods is likely to include complex collection of data. If you're assigned a methods heading in a first-year paper, don't question it, follow the advice of the commercial and just do it.

Abstract or executive summary

Think of an abstract or executive summary as an introduction to the introduction. They're usually required for papers exceeding eight to ten pages. But you may be assigned one for the experience of becoming familiar with writing them.

An *abstract* is a summary or overview of the topic, and an *executive summary* is a short analysis of the topic. Here's a dive into each.

Abstract

Abstracts frequently include a description of the topic, the importance of the topic, and identification of research questions. Common requirements for an abstract include the following:

>> Purpose of research

>> Topics covered in the research

>> Brief summary of major sections

>> Inclusion of key terms making the abstract searchable

>> Factual information that avoids discussing options

Abstracts (see Figure 16-3) range between 150 to 200 words. They're written in one paragraph and exclude indentation. They begin at the top of a new page and are positioned immediately preceding the introduction.

REMEMBER

Ask professors if they require sources and citations in abstracts. Professors' preferences vary.

Abstract

This paper investigates the value of emotional support animals on college campuses and its effect on improving students' mental health and GPA. A recent report showed a 25 percent increase in emotional support animals on campuses in the past two years, with dogs being the most popular animal, especially Golden Retrievers. Verification of animals on campus requires documentation from a mental health professional. But approval from online sites in past years has compromised authenticity with many sites primarily interested in selling certifications. Students are ensured the right to verified animals through the Fair Housing Act. This paper argues that emotional support animals are an asset on campus and moderately improve students' mental well-being.

FIGURE 16-3: A sample of abstract language.

Executive summary

An executive summary serves a similar purpose as an abstract and is frequently used for research reports in business and education. They frequently include sub-headings and paragraph structure. Structure ranges between four and five double-spaced paragraphs, and ideal length is about a page to a page-and-a-quarter.

Their organization varies according to the type of report they precede. When executive summaries are required, professors frequently provide writing guidelines. If they're not offered, ask about them. Here are a few guidelines for a generic executive summary:

>> Begin with a short engaging story.

>> Transition into a brief explanation of the problem.

>> Support the urgency of solving the problem at this time.

>> Offer a few brief solutions to solve the problem.

>> Include financial implications of the problem and solution.

Methods

At the undergraduate level of research-paper writing, the methods section describes how you gathered your information. In former decades of research, the methods (frequently used interchangeably with methodology) section was titled "methods and materials" because it required researchers to identify procedures and materials used in their research experiment.

The purpose of a methods section is to provide enough information for another researcher to duplicate your study.

The student model in APA's 7th Edition doesn't show a methods section. MLA's 9th Edition doesn't emphasize it either. But professors who were required to describe methods in their degree programs sometimes require it.

A methods section is common in original research where collecting data exceeds searching documents. You most likely won't be conducting original research requiring participants; therefore, your methods section will be limited. If your professor doesn't require a methods section, avoid it like long Covid. Methods isn't an option you want to choose.

If you're required to write one, explain types of sources you researched: journal articles, YouTube videos, websites, news sources, and so forth. Identify names of databases you downloaded documents from. You may also explain sources you didn't choose and why.

Here's sample language commonly found in an undergraduate methods section:

> My research began meeting with a reference librarian. After discussing my topic of emerging technologies and sports betting websites, she recommended websites and podcasts that explained designs using these new technologies. These sources offered documents explaining complex descriptions of technologies that built websites to attract and sustain college population sports betters. In addition, I examined sports betting sites that included features such as incentives, high stimulation, and credit card conveniences.

List of figures

When you use more than three figures, include a list of figures as a heading in your paper and position it immediately before the introduction of your paper (or before an abstract if one is required). Chapter 5 explains the use of figures (photos, maps, drawings, and so forth).

Here are tips for creating a list of figures (Figure 16-4 shows an example):

>> Bold and center "List of Figures" [without quotation marks] at the top of a page.

>> Bold figure numbers and position flush left, followed by a colon and the title.

>> Italicize the title of the figure.

>> List the page number where the figure is located.

List of Figures
Figure 1: *Reported Income of Sports-Betting Companies*..............3
Figure 2: *Photo of 1990 College Common Area*..........................4
Figure 3: *Average Tuition Costs of Top-Rated Colleges*...............6
Figure 4: *Student Loan Comparisons Across Decades*.................7

FIGURE 16-4: A generic list of figures.

Completing Optional Middle Headings: Body Parts

Similar to good exercise practices, a healthy research paper begins by strengthening the core or middle section. The middle section, the evidence section of your research, is all business and includes no major options. Minor options, subheadings for your evidence and rebuttal, offer choices to structure the middle section into a reader-friendly format. The following sections explain options in the core section of your research paper.

Middle-content subheadings

The dense evidence section of your research becomes more accessible to your readers by adding a few subheadings. For example, if you're arguing the advantage of post-Covid's work-from-home trend, subheadings for your evidence can include the following:

- Commute savings
- Wardrobe savings
- Entertainment office-related savings

Here's an example of language that supports evidence in the middle section of your research:

> U.S. Workplace Data (2023) reported that in the first year following Covid restrictions, a survey of Office 100 Workplaces said that business production from work-at-home employees increased between 20 and 25 percent. The source also said that employees recognized higher spending income as a result of decreasing wardrobe costs, travel costs, and office-related entertainment costs.

Rebuttal subheadings

Without subheadings, the rebuttal section to your evidence can easily become misaligned in the middle section.

Subheadings for the rebutting advantages of a topic such as working from home can include the following:

» Employees lack face-to-face opportunities to develop rapport with colleagues.

» Working from a home environment encourages an informal, non-business attitude towards work.

» Home environment provides work distractions not found in workplace setting.

For more information on the rebuttal section, see Chapter 7.

Here's an example of language commonly found in the rebuttal section:

Krypton identifies a liability of employees working from home, arguing that "managers' influence on employees has significantly declined with the work from home model" (2023, p. 136). He explains that employees' independence working from home, combined with their increased production, has the potential to change a manager's role. He added that employees have "succeeded in a nonmanagerial environment" (p. 142). Stimetz believes that the post-Covid workplace represents an opportunity to revise the role of managers in the workplace (2023).

Fulfilling Final Options: Rear Views

The end of your research paper is your last call to play options and score points — and high-scoring options are available. Chapter 15 explains writing the conclusion, a major required section of your research. These sections discuss point-producing options in your paper's last section.

Conclusion subheadings

Subheadings in your conclusion highlight final points for readers. Here are examples of subheadings in the conclusion that can appear on the topic of emotional support animals on campus:

>> Increases socialization among students

>> Reduces crime on campus

>> Offers opportunities for veterinary research

TIP

Notice parallel structure of the previous subheadings. Each subheading begins with a verb (*increases, reduces,* and *offers*) followed by a noun (*socialization, crime,* and *opportunities*). See Chapter 11 for more information on parallel structure and be sure to structure subheadings parallel.

REMEMBER

Use the word "Conclusion" [without quotation marks] as a major heading at the beginning of the conclusion section.

Implications beyond classroom

The conclusion includes extended application of the evidence beyond the classroom. What's the big picture of your research? Here's an example of subheadings that represent extended implications on the topic affordable solar power:

>> Increases pay 15 percent across the board

>> Increases solar-power vehicle development

>> Reduces housing energy costs

>> Reduces public energy costs

>> Provides employment opportunities

Topics for future study

Professors anticipate reading this subheading because it reflects your original thought on the topic. It's an opportunity to demonstrate thinking beyond what professors know is standard on the topic.

Suggested future studies on the topic of AI and writing can include the following:

>> Can professors identify AI writing in traditional college assignments?

>> Can assignments be AI-proofed?

>> How does AI writing style compare with typical college writing styles?

>> How will the absence of writing affect education?

>> Will AI writing increase acceptance of less standard written language?

Annotated bibliography

A list of references is a requirement; an *annotated bibliography* is a replacement requirement for references (or works cited or bibliography).

Professors assign annotated bibliographies to require you to analyze your sources and your use of them in your research, which is a good experience for you. Regardless of which major style your using, the wording "Annotated Bibliography" (centered and bolded) is the heading for a list of sources that includes two or three sentences describing their use in the paper.

If you write an annotated bibliography and aren't required to write one, your professor will assume you thought one was required. Don't annotate your list of sources as an option. See Chapter 8 for an example of an annotated bibliography.

Appendixes

An *appendix* is an add on, just like your appendix (if you still have one) is an add on to your small intestine.

An optional appendix in your research paper provides an opportunity to supplement information such as the following:

>> Detailed description of a topic for further research

>> Questionnaire or survey used in the research

>> Copy of a document or artifact related to the research

>> Summary of a related interview

Your professor may require you to create an appendix on a topic related to your research and writing process. The purpose of these assignments is to evaluate your writing, thinking, and research processes. Examples of those topics include the following:

>> Personal reflection on the process of revising your research

>> Diary entry of a researching session

>> Description of how you revised at the structural level (see Chapter 17)

>> Evaluation of a peer-feedback experience

>> Evaluation of a session at the writing center

>> Description of experience with a reference librarian

Appendixes rarely exceed one page (see Figure 16-5 for an example of language in an appendix evaluating a session at the writing center).

Appendix A: Writing Center Evaluation

Within a week of the paper being assigned, I walked into the library and met with a reference librarian. I explained my topic (music and exercise) and she suggested numerous approaches to the topic and types of sources that would ensure an academic approach as described in the assignment.

We discussed key words in the assignment that helped me focus on what I was required to do.

She asked me if I was familiar with the library's main catalogue. I said "no," and she guided me through searches on the topic of music and exercise. In the search parameters, we used Boolean operators and eliminated non-academic sources on music and exercise.

When we located sources, she showed me how to email them to myself. The experience showed me the benefits and time-saving results of meeting with a reference librarian before the start of every assignment.

FIGURE 16-5: An example appendix.

Tables and figures

APA recommends listing tables and figures on a separate page following the list of references. (The list of figures option that I discuss earlier in this chapter in the section by the same name represents an option for using figures such as maps and photos for the type of research for students such as you.)

If your research includes one or two tables and figures, embed them into your text. If you're using three or more, include an optional "Tables and Figures" page following references.

Glossary

A limited number of technical terms can be explained in the content of the paper. When a topic requires explanation of approximately a half dozen new terms, a glossary of new terms is more reader-friendly than individual definitions with context of the paper.

A *glossary* (see Figure 16-6) lists terms specific to the research topic. Topics, for example, may include art, science, business, literature, or nutrition.

	Glossary	
Terms	**Definitions**	
Amino acids	Building blocks of protein	
Blood glucose	The main sugar found in blood	
Electrolytes	Minerals in body fluids	
Gluten	Protein found in wheat	
Polyunsaturated fat	Fat that remains in liquid form at room temperature	
Saturated fat	Fat that turns solid at room temperature	
Trans fat	Created when liquid oils change into solid fat	
Triglycerides	Type of fat found in blood	

FIGURE 16-6:
A sample glossary
of terms.

© *John Wiley & Sons, Inc.*

Footnotes and endnotes

APA designates footnotes as a reference to text with a superscript and corresponding reference at the bottom on the page. APA's format is similar to Chicago's footnote and endnote format. When footnotes are listed on a separate page following the reference page, they're called endnotes. Figure 16-7 shows an example of a footnote in a paragraph of text, followed by the corresponding footnote at the bottom of the page.

FIGURE 16-7:
Numbered
footnote in text
and bottom of
page note.

> The building history included several witnesses who reported seeing "dancing translucent" figures[1] in a smoky mirror above a fireplace.
>
> [1]From the chapter "Haunted Histories," in *Buildings Needing Further Exploration* by J. Becca (Milestone Publications, 2023), 248-260. Reprinted with permission.

© *John Wiley & Sons, Inc.*

Footnotes and endnotes represent another option for including supplementary information into your research. They rarely appear in college research, and I've seen them in student research papers as frequently as Halley's Comet — once every 75 years.

Chapter 17

Revising and Editing in Three Layers

How important is revising? Committing to revising is a grade changer. It helps professional writers sell their work, and it helps college writers earn the grades. It can increase your writing grade one letter and your GPA almost a full number. Ask a summa or magna student how much they revise their writing.

Educational studies endorse the value of revising and other practices related to the process of writing. But many students today aren't acting on the research. Recent studies show that students underestimate the importance of revising, neglect to commit the time, and believe revising is equivalent to editing for spelling.

One of the goals of this chapter is to change your thinking about revising and convince you that revising is a grade changer. It's what professional writers do to clarify their writing. I explain three layers of revising: structural layer, sentence and paragraph layer, and word layer. Furthermore, I detail why your professor likes revising and the role of feedback in the revising process.

Just remember not to fall in love with your first draft — it's like a first date.

MODELING LEGENDARY WRITERS: EXPERTS KNOW BEST

When you want to learn something new, you go to the source of expert advice. You're in college because your professors have accumulated the knowledge you need to succeed in your field of study. Professors obtained their knowledge from studying the experts.

The writing advice experts, the writing practitioners whose works represent some of the best writing in the world and their analysis of what made them successful, offer is limited, but what remains recorded shows their passion for the revising process. The following table lists examples and lessons from their words that apply to revising and college writers today.

Writer	Revising Reference	Lessons
Vladimir Nabokov	"I have rewritten — often several times — every word I have ever published."	The extent of revising is determined by the writer. Many writers commit more time to rewriting than writing their first drafts.
Neil Gaiman	"The best advice I can give you is this . . . If there are things you aren't satisfied with as a reader, go in and fix them as a writer."	Identify issues as a reader and improve them as a writer. Review your writing through the eyes of the reader.
Judy Blume	"I'm a rewriter. That's the part I like best . . ."	Some writers identify themselves as rewriters first, and some writers enjoy revising more than writing.
Michael Crichton	"Books aren't written — they're rewritten."	For some writers, revising supersedes writing. Here's another example of revising emphasized more than writing.
Robert Stone	"I'll write a very rough first draft of every chapter, then I will rewrite every chapter."	The goal of many writers is to complete a first draft from which they can develop an improved draft. This chapter explains how to improve a first draft.
Ha Jin	"I work hard, I work very hard. All the books at least 30 revisions."	Writing, like other worthwhile accomplishments, requires hard work, especially revision. The harder you work, the smarter you become.

Writer	Revising Reference	Lessons
Henry Green	"The more you leave out, the more you highlight what you leave in."	Your best writing stands out by revising what's unsuccessful. The major decision of successful writers is what to cut, not what to add.
Robert Cormier	"The beautiful part of writing is that you don't have to get it right the first time."	You have unlimited opportunities to improve writing.
J.K. Rowling	Revised first *Harry Potter* series book for years and rewrote manor sections multiple times.	Writing improvement results from extensive revision of content.

Comparing Editing and Revising

Many students incorrectly associate editing with revising, and they believe that when they're editing, they're revising. They unfortunately aren't the same.

Here's the difference between editing and revising (see Table 17-1):

>> Editing is a lower-order skill; revising is a higher-order skill.

>> Editing is like sitting on the beach; revising is like making an ocean rescue.

TABLE 17-1 ## Contrast of Editing and Revising

Editing	Revising
Replacing a comma with a semicolon	Revising paragraph order into a logical sequence
Deleting an unnecessary hyphen and unnecessary italics	Deleting unnecessary words in a sentence and unnecessary paragraphs in a section

Answering Revision's Why: Grade Changers

Evaluating and revising, such as your writing, applies to almost every developmental process: studying, performing, cooking, building, knitting, skiing, raising children, and improving relationships. If you want to improve your writing, grades, and GPA, invest your time and commitment into revising. The following sections explain why revisiting your writing makes a difference.

Why revising makes a difference

The revising process (encouraged by professors and explained in the section "Why your professor likes revising" later is this chapter) is like cleaning broken glass from a tile floor. First you carefully pick the large pieces, then you safely gather medium-size shards, and finally you vacuum the slivers. Glass splinters always remain and you eventually find them with bare feet. It can be a painful and bloody process.

And similar to revising, cleaning up minor issues is never perfect. You do the best you can and learn from your experience.

The glass-cleaning process mirrors the process of three-layer revising. Revising writing is reimagining your writing as you think your audience would imagine it. It's clarifying, condensing, and preparing information for your reader. It's the process of performing "re's" such as demonstrated in Table 17-2.

TABLE 17-2   **"Re's" for Revising Writing**

"Re . . ."	Explanation	"Re . . ."	Explanation
Restructure	Position paragraphs into more logical sequences.	Rebuild	Develop paragraphs with specific details.
Resist	Avoid irrelevant information.	Recall	Generate ideas from previous information.
Reconnect	Improve relationships and connections among ideas.	Refute	Explain another side of the issue.
Realign	Change the sequence of information.	Redefine	Offer additional explanations of ideas.

Why your writing needs revising

Brain scientists state that one of the brain's most difficult challenges is acclimating to a new culture, such as someone immigrating to a foreign country, an adjustment spanning a full generation.

Written ideas also require a period of adjusting before ideas become clear to readers. Writing is a highly intellectual activity that requires the intensity of multiple sessions and multiple effort.

Here's a look at why writing needs revision and requires more than one draft. It requires the following:

- >> **Persistence:** It's a complex mental process that requires multiple tries to complete.

- >> **Fresh eyes:** Periods of refreshing are required to energize a fatigued brain and depleted working memory.

- >> **Focus on the reader's needs:** Initial drafts are frequently written to the writer as the audience, and revised drafts are written to the reader as the audience.

- >> **Brain prompting:** Writing ideas are generated from previous drafts, with previous ideas prompting new ideas.

Why many students dislike revising

Writing is physically and mentally demanding and requires time and energy. It's challenging, but rewarding because it creates original ideas never previously recorded. Academic writing produces new insights from previous ideas.

Much of students' dislike of writing is based on their misunderstanding of the process of writing. Here's a look at common student misconceptions:

- >> **Not worth effort:** Revising is physically, mentally, and academically challenging and they don't think it's worth the effort. Someone once said the harder you work, the luckier you get.

- >> **Importance undervalued:** Students don't identify revising as an integral component of the writing process — a process that many legendary writers identify as more important than writing itself (refer to the nearby sidebar for examples).

- >> **Requires planning:** Students lack a plan for exclusive revising, and lack of a revising plan is a plan for a poorly written assignment.

- >> **Can't be performed sporadically:** Students haven't developed a revising habit. Any academic behavior practiced regularly can become a habit. Revising becomes successful when it's habitually performed.

- >> **Equated with editing:** Revising, a higher-order skill, is often equated with editing, a lower-order skill. Revising and editing are two different skills as I explain in the section "Comparing Editing and Revising" earlier in this chapter.

- >> **Not ingrained:** Revising wasn't integral to the high school writing process because of high school teachers' excessive student load and teachers' lack of allocating time for evaluating interim revised papers. College students are more academically committed than high school students, and revising is integrated into the college classroom. Professors are routinely allocated time for teaching revising and evaluating papers.

Why your professor likes revising

Most professors experienced revising when they were students and recognize the importance of it, especially professors with a background in writing instruction. Here are some of the reasons professors like revising:

>> **Visualizes student thinking:** Professors can see your thinking on revised drafts similar to how a math teacher can see your computation to solve a problem.

>> **Identifies writing progress:** They can use drafts to evaluate your writing progress monthly and annually.

>> **Shows patterns of improvement:** Drafts provide an opportunity to identify patterns of writing issues.

>> **Provides instructional tool:** Professors can use drafts as a teaching tool to assess skills such as analyzing, evaluating, and summarizing.

>> **Teaches accepting constructive criticism:** Revising gives students an opportunity to respond to constructive criticism, a skill necessary for career success.

Benefiting from Partnerships: Feedback and Revising Loops

Similar to many of your favorite activities on campus, writing is a team sport. Yes, you're individually responsible for your writing, but you have a back-up team to support you with structure, support, detail, revising, and editing. The value of your team is that any three of you are smarter than any one of you. Your writing team members include your peers, professor, and writing center.

The following sections explain the role of feedback as part of your writing partnership. Go team; write team write!

Giving and receiving feedback

You've heard the expression "quality in, quality out," referring to the idea that the value put into a product or project equals the quality that comes out. For example, a recipe that lacks quality ingredients will lack quality taste.

That same advice applies to your writing planning (see Chapter 14) which produces a productive first draft. It also applies to the feedback you receive that determines the quality of your revising. You have opportunities to receive feedback from other students, your writing center, and your professor — all sources of quality input, especially your professor.

WARNING

Feedback from your peers assumes your professor's assignment guidelines allow it. See Chapter 3 for occasions when working with others may constitute plagiarism.

Another excellent source of receiving feedback is a trusted friend in another course who can serve as a feedback exchange partner. Be sure to establish guidelines for mutual feedback such as providing three days for completing feedback.

TIP

When you're asked to give feedback, take it seriously and give it your best writing effort, and capitalize on the opportunity to study another piece of writing. When you're receiving feedback, evaluate it and analyze what can contribute to improving your writing. You're not obligated to accept all feedback (except from your professor, which I discuss in the section "Receiving professor feedback" later in this section).

These sections explore the benefits of giving and receiving feedback.

Giving

Your parents taught you that giving is better than receiving. But with feedback, giving and receiving is better than not giving and not receiving.

When you're giving feedback, remember that you're invited into the personal space of another student. (And remember the respect for people your parents taught you.) Be sure to clarify directing feedback toward the writing — not the writer.

TIP

Also, when you're asked for feedback, ask the recipient the intensity of the feedback they want from you, ranging from soft and easy to hot and spicy. Regardless of what they request, use a respectful tone and language.

In other words, avoid feedback with tone and language such as the following:

> » You should . . .
> » I don't like how you . . .
> » Don't . . .
> » You need to . . .

Prefer tone and language such as the following:

>> Have you also considered . . .

>> Consider . . . for explaining . . .

>> Have you thought about a stronger connection of . . . to your thesis?

>> I am not getting your meaning about . . . . Can you clarify . . .

I often use a classroom feedback activity having students complete the prompt: I like what you said about . . . . Have you also thought about . . .

The value of giving peer feedback includes the following:

>> Offers examples of language that also addresses your assignment requirement

>> Shows common issues with the assignment

>> Opens common ground for conversation about the assignment

>> Makes learning a social activity

Receiving

Receiving feedback is a gift of a person's time and knowledge. It's an excellent opportunity to learn from someone who speaks from similar experiences.

When you ask for feedback, explain "wit or witout" (an expression used in Philadelphia to order cheese on your cheesesteak). Ask your peer to give you feedback with or without editing, in addition to feedback on your content. Also don't forget to order your feedback "soft and easy" or "hot and spicy." (And don't forget to add South Philly to your bucket list so you can correctly order a Philly cheese steak.)

For editing (see the section "Eagle-Eying Your Editing: Reaching New Heights" later in this chapter), coordinate with a peer to review each other's papers exclusively for editing. You also have the option of having your paper reviewed for editing at the writing center.

The value of receiving peer feedback includes the following:

>> Provides stress-free feedback because it's not from your professor

>> Shows how another student problem solves

>> Helps keep both students on track

>> Helps identify similar issues on the assignment

Receiving professor feedback

Unlike receiving feedback from your peers, professor feedback comes with a reverse warranty — don't do it and you're liable for what you don't address. Professors not only expect you to address their feedback, but they're also annoyed if you don't because you decided to ignore their time, effort, and advice to improve your grade.

REMEMBER

Professor feedback may include submitting a section of the assignment weeks in advance to give the professor a sense of your progress. (If you're not required to submit a sample section, ask your professor if you can submit one in advance or the deadline.) Professors' feedback may include comments such as the following:

>> **"Needs development"**: Interpret this comment to mean you didn't provide adequate information on the topic, such as developing your background on the topic, evidence, or thesis. This comment usually indicates your paper hasn't reached a B grade.

>> **"Needs more reliable research"**: The key word here is "reliable" (see Chapter 6), meaning quality sources such as peer reviewed or more recently published.

>> **"Needs organization"**: Address this comment by restructuring the boundaries of your introduction, body, and conclusion. Your research paper needs major reorganization. It's a serious issue that requires talking with your professor and visiting the writing center.

>> **"Needs 'so what?'"**: This comment indicates the need to connect evidence to the thesis and to conclude with the significance of your argument.

>> **"Please see me"**: This doesn't mean a public flogging. It means your professor has a question about your paper that's too complex to comment on your paper. It usually means a misunderstanding such as using the wrong documentation style or misusing a source.

>> **"Language and sentence structure issues"**: This comment needs immediate attention. Camp outside your professor's office and wait for the next office hours. You may be studying English as an additional language, and your professor may suggest visiting the writing center for support with language fundamentals. English is a difficult language to learn and requires practice and support that's available at the writing center.

REMEMBER

Professors' comments aren't suggestions; they're requirements that need addressing to improve your paper. They're also opportunities to visit your professor and ask for clarification how to address comments. You're also showing your initiative to help yourself, which professors appreciate.

Identifying the importance of self-feedback

Giving and receiving feedback provides experience for applying your own feedback. An advantage of self-feedback is that you're available on your own schedule, compared with adapting to someone else's schedule. Coordinate self-feedback with other feedback. Self-feedback and revising is a recurring process to complete throughout your writing.

Tips for applying self-feedback include the following:

>> Follow the revising three-layer approach explained in the next section.

>> Familiarize yourself with your own patterns that need revising.

>> Use campus resources for issues you can't problem solve yourself.

>> Practice and use self-feedback as your final form of feedback and revising before submitting your paper.

Evaluating the Organizational Layer: Structural Elements

Revising an essay is like building a dorm room loft. Begin with the foundation, the vertical uprights that support it to the floor. Then add the horizontal cross supports for the bed base, and finally add the diagonal supports, bed rails, and ladder.

Loft-building duplicates the process for revising your research paper. Begin revising the foundation, your paper's structure. Then follow with the cross supports, supporting paragraphs and sentences. Finally, add the accessories, the words that have so much to say.

These sections explain three layers of revising research papers — assuming you're not obsessed with building a loft.

Revising structural elements

Without a supporting foundation, you don't have a grounding for a piece of writing. But revising offers you multiple opportunities to strengthen the foundation and strengthen your writing. Structural reviewing revisits the major elements that build the writing, from the framework through the writing style. The following sections offer more detail for revising structural elements of your research project.

Review structural framework

Prioritize revising your writing structure — the placeholder of content.

Consider the following elements for revising structural framework:

>> Define boundaries of the major sections: introduction, body, and conclusion (see Chapter 15).

>> Contain required and necessary optional parts (see Chapter 16).

>> Include a framework to answer required questions (see Chapter 9).

>> Demonstrate writing with an academic style (see Chapter 11).

Review assignment requirements

Review your assignment checklist for deliverables (see Chapter 16) to insure you're prepared to submit requirements and include necessary sections.

Consider the following elements for revising assignment requirements:

>> Prepare and format deliverables for submission.

>> Answer major and minor questions in the assignment.

>> Align deliverables with the assignment rubric.

>> Reference course content in deliverables.

Review topic selection

Review that your topic addresses the question your professor asked in the assignment, not research you found describing the topic.

Consider the following elements for revising the topic (refer to Chapter 5):

>> Include an innovative approach to the topic that attracts professor and reader interest.

- » Reference background on the topic in the introduction.

- » Avoid topics that are too broad or too narrow.

- » Include references to course content.

Review audience and purpose

Think of your audience as you write, readers who are representative of your professor and your school faculty. Write with language that fulfills the purpose of the assignment. Chapter 10 discusses what you need to know about your audience.

Consider the following elements for revising audience and purpose:

- » Include academic language appropriate for the audience.

- » Interest your audience with new curiosity about the topic.

- » Anticipate audience questions.

- » Respect your audience and demonstrate an academic tone.

Review paragraph flow and coherence

Good paragraph flow is like smooth movement of traffic on a country road with enough curves to keep interest.

Consider the following elements for revising paragraph flow and coherence:

- » Connect paragraphs with those preceding and succeeding.

- » Apply transitions that are seen and not heard.

- » Implement paragraphs that fulfill their purpose.

- » Avoid paragraphs that sound like thunder on a sunny day.

Review style

The academic audience expects an academic writing style.

Consider the following elements for revising style:

- » Vary sentences in length and structure.

- » Emphasize the active voice and active verbs.

>> Ensure paragraph lengths vary.

>> Include sentences and paragraphs that play well together.

Revising research elements

Research elements within your paper are like their own little police district within a research paper that contains its own enforcement codes. These sections offer more detail for revising research elements of your research project.

Review introduction, body, and conclusion

These three main structural sections are like safe rooms for your research paper. They're protective containers for proprietary properties for each section. Ensure that each section is well maintained.

Consider the following elements for revising the introduction, body, and conclusion:

>> Include research opening with an appealing title, first sentence, and opening (see Chapter 15).

>> Begin with a title that references the topic and the paper's position on the topic.

>> Develop the body section with the argument and reliable evidence.

>> Conclude with the importance of the research and its significance beyond the classroom.

Review argument and evidence

Argument and evidence are the fuel and lubrication of your research purpose.

Consider the following elements for revising assignment requirements:

>> Include reliable and timely evidence supporting the argument (refer to Chapter 7).

>> Reference an argument that contributes to the available body of evidence on the topic (see Chapter 7).

>> Organize evidence logically and absent of illogical fallacies (refer to Chapter 6).

>> Connect evidence to the thesis (Chapter 6).

Review documentation

Revising documentation requires attention to detail — it's a research paper.

Consider the following elements for revising documentation:

- **»** Document all sources used in the research.
- **»** Follow required documentation style.
- **»** Include accurate punctuation of documentation.
- **»** Coordinate citations and references.

Review formatting

Formatting requires adherence to the required documentation style.

Consider the following elements for revising formatting:

- **»** Follow requirements for documentation style.
- **»** Sequence major sections and pages accurately.
- **»** Format levels of headings.
- **»** Position page numbers correctly.

Rethinking the Paragraph and Sentence Layer: Point Makers

Paragraphs and sentences are information carriers; they're the circulatory system that carries ideas throughout your research paper. They're part of a complex network of ideas that need reviewing. Revising is their health-check. The following sections suggest revising at the sentence and paragraph layer.

Revising paragraphs

Paragraphs fulfill organizational purposes of your research such as introducing a major topic, presenting pieces of evidence, and providing supporting detail.

Review the purpose of each paragraph by evaluating answers to the following questions:

>> Does each paragraph transition smoothly at the beginning and end?

>> Within paragraphs, can you substitute better reasons and explanations?

>> Does each paragraph develop only one idea?

>> Can you combine or delete any ideas in different paragraphs?

>> Do paragraphs flow in a logical sequence?

>> Is any paragraph awkwardly too short or too long?

>> Does each paragraph fulfill its purpose?

Review topic sentence integrity

Topic sentences may not be the most important sentences you write as a college student, but they're as important to your academic life as a reliable laptop. Revising topic sentences offers additional opportunities to keep your paragraphs on track.

Consider answers to the following questions to help you revise topic-sentence questions:

>> Do topic sentences in body paragraphs contribute to developing the thesis?

>> Do topic sentences in the conclusion highlight importance of the evidence?

>> Are topic sentences followed by supporting information?

>> Do topic sentences predict development of the paragraph?

Paragraph development

Research paragraphs are developed with evidence from sources as explained in Chapter 11. Revise paragraph development with consideration of answers to the following questions:

>> Does paragraph development include attributions to sources?

>> Does paragraph development accurately reference the source?

>> Is paragraph development accurately cited?

>> Does paragraph development smoothly transition?

Revising sentences

Sentences are the building blocks of paragraphs, like the toy plastic blocks that snap into small structures and support larger structures. When the smaller structures fail, the larger structures fall. But revising offers you the opportunity to prevent a failing structure. These sections suggest revisions for sentence elements.

Revise sentence structures

When you revise sentence structures, check that variety includes the following elements as explained in Chapter 11:

>> Grammatical variety

>> Length variety

>> Branching variety

>> Purpose variety

Revise sentences that stand out like high-rises in the desert and sand dunes in the city.

Revise sentences starters

A sentence that begins without reference to a subject is like a video that begins with a blank screen. Avoid sentence constructions that begin delaying identification of the topic and action — constructions such as

>> There is (are) . . .

>> It is (are) . . .

>> It has . . .

>> It becomes . . .

>> It seems . . .

>> It appears . . .

These constructions are like default sentence starters because they can be used to begin almost any thought. To readers, "It" lacks reference to a sentence topic, a specific object or person. Sentence starter constructions can be revised by looking into the sentence and identifying the topic talked about.

Here's an example:

Sentence starter: *There's* a reason students dislike revising.

Revised: Students dislike revising because it requires additional time.

In this example, the sentence topic (student) appears near the end of the sentence. The revised sentence positions the topic at the beginning of the sentence.

Revise spoken-language wordiness

Words have their place, but some words talk too much. For example, words that belong exclusively in the spoken language infiltrate into the written language where they don't belong.

Here are examples of words that serve no purpose on the page:

» By the way . . .

» Permit me to say . . .

» And I want to tell you . . .

» It's no wonder . . .

» In my humble opinion . . .

Look at this example and its revision:

Wordy: *In my humble opinion,* the Eagles should have won the game.

Revised: The Eagles should have won the game.

The revised sentence eliminates four unnecessary words common to the spoken language that reduce conviction of the stated opinion.

Revisiting the Word Layer: Choosing Wisely

American poet Emily Dickinson (1830–1886) is known for writing that a word is dead when said. But in today's language environment, written words have unlimited lives because they can be revised multiple times and brought back to life. These sections discuss revisions for words that deserve to be resurrected — and also words that should remain silent.

Emphasizing action verbs

Active verbs are the energy drinks for your sentences. End your revising with a dedicated reviewing of all action words. Circle verbs and revise them as actively as possible as I explain in Chapter 11.

Here are examples of a few revisions as a reminder:

Inactive	did	went	got	made
Active	finished	jogged	purchased	roasted

Selecting specific nouns

Nouns, along with verbs, are the nitrogen and oxygen of the sentences you breathe. Revise general nouns into specific nouns that I also explain in Chapter 11. Here are a few reminders:

General	seat	tool	book	vehicle
Specific	recliner	wrench	novel	limousine

Avoiding redundancies

When you're learning new ideas, repetition is your best friend. When you're writing new ideas, redundancies are your worst enemy. Avoid word combinations (see Table 17-3):

TABLE 17-3 **Revising Redundant Words**

Redundancy	Revised	Redundancy	Revise
month of May	May	repeat again	repeat
adequate enough	adequate	separate apart	separate
round circle	circle	added bonus	bonus
two twins	twins	baby puppy	puppy

Reducing wordy phrases and clauses

Wordy phrases and clauses have too much to say. They need a word count. Table 17-4 lists some examples of wordy expressions that need some silencing:

Here's an example of a revision in a sentence:

Wordy: *At the present time*, many people distrust authority.

Revised: Today, many people distrust authority.

TABLE 17-4

Revising Wordy Expressions

Wordy Expressions	Condensed Revisions
first and foremost	first
on a daily basis	daily
as per	per
do damage to	damage
during the course of	during
at the present time	now

Avoiding cliches

Cliches are worn-out expressions that should be permanently retired and replaced with fresh wording (the following shows common cliches in college writing):

a prime example	in this day and age	the bottom line
at the end of the day	little did I know	the time of my life
proof's in the pudding	live up to the hype	pie in the sky
the powers that be	sit tight	hold your horses
since the beginning of time	when all is said and done	every cloud has a silver lining

Here's an example and revision in a sentence:

Cliché: *The powers that be* voted a tuition decrease.

Revised: The board of trustees voted to decreased tuition.

Revising overused and unnecessary words

Avoid words that have worn out their welcome and other words that don't deserve a home.

During word revision, you can almost always find a replacement for the following words:

Adjectives: amazing, great, nice, wonderful, tremendous, amazing, great, fantastic, awesome, and super

Adverbs: fine, truly, superbly, very, and really

Nouns: gadget, thing, stuff, factor, aspect, and case

Verbs: claims, seems, appears, got, went, and did

Some words just show up where they're not needed. In the sentence that follows, you can eliminate unnecessary words and condense other wordy expressions:

Unnecessary words: No texting while driving is strongly enforced in all fifty states. (11 words)

Revised: Texting while driving is prohibited nationally. (6 words)

PROFESSORS' EXPECTATION FOR STUDENT REVISING

Your professors are well-experienced with every process you experience as you revise your writing. They've had their writing criticized, been asked to meet unreasonable deadlines, and may have failed a paper. They also know the occasional unrealistic pressures of meeting academic deadlines.

Professors' must find the intersection between how much they can demand from you without crushing you. They're demanding, but they know limits from teaching previous courses. They also know that their success in the classroom is dependent on your success.

Here's a list of what professors expect from your revising, your additional opportunity to clarify your writing and improve your grade:

- Clearly defined major sections of your paper: introduction, body, and conclusion (see Chapter 15).

- Language that addresses the academic audience with a purpose that fulfills the major question in the assignment.

- Proficiency citing and referencing sources (see Chapter 8).

- Understanding of the formatting required by your documentation style.

- Sentences that reflect the academic writing style (see Chapter 11).

Planning your revising

My goal in this chapter is to convince you to prioritize revising as a necessary element of your writing success and a difference-maker for your grade. Unless you're a writing major, you may not develop an obsession with revising. But a revising obsession isn't a prerequisite for success — only a commitment. Here's a revising plan guaranteed to improve your writing (all you need to add is your commitment):

>> Begin writing assignments as soon as they're assigned.

>> Allocate 35 percent of your writing budget to revising and 5 percent to editing.

>> Emphasize revising at the structural layer that accurately positions content into the introduction, body, and conclusion.

>> Revise accuracy of citations, references, and formatting.

>> Develop a habit of revising almost every day, such as previous papers, other students' papers, signs on campus, and so forth.

>> Review instructor comments on past papers.

>> Read online articles about revising college writing.

>> Utilize campus revising resources, whether you think you need them or not.

Your evidence of success is comparing former writing drafts with present drafts.

Eagle-Eying Your Editing: Reaching New Heights

Editing is like looking for a lost contact lens on a hard surface. You can't see what you're looking for, but you know it when you find it. Most people search for a lost contact lens by designing a plan, a strategy to examine square inches in the area where the lens was lost.

Here's a few of the top editing errors made by college students:

>> **Missing comma after an introductory element:** Here's an example of the correct use: Determined to earn a good grade on her research paper, Elisa visited the writing center.

>> **Missing comma in a compound sentence:** Here's a correct example: Gas prices increased, and people began walking more.

>> **Its and It's:** *Its* is a possessive form, as in the example: The dog found *its* toy. *It's* is a contraction for it is (or it has). Here's an example: *It's* been twenty years since the last measurable snowfall.

>> **Sentence fragments:** A fragment is an incomplete thought and not a complete sentence. Here's an example of a fragment: *Where we began studying for the test.* Here's an example of changing a fragment into a complete thought: *The library is where we began studying for the test.*

>> **Then and than:** *Then* indicates time, and *than* indicates a comparison. Here are examples: We *then* decided to go to the coffee shop. The time was later *than* we thought.

>> **Allusion and illusion:** *Allusion* is a casual reference as in the example: The title was an *allusion* to Shakespeare. *Illusion* is a misleading impression, as in the example: We were under the *illusion* that class was cancelled.

Here's a list of tips for better editing:

>> Read through your paper separate times for the exclusive purpose of correcting errors in grammar, punctuation, and spelling.

>> Keep a list of editing errors common to your writing.

>> Edit when your eyes are fresh, not when you're tired.

>> Carefully edit spelling of words related to your course, including your professor's name.

>> Give extra care to editing words that include apostrophes.

TIP

If language errors have been common to your writing, plan ahead and have your paper reviewed and discussed at the writing center.

If you haven't had language issues in the past, Table 17-6 is an editing checklist that's a reminder of editing issues common to college students. See Chapter 12 for more explanation of editing errors.

TABLE 17-6 **Your Editing Checklist**

Grammar	Spelling	Punctuation	Conventions
Subject/verb agreement	Proper nouns	Possessives	Italics
Pronoun agreement	Plurals	Colons and semicolons	Major works of art
Confused pairs	Brand names	Proper nouns	Minor works of art
Description positioning	Personal misspellings	Commas and end punctuation	Quotation marks

IN THIS CHAPTER

» **Wrapping up research reminders**

» **Pursuing opportunities for writing and presenting**

» **Post-writing for future gains**

Chapter **18**

Finalizing before Sending: Checking the Presentation

oes appearance matter? Does the presentation of the product influence the perceived value of what's inside the package? The world's largest computer company thinks it does and that's why every tech product you buy from them has the appearance of a red-carpet opening.

Appearance also matters in the packaging of your academic product. In other words, when you're submitting a research paper, appearance matters, including documentation, page formatting, and language accuracy.

In this chapter I explain pre-submission procedures for finalizing major parts of your paper, quickly reviewing your academic writing style, and a last call for checking what's missing. I also suggest publishing and presenting opportunities for your work, and a final review for improving your writing.

Let the checking begin. The finish line's around the corner.

Avoiding Crash Carts: Your Grades' Golden 60 Minutes

In the medical profession, the 60 minutes after patient trauma is identified as the golden hour, the critical minutes that determine the patient's outcome. In the academic world, the golden hour before submitting your paper frequently determines your paper's first impression and sometimes lasting impression. Pre-submission of your research paper isn't life or death, but it can determine the health of your grade.

These sections review the final reminders for organizing major parts of your research and packaging deliverables for your professor.

Positioning parts in their place

You probably have heard the expression "a place for everything, and everything in its place." One of your final checklists before submitting your project includes identifying pieces of your research paper along with subheadings for each heading.

REMEMBER

Style guides offer limited support for identifying and sequencing optional sections, major headings, and subheadings. Follow your professor's guidelines. If they don't provide any, then follow the guidelines in this book.

Table 18-1 shows a checklist for research parts required by almost all professors, along with frequent options.

TABLE 18-1   **Research Parts' Checklist**

Major Parts	Subheadings Frequently Required	Common Options/Student Choices
__Introduction	__Statement of problem	__Methods
	__Background on topic	__Limitations of study
	__Description of argument	__Results
__Body	__Evidence	__Content subheadings
	__Rebuttal	__Analysis of data
__Conclusion	__Implications	__Discussion
	__Future studies	
__References		__Annotated bibliography

Use this table as a checklist to review required and optional research parts. Place a checkmark next to paper parts when they're completed, reviewed, and ready for submission to your professor.

Chapter 15 explains the major sections of research papers and Chapter 16 discusses optional headings.

REMEMBER

APA requires a title page. MLA and Chicago don't require a title page, but many professors do require a title page. See samples of title pages in Chapters 5 and 16.

Additional front and back options include the following:

- ❏ Table of contents (positioned between the abstract and introduction)
- ❏ Abstract
- ❏ Appendix
- ❏ Figures and tables
- ❏ Notes

Styling for success

Reviewing style is like your parents telling you to clean up after yourself — it's a recurring process, and like editing you're never finished.

Finalize your academic style with the following checklist:

- ❏ Primarily uses active voice sentences.
- ❏ Emphasizes action verbs and specific nouns.
- ❏ Varies sentence structure and length.
- ❏ Focuses on right-branching and middle-branching sentences.
- ❏ Varies word patterns, including content words.
- ❏ Uses smooth-flowing transitional ideas.
- ❏ Contains respectful language.
- ❏ Structures related ideas parallel.

See Chapter 11 for detailed information on building an academic writing style.

Checking Them Twice: Deliverables

Forgetting a deliverable is like forgetting a friend's 21st birthday celebration. It just can't happen. Finalize your deliverables with the following checklist:

- ❏ Reviews an assignment for verification of deliverables.
- ❏ Verifies internal assignment deliverables such as "include references to class readings and class discussion."
- Double-check your to-do list for deliverables when analyzing the assignment in Chapter 14.
- ❏ Validates deliverables with another student in the course.

TIP

See Chapter 14 for more information on deliverables.

Wrapping Up: Finalizing Hello and Goodbye

The introduction and conclusion are like the appetizers and dessert of your research paper. They're your first and final message to your readers. The following sections explain that hello and goodbye.

Making a first impression: Introduction

Your writing goal includes an opening that creates reader curiosity.

Use the checklist that follows to finalize your opening impression:

- ❏ Flows from the title into the first sentence (see Chapter 5).
- ❏ Establishes a connection with the reader.
- ❏ Identifies purpose to read (see Chapter 10).
- ❏ Maps out the direction of the paper.
- ❏ Offers background on the topic.
- ❏ Introduces the argument (refer to Chapter 7).
- ❏ Reviews research on the topic (see Chapter 5).
- ❏ Ends with a thesis (check out Chapter 5).

Leaving a lasting impression: Conclusion

Most people dislike goodbyes, especially ones that end relationships. But you can celebrate finishing your paper with your conclusion and ending a possibly weeks' long relationship with your research paper.

Finalize your conclusion with the following checklist:

- ❏ Transitions from the body to the conclusion.
- ❏ Summarizes the argument (see Chapter 7).
- ❏ Summarizes the evidence (refer to Chapter 6).
- ❏ Explains the importance of the argument and supporting evidence (see Chapters 6 and 7).
- ❏ Suggests the need for future research on the topic.
- ❏ Provides closure for the reader.

For more information on conclusions, see Chapters 14 and 15.

Formatting Firsts and Lasts: Titles through Reference Page

Your paper's first impression becomes successful when it's lasting — which also includes accurate formatting.

The following checklist finalizes formatting for the "firsts" on your paper's openings and includes the following:

- ❏ Title centered and bolded
- ❏ Title repeated on first page of text
- ❏ Page numbers positioned in upper right corner
- ❏ Author's contact information and affiliation included
- ❏ Text double-spaced throughout
- ❏ Reference page reverse indented (see Chapter 8)

For more information on formatting, see Chapter 13.

Minding Your Middle: Finalizing Evidence

Your research paper isn't about the money, but it's about the evidence that supports the argument.

These sections offer a checklist for elements of evidence.

Arguing your case

The word that defines your college writing is "argument," defending a position on an issue.

Finalize your argument with the following checklist related to your supporting evidence:

- ❏ Supports the argument (see Chapter 7).
- ❏ Appeals to logic of the audience.
- ❏ Contains most current information available (see Chapter 6).
- ❏ Develops logically.
- ❏ Fulfills the purpose of the assignment (refer to Chapter 10).
- ❏ Connects to them thesis (check out Chapter 5).

Engaging with sources

In college writing sources have conversations with each other — they engage with each other.

Finalize source engagement with the following checklist:

- ❏ Sources engage with each other.
- ❏ You, the author, engage with each source.
- ❏ Each source speaker is clearly distinguishable.
- ❏ Engagements begin with signal words.

For details of source engagement, see Chapter 6.

Asking What's Missing: Last Call

Describing people as obsessive compulsive frequently carries a negative connotation. But when you're submitting a major assignment, such as a research paper, it's an asset. When you produce your best effort, you want to assure yourself that you don't lose points for oversights such as omitting a page or submitting a file that doesn't open.

These sections offer final checklists for documentation, editing, and final submission.

Final documentation reminders

Documentation is the lifeline of academic papers. Research papers without documentation aren't ready for prime time.

Review this final checklist of documentation reminders (see Chapter 8):

- ❏ Associates citations with every author and publication.
- ❏ Coordinates reference entries with citations.
- ❏ Connects page numbers with every quotation.
- ❏ Affiliates source recognition with every summary and paraphrase.
- ❏ Maintains documentation style consistency.

Final editing reminders

Editing errors attract reader and professor attention — for the wrong reason.

Use this checklist to ensure your editing includes language accuracies such as the following:

- ❏ Spelling (including capitalization) on the title page, including your name, your professor's name, and words related to your course affiliation.
- ❏ Spelling and formatting of major headings throughout your paper.
- ❏ Punctuation within parenthesis.
- ❏ Accurate formatting of the reference list.

Final submission reminders

As you review your final checklists, avoid the natural inclination to quickly make adjustments and hit send. Schedule final review time into your planning and work patiently. The human brain shows a sense of humor by revealing editing errors immediately after hitting send.

REMEMBER

As you're preparing your paper for submission, update your back up copies as you make final editing and adjusting.

Finalize the following items prior to submitting your paper:

- ❏ Meeting the deadline date.
- ❏ Submitting in the required file format for electronic submissions or print requirements if hard-copy submission is required.
- ❏ Inserting hard-page breaks for both print copies and electronic submission copies.
- To verify stability of formatting, email your paper to yourself prior to submitting it to ensure reliability of formatting.
- ❏ Emailing to the required email address (don't assume it's your professor's class email) uploading to a class portal, or dropping off a hard copy at an identified location.

NEAR-PERFECT PRESENTATION: PROFS' EXPECTATIONS

From the professors' perspective, near-perfect presentation is an expectation. "Near-perfect" means some parts of your paper are required to be perfect such as the following: inclusion of all major research parts, deliverables, basic page formatting, spelling of your professor's name, spelling of common words, basic comma use and end punctuation, word conventions, apostrophes, and key words related to the course.

And some parts may include a few minor errors such as the following: an occasional misspelling of technical terms and non-English terminology, a citation punctuation error, or a reference entry punctuation or abbreviation error.

You're expected to use near-perfect English language skills and accurately distinguish commonly confused words such as affect and effect, allusion and illusion, its and it's, and there, their, and they're. See Chapter 12 for a basic language review of principal parts of verbs, positioning description, word conventions, and apostrophes.

☐ Reviewing print appearance of every page if print copy is required.

☐ Reviewing the complete paper for passing the eye test of looking like a college research paper.

Publishing and Presenting: Wider Audiences

This is my sixth book, and seeing my words in print still excites me. If you have a passion to see your words published, the only obstacle stopping you is you. Writing and presenting are excellent credits for applying to grad school — and they're also impressive resume credits for almost any career.

The following explains how to pursue publications and also opportunities for presenting your research. The following also explains opportunities for presenting your research as an undergraduate.

Student publication opportunities

As a college student, you live in a world that values publishing and not exclusively research. You can submit for publication almost any topic you feel strongly about: research, essays, and variations of class assignments. Submitting fiction is yet another opportunity.

Here are a few guidelines for submitting your writing for publication.

REMEMBER

>> Never pay to have your writing published.

>> Review submission guidelines on sites that accept writing.

>> After you submit one article, forget about it and work on the next one.

Writers' guidelines tell you topics that the source publishes, article lengths, and authors' backgrounds.

>> Submit your writing to newspapers, magazines, and online sites you read.

>> Submit articles on topics outside the classroom such as music, sports, travel, hobbies, political opinions, and special skills and interests.

REMEMBER

Writers with no professional publication credits are unlikely to earn payment for writing. Payment usually follows years of experiences and then it usually comes in small amounts, about equal to snowfall in South Florida. Universal advice for writers includes never quitting their day job. Think of writing as an inexpensive hobby.

Consider the following sources for submitting your writing for publication:

>> **On-campus opportunities:** This represents your best chances to publish your writing. Almost all campuses have a newspaper, literary magazine, poetry magazine, and a half dozen newsletters. They're usually looking for student work. Contact respective editors.

>> **Newspapers:** Consider campus community and other newspapers for writing opportunities. Review any guidelines that may be available and contact editors.

>> **Contests:** Writing contests are common to college campuses, and they frequently award cash prizes. You can earn as much as a week's payment of your favorite morning beverage.

>> **Blogs:** Blogging is another good starting point to begin writing. Start your own or submit writing to blogs you read.

>> **Undergraduate literary journals:** For a list of undergraduate literary journals for submitting your writing, search National Undergraduate Literary and Scholarly Journals (see https://altoona.psu.edu/academics/bachelors-degrees/english/national-undergraduate-literary-scholarly-journals).

Student presentation opportunities

Scholars, such as your professors, share their research at symposium (more informal than a conference) and conferences. Many universities have an office of research for coordinating professors sharing their work.

Here's a list of reasons why you can present your research:

>> Contribute to the body of research in your field of study.

>> Familiarize yourself with speaking discourse of your field of study.

>> Immerse yourself in the academic environment of your field as a presenter and speaker.

>> Network with student and professional researchers.

>> Learn about future research presentation opportunities.

In addition to an office of faculty research, some schools have an office of under-graduate research for coordinating undergraduates who wish to share their work. As a student, visit the undergraduate office (or the faculty office if an undergrad-uate office is unavailable) for direction for presenting your research. You may also contact The Council on Undergraduate Research (see www.cur.org).

Presenting and speaking in public are resume credits valued in the workplace.

Reflecting Future Gains: Post-writing

Reviewing performances is a common practice among sports teams and musical groups such as university marching bands.

Reviews also improve writing performances. Your review can be performed within the days following submission or when you receive your paper back with your professor's comments.

The following sections offer you reflections for evaluating past writing perfor-mances and improving writing in future projects.

Writing

Writing is a growth mindset activity that improves with evaluation and practice. Evaluate your writing process by reflecting on answers to the following questions:

>> How could you have improved your planning, outlining, and gathering of information before you began writing?

>> How could you have increased productivity of your writing sessions?

>> Did you meet with your professor at least once at the beginning of the writing? If not, why not?

>> Did you utilize the writing center and your peers? If not, why not?

>> What part of the writing challenged you most, and did you utilize resources for support?

>> What parts of the writing did you feel most successful and least successful about? How can you strengthen your writing assets and improve your weaknesses?

>> If you had unlimited time, how would you have utilized it on the assignment?

>> Did you complete adequate background reading prior to identifying your topic, creating your research questions, and determining your thesis?

>> What are your goals for writing your next paper?

Revising

Revising hasn't as yet become habit-forming among many student writers. It's a major skill that improves with evaluation and practice. Chapter 17 explains revising in detail.

Evaluate your revising by reflecting on answers to the following questions:

>> Did you commit to, plan, and schedule adequate time frames for revising?

>> Did you follow the three-layer approach for revising: Structure, paragraphs and sentences, and words?

>> Did you elicit feedback for revising?

>> Did you utilize resources for revising?

>> Did you focus on action verbs and specific nouns?

>> What part of revising do you need practice with?

>> What are your goals for revising your next paper?

TIP

A research-supported strategy for improving your writing and revising is teaching it to another person. Consider volunteering as a tutor on campus or helping high school students with their writing. Don't exclude tutoring as an entrepreneurial opportunity.

Researching and documenting

Research and documentation skills also improve with practice. Evaluate researching and documenting by reflecting on answers to the following questions related to each topic:

>> **Research librarian:** Did you meet with a reference librarian prior to beginning your research (see Chapter 5)? What did you find out that resulted in efficient researching? If not, what prevented your from meeting?

>> **Research questions:** Did your research questions result in the information you needed to develop your argument? Could your questions have been improved? Did you consider using the writing center to help develop your questions?

>> **Documentation style:** Did you utilize resources to learn about your required documentation style? Are you confident that your documenting avoids plagiarism?

>> **Sources:** Did you research primarily through your library, using library databases and similar resources? Were your sources successful for your paper? Were sources easy to locate? Did you improve your research skills?

5

The Part of Tens

Examine common research problems and how to fix them including thesis and argument failures, research question transgressions, planning deficiencies, and style misguidance.

Familiarize yourself with campus resources for improving your research paper such as meeting with your professor during office hours, applying content from other courses, attending topic-related events on campus, and reviewing your paper at the writing center.

Chapter 19

Ten Common Problems and How to Fix Them

Y ou became a successful college student by learning to adapt, improvise, and occasionally search a self-help YouTube video. And you most likely have searched self-help videos to improve your research paper writing.

The purpose of this chapter is to show you how to help yourself and self-repair your research paper problems before they become point deductions. Here I explain the most common research paper problems I've seen and how you can repair them. The sections that follow show you how to avoid small point loses and earn big point gains.

Missing Assignment Details

Problem: My paper appears to be bleeding to death with small assignment point loses that will eventually lead to cardiac arrest, and even worse a failing grade.

Solution: A saying among college athletic coaches is that if you take care of the small points, the big points will take care of themselves. Coaches may not have been thinking classroom assignments, but neglecting assignment details can result in a grade that ruins your day.

REMEMBER

You can't earn good grades if you neglect assignment detail, especially when details are spelled out in the assignment. (Chapter 14 explains analyzing assignments.) You can easily remember that you're required to submit a research paper and that it needs ten sources in APA style. But for example you can easily overlook that the sources must include at least one website, one book, one academic journal, one artifact, and one expert reference.

Students frequently perform poorly on assignments because they don't prioritize details. Approach research paper assignments with a focus on the detail points, the difference-makers on your grade that your professor thinks are important enough to list on the rubric and the assignment. Research paper details include requirements such as the following:

>> Title page and headings (see Chapter 13)

>> Table of contents (see Chapter 16)

>> Accurate sequence of required parts (see Chapter 18)

>> Evidence of peer feedback (see Chapter 17)

>> Evidence of three-level revising (see Chapter 17)

>> Evidence of planning and organizing (see Chapter 14)

>> Annotated bibliography (see Chapter 5)

>> PDF formatting for submission (see Chapter 18)

REMEMBER

You can avoid small point losses by focusing on what your professor tells you not to do, such as enclosing hard-copy pages in plastic sleeves, submitting your assignment on a thumb drive, and not emailing to a specific address.

TIP

Create a to-do list titled "details" and continue to build your list as you work through the assignment. Keep lists visible as you're working and ask your professor and peers questions to clarify items as you create them.

Failing to Follow the Rubric

Problem: I lost points because my professor said I didn't follow the rubric. I want to fix the problem.

Solution: The *rubric* explains point values for different parts of the assignment whereas the *assignment* tells what's required. See Chapter 14 for a detailed explanation of rubrics.

For example, a letter grade can be lost for lack of attention to assignment details such as a title page, table of contents, annotated bibliography, and emailing to the wrong address.

TIP

Dedicate a to-do list exclusively for the rubric. Identify items the rubric requires and the point value for each requirement. To help you prioritize your work, list items from the highest point value to the lowest.

Neglecting to Tie the Thesis to the Evidence

Problem: My thesis appears to malfunction and doesn't cooperate with the evidence.

Solution: Imagine if thesis sentence failures were as simple as an engine warning light. But they're not and they lack an early-warning fail-safe system. Chapter 5 explains how to create them, and this section shows how to repair them.

Be sure you dedicate the time to develop them. Thesis development includes the process of analyzing the assignment and reading background information. You're thinking argument, not a feel-good description of a problem.

TIP

Here's how to fix them:

>> If you're experiencing thesis paralysis, focus on an academic discipline approach, such as economically, politically, legally, or culturally.

>> If your thesis doesn't exactly hit the mark, look to make minor adjustments based on the evidence and counter-evidence.

>> If you can't find evidence to support your thesis, check with your reference librarian before you abandon it.

>> If you can't locate counter-evidence for the rebuttal, check that you have a debatable issue in your thesis.

>> If you can only locate counter-evidence, consider making your rebuttal your argument.

Transgressing with Your Research Questions

Problem: The idea of research questions is new to me, and I'm not sure how to practice them.

Solution: Chapter 5 explains how to develop your research questions and their importance for developing your argument. It's a skill as basic to research as adaptability is to college.

Stop trying to figure out answers and start creating questions. Here are some answers for you to practice developing questions:

>> If the answer is the reason why you're in college, what's the question?

>> If the answer is the content of each of your courses, what's the question?

>> If the answer is what you want to do with your life, what's the question?

>> If the answer is the reason you went to college, what's the question?

>> If the answer is your preparation for a major test, what's the question?

Lacking Research Paper Value

Problem: My professor wrote a comment on my research paper saying my topic lacks reader value. I'm not sure how to fix it.

Solution: The reader value part of the assignment is developed through making the topic relevant to readers' lives. Address reader value by answering questions such as: What information does the argument offer that adds meaning to the lives of the readers? What are the benefits of the topic? What's the big picture meaning? How does the topic make the world a better place to live?

Reader value appears in the conclusion section of your paper.

Fearing Where to Begin

Problem: I don't have much experience writing research papers, and this is my first in college. I don't know where to begin.

Solution: The task can be overwhelming emotionally and academically, but your university believes in you academically or you wouldn't have been permitted to enroll in the course.

Get some background information before talking with your professor. Talk with the writing center to help develop your topic, thesis, argument, and research questions. Look at a completed model research paper (see page 61 in the APA's 7th edition).

Next, meet with a reference librarian for suggestions on databases related to your topic. You can do this and you have the resources on campus to help you do it well. If you're experiencing anxiety, visit the health center. They help students like you every day.

After locating evidence with the help of a reference librarian (see Chapters 5 and 6), begin the writing process (see Chapters 14 and 15), followed by the revising process (see Chapter 17).

Messing Up Your Citations

Problem: I don't understand citations and have difficulty getting a handle on when and what to cite.

Solution: If you take an idea, reference, quotation, infographic, image, photo from another source, you're required to cite it. In other words, ideas from others — that you didn't create — require citations. And if you cite it, you're required to list it in the reference section at the end of your paper. Chapter 8 gives the lowdown on citation basics. Think of citations as a two-part process: citing text and listing the source at the end of the paper.

Information you're not required to cite — called common knowledge — includes information known to most people that can easily be retrieved from an encyclopedia or AI.

Error on the side of citing rather than not citing and avoid citing everything. About 90 percent of your citing will appear in the body section of your paper. One or two citations are likely to appear in the introduction as background information on your topic. Don't introduce new sources in your conclusion, but reference previous sources.

Deserting an Academic Writing Style

Problem: I never think much about my writing style. I just write. I'm not sure of the importance of learning the academic writing style.

Solution: As you increase your time in college, you'll learn more academic discourse — more language and vocabulary of higher education. You'll develop the academic style as you complete your required writing assignments.

Here are a few tips to help you (refer to Chapter 11 for more complete list):

>> Prefer the action verbs of academic writing: *argue, analyze, synthesize, apply document, reference, cite,* and so forth.

>> Prefer the specific nouns: *argument, evidence, rebuttal, counter-evidence, syntax, feedback,* and so forth.

>> Write with formal language, words you would use in a conversation with your professor.

Failing to Plan Accordingly

Problem: I'm not a good planner. I wrote my high school research papers two days before they were due.

Solution: As Chapter 14 details, successful people plan almost everything they do. Big projects, like research papers, require major planning; smaller projects, like registering for a new semester, require less planning.

Think of planning a research paper as planning to start a new year of college. Planning decisions (Chapter 18) include listing requirements, accessing information to complete requirements, and determining completion dates that allows time for addressing problems that will occur. Remember the saying: Lack of a plan is a plan for failure.

Screwing Up Styles

Problem: I'm assigned to write two different research papers, in the same semester, with two different documentation styles.

Solution: You identified a problem that students sometimes need to face and conquer. It's similar to some things in life that you need to find a way and give it your best effort. Most likely your two required styles are APA and MLA. And the MLA paper is most likely a literature course requirement.

TIP

The conflicting areas of styles are citations, references and bibliographies, and formatting. See Chapters 8 and 13.

Chapter **20**

Ten Resources for Improving Research Writing

You're immersed in an academic environment where a wealth of research sources surrounds you. But those research opportunities are like the forest blocking the trees — research resources are engulfed by the consuming campus environment. This chapter illuminates resources you may not be familiar with on your own campus.

Here I explain ten campus resources awaiting your discovery of information that can improve your research paper. Those resources include content experts, support services, and campus initiatives — and assumes you discovered library databases.

Leave no advantage unturned, search out sources that can improve your research writing grade, and be sure to meet with a reference librarian (see Chapter 5).

Professors

You don't earn personality points in college, but professors recognize students who take initiative to locate the help they need. Learn to utilize academic resources available to you — a sign of determination to improve and not a sign of deficiency.

REMEMBER

Professors offer you the best resource for help with your research or other course issues. You not only receive clarification of research issues, but you also show your professor your determination to succeed academically. You have three regular opportunities to capitalize on professor help: office hours, before classes, and after classes.

Professors are required to be available in their offices for student help approximately 90 minutes weekly when students can walk in and ask questions. Professors' office hours are the most underutilized resource on campus — except at the end of the semester when students have grade concerns. Times and locations of office hours are posted in your syllabus.

Other Courses

Sometimes students overlook the obvious. Your courses, in addition to your research paper course, offer you dozens of research paper topics every time you attend a class or complete an assignment. You also see topics through other disciplines. For example, an economic course helps you see the finances of topics, a sociology course helps you see the societal influence of topics, and a math course helps you see the mathematical concepts of the topic.

In addition, professors in those courses are possible experts for your paper. Don't assume that professors' expertise is limited to the content they teach. Almost all professors have academic interests beyond their field of study. Their interests beyond their content areas will surprise you.

Chair of Your Major

College campuses proliferate with professor expertise in a variety of fields, including areas of study for research topics. The chair of your major offers often-overlooked sources of information for your research. Chairs are usually multitalented people with extensive academic interests. That's why they're elected to department leadership positions.

TIP

Search the chair's background for topics that apply to your topic. Look for broad connections between their area of interest and your research topic.

You're usually required to schedule an appointment with a chair and give a reason for your meeting. Your reason includes the chair's expertise on a topic related to your research paper.

Also consider any staff member on campus as a resource for your research. They're almost always willing to help students with a project. And be sure to follow up with a thank you.

Lectures and Events on Campus

In addition to the rich deposit of intellectual capital on your campus, visiting experts bring additional topics each semester. Many guest lecturers speak on topics related to research. Also, a lecturer topic can provide background on your research or suggest an idea for your conclusion. For example, a speaker on the topic of addiction can be a resource for topics on health, mental health, diet and exercise, community outreach, education, and so forth.

Campus Organizations

Your campus is a beehive of intellectual activity with organizations appealing to the eclectic interests of students. Your campus likely has an organization that begins with almost every letter of the alphabet. Some organizations are affiliated with national sponsorships with access to a large body of resources.

Many campus organizations are associated with an academic discipline such as education, philosophy, political science, technology, and engineering. Most organizations have access to resources unavailable through traditional methods of researching.

TIP

Search organizations' by-laws and other documents to determine if resources are available for your research. And if an organization appeals to your interest, consider joining.

Writing Center

If your assignment includes writing or speaking, your campus writing center is your primary resource. They offer enough resources that they're worth visiting two or three times for parts of your project such as planning, organizing, writing, revising, editing, reviewing documentation, and so forth.

Visiting the writing center requires planning on your part to complete assignments before your deadline. Your writing center is your second-best resource behind your professor's office hours.

Career Center

Your campus career center is another overlooked resource for research topics related to careers, career planning, business, studies of companies, workplace issues, and career opportunities. If your topic connects to careers and companies, utilize career center resources. Many research paper topics incubate from the career center.

REMEMBER

You don't need an appointment to visit most career centers. You can usually walk in and ask questions on a variety to topics and be directed to resources for additional information.

Travels Abroad

Travels abroad offer an experience that not only complements almost any field of study, but also provide sources of research for topics such as cultural studies, history, technology, transportation, sports and recreation, and food and nutrition.

If you had the benefits of foreign travel, you can apply experiences to your research as comparisons, contrasts, or analysis. If you're planning travel abroad, your planning experiences may apply to your research.

Suggested Campus Innovation

Explore campus innovations for connections to your research. Ongoing campus innovations may include alternate energy projects such as solar installations, technology upgrades, campus housing upgrades, and facilities improvements.

Campus innovations offer research opportunities for connecting topics, applying topics, and contrasting and comparing topics.

Extended Campus Community

Many campuses have close affiliation with an off-campus community that shares common resources and requires peaceful co-existence. As a result, colleges and extended communities share resources such as housing, transportation, open spaces, public safety, parking, and sometimes infrastructure.

Index

as resource, 348
revising paper and, 306
role in stopping plagiarism, 45–46
rubric requirements, 262
scholarships and, 16–17
sources displeasing to, 90
topic ideas and, 66
writing purpose and, 186
project management skills, 18
pronouns, 210, 213–214
PsycINFO database, 79
public domain, 135–136
PubMed database, 79
punctuation
apostrophes, 224
brackets, 219
colons, 215–216
commas, 214
dashes, 217
ellipsis, 218
en/em dash, 217
hyphenation, 224–225
lists and, 238–239
parentheses, 219
quotation marks, 221–222
semicolons, 216–217
slashes, 217–218
spacing, 229
Purdue OWL (Online Writing Lab) website, 265

Q

questions
asking professors, 256–257
developing, 70–72
fixing common problems regarding, 342
focusing on, 83
subquestions, 83
quotation marks

notetaking and, 96
using, 99–100, 221–222
quotations, citing, 129–130

R

race, respectful writing language, 182–183
reaction papers, 156, 172
reader's unspoken purpose, 186
reading, dedicating time to, 255
rebuttals
defined, 108
identifying counter-evidence for, 84
overview, 114–115
planning and organizing, 263
subheadings, 296
Red Book documentation style, 24
reference librarians, 75–76, 83
reflective statements, 52–53, 58
RefWorks app, 86
regular verbs, 208
relevance of topic, 109
reports, 154–155, 172
research
argumentation, 113
backing up, 67
developing questions, 70–72
focusing on research questions and subquestions, 83
handling, 85
heading, 290
identifying counter-evidence for rebuttals, 84
Internet and, 11
overview, 63–64
plagiarism and, 42
planning and organizing, 84–85
preparing findings for writing, 274

revising, 313–314
skills, 11, 18
source management tools and, 86
steps for, 83–84
strategic, 82–83
thesis statement, 67–70
topics
avoiding common mistakes, 66–67
focusing thesis on problem within, 68
generating ideas, 65–66
recognizing elements, 64–65
selection, 64–67
Research Gate database, 78
research papers
building research skills, 18
careers and
career center, 350
opportunities, 333–335
overview, 9
portfolios, 59–60
classifying skills, 12
essays vs., 13–14
ethics and, 281–284
excelling at, 13–15
first-year college, 10–13
importance of, 9–10
mindset and, 15–16
overview, 7–9
publishing, 331–333
requirements from professors, 16–17
resources for, 348–351
submitting, 326, 330–331
undergraduate mentored research, 17
writing across disciplines, 13
research vocabulary, 201
research writing. *See* writing

About the Author

Dr. Joe Giampalmi, a lifetime learner and teacher, has more than half a century classroom teaching experience from middle school to graduate school and consulting classroom experience from K to 12. He taught at Nether Providence Schools (Wallingford, Penn.), Sun Valley High School (Aston, Penn.), and on the collegiate level at Neumann University, Immaculata University, Widener University, Delaware County Community College, and recently Rowan University for two decades.

His publications include six books, the recent *College Writing For Dummies*, *APA Style & Citations For Dummies*, a dozen articles for national magazines, and a 34-year twice-monthly newspaper column. He received numerous academic awards and was named to a number of area halls of fame.

He earned his B.A. and M.Ed. from Widener University and Ed.D from Temple University. He writes from Florida's Gulf Coast and Center City Philadelphia. He's inspired by warm weather, whispering palms, and white-sand beaches. His favorite writing locations in Philadelphia include the atrium at Liberty Place and Rittenhouse Square when he greets Golden Retrievers during writing breaks.

Dedication

This book is dedicated to the undervalued skill of the writing process — revising. If you aspire to be a writer, first aspire to be a re-writer. My *For Dummies* books have been successful — not primarily because of my writing — but because of the perceptive revising recommendations by Chad Sievers, project manager and editor. Chad has been my best writing teacher.

To K-12 classroom teachers, your dedication to your students is appreciated.

To Carole Anne, thank you for making every day enjoyable, and every day an adventure that's usually centered around good food.

To a safer and smarter America. We can achieve both if we have the will.

To every college student who earns a degree in 2023, including grandson Grant from Boston College.

Author's Acknowledgments

Thank you, to the following:

Margot Maley Hutchison, my literary agent at Waterside Productions, and Bill Gladstone, founder.

John Wiley & Sons, Inc. editorial team, thank you for your editorial expertise and your belief in my writing: Lindsay Lefevere, executive editor; Elizabeth Stilwell, acquisitions editor; Vicki Adang, editor; technical editor Dr. Amber Chenoweth for the instructional expertise and validation of instructional strategies — and, of course, Chad.

Proofreaders, daughter Lisa (her sixth book proofreading), wife Carole Anne, and West Chester University adjunct professor, Michelle Guinam.

To family members who regularly ask how the book was going. You're reading the answer.

John Mooney and Joe Logue (teachers and coaches at St. James High School) who taught me that any accomplishment is possible.

Former students at Nether Providence Junior High School, Sun Valley High School, and Rowan University — you motivated me to continue challenging you.

Former colleagues at Rowan University's Department of Writing Arts.

Former newspaper editors Dottie Reynolds, Chris Parker, and Peg DeGrassa at Delco News Network. Thank you for the start of my writing career.

And to the Golden Retrievers who were a welcomed distraction during writing time at Rittenhouse Square: Murphy, Daisy, Octavia, Lola, Scout, River, Olive, Docs, Winston, Max, George, and J.J. I hope your loyalty exceeded receiving a treat.

And you — readers.

Publisher's Acknowledgments

Acquisitions Editor: Elizabeth Stillwell

Project Manager and Editor: Chad R. Sievers

Technical Editor: Amber Chenoweth, Ph.D.

Mangaging Editor: Ajith Kumar

Production Editor: Saikarthick Kumarasamy

Cover Image: © Marco VDM/Getty Images